We shall not be moved

I0809691

MANCHESTER 1824

Manchester University Press

We shall not be moved

How Liverpool's working class fought redundancies, closures and cuts in the age of Thatcher

Brian Marren

Manchester University Press

Published by Manchester University Press
Altrincham Street, Manchester M1 7JA
www.manchesteruniversitypress.co.uk

British Library Cataloguing-in-Publication Data
A catalogue record for this book is available from the British Library

ISBN 978 0 7190 9576 4 hardback
ISBN 978 1 5261 3296 3 paperback

First published by Manchester University Press in hardback 2016

This edition first published 2018

Typeset by Out of House Publishing
Printed in Great Britain
by TJ International Ltd, Padstow, Cornwall

I wish to dedicate this work to my parents, Joseph (1920–92) and Dorothy (1924–83). For my mother, who taught my older brothers and me the beauty of learning, books and knowledge; and for my father, who taught us such wonder belongs to all, not just the privileged.

Contents

Figures and tables

Figures

Tables

Acknowledgements

I would like to begin by thanking my many friends and colleagues who gave me their unreserved support and encouragement. I am especially grateful to Jon Hogg, Pete Millward, Mark Lawrence, Niall Carson and Christoph Laucht, who lent excellent advice regarding the preparation of the book proposal and manuscript. I would also like to thank my dear friends and relations, Keith Constable, Casey Beaumont, Rhian Wyn-Williams and Samuel Hyde, for their moral support throughout this project. And a special thank you to my old friend, John Cummins, who gave me my first guided tour of Liverpool nearly thirty years ago.

May I also extend my appreciation to the various archives, libraries and librarians throughout Britain who helped make this research experience a most enjoyable one, especially the Liverpool and Merseyside Records Office, the Working-Class Movement Library in Salford, the People's History Museum in Manchester, the archives of Unite the Union in Holborn, London and the Modern Records Centre at the University of Warwick.

However, above all, I wish to offer my utmost gratitude to my mentor and friend, Dr Alan Campbell, Reader Emeritus at the University of Liverpool, for his continuous support and guidance with this project. His warmth, geniality and sense of humour sustained me in this work and gave me the confidence needed to carry this tome on to its conclusion. May I also express my sincere thanks to Dr John McIlroy, Professor Keith Laybourn and Dr Nigel Swain for their sound advice in strengthening the argument and structure of this work.

Finally, I am eternally indebted to the many people who agreed to be interviewed for this book, as it was their revelations of such intensely personal experiences, which I hope has lent some degree of humanity to this research. Thank you all!

Abbreviations

AUEW	Amalgamated Union of Engineering Workers
BBC	British Broadcasting Corporation
BDC	Biennial Delegate Conference
BL	British Leyland
BLMC	British Leyland Motor Corporation
Confed	Confederation of Shipbuilding and Engineering Trade Unions
CSEU	Confederation of Shipbuilding and Engineering Unions
DLP	District Labour Party
DOE	Department of Education
EEC	European Economic Community
GM	General Motors Corporation
GMB	General, Municipal, Boilermakers and Allied Trade Union
IMF	International Monetary Fund
IRC	Industrial Reorganisation Commission
ITF	International Transport Workers' Federation
IWC	Institute for Workers' Control
LCC	Liverpool City Council
MCC	Merseyside Coordinating Committee
MDHB	Mersey Docks and Harbour Board
MDHC	Mersey Docks and Harbour Company
MDW	Measured Day-Work System
MRC	Modern Records Centre, University of Warwick
MSC	Manpower Services Commission
MTUCURC	Merseyside Trade Union Community and Unemployed Resource Centre
NALGO	National and Local Government Officers' Association
NASD	National Amalgamated Stevedores and Dockers Union

NDLB	National Dock Labour Board
NDLS	National Dock Labour Scheme
NEB	National Enterprise Board
NEC	National Executive Committee
NUM	National Union of Mineworkers
NUPE	National Union of Public Employees
NUT	National Union of Teachers
NUWM	National Unemployed Workers' Movement
NWRTUC	North West Regional Trade Union Council
OFFA	One Fund for All
PEP	Protected Earnings Plan
RTS	Reclaim the Streets
RSL	Revolutionary Socialist League
TGWU	Transport and General Workers' Union
TUC	Trades Union Congress
UCATT	Union of Construction, Allied Trades and Technicians
UCS	Upper Clyde Shipbuilders
VSEL	Vickers Shipbuilding and Engineering Limited
WOW	Women of the Waterfront

Introduction

At a recent academic conference dedicated to labour history, one participant posed a final question at the end of her paper. Pondering why popular protest erupts in some areas but not others, despite the prevalence of similar economic conditions and common demographics, she concluded that the historiography was lacking on this topic and in need of further research. While her query was in relation to the Swing Riots of the early nineteenth century, this question could easily have also applied to late twentieth-century Britain, during the painful period of de-industrialisation, a time when mass unemployment erupted to record levels and was particularly damaging in the manufacturing belts of northern England.

The last quarter of the twentieth century was most certainly an alienating age for a large percentage of the British working class. Many within this group had gone abruptly from living the promise of upward mobility in the immediate post-war years to suddenly confronting the cold slap of rising unemployment and record level inflation in the 1970s. The remedy prescribed by the City for this malaise was left to the devices of market forces and placed in the care of Margaret Thatcher. Some would argue that the result which followed for much of the British working class was a marginalised world of displaced communities and an end to meaningful work. Furthermore, they would submit this period signalled the parting of a set of values held in common by working-class people and a decline in what was once a pervasive collective class consciousness.

Yet just as in the era of Captain Swing, a time when some agricultural labourers from random rural areas banded together in armed rebellion, while others from nearby and similar localities accepted their fate with quiet despair, the question arises, can a comparable fragmented pattern of resistance also apply during the callous days of de-industrialising in 1980s Britain? This question is raised in light of how certain heavily industrialised British conurbations struggled against the neoliberal economic policies of Thatcher with ferocious abandon, while populations in comparable cities remained noticeably silent. Indeed, why was the right-wing economic agenda under Thatcher even welcomed by some segments of the British working class, but fervently obstructed by blue-collar workers in other areas?

There will be an attempt at answering such questions by highlighting the often contentious role that the city of Liverpool played during this age of Thatcher and in the immediate years which followed. Such answers must be pursued in order to determine why it was in Liverpool that much of the war against Thatcherism was centred and so fiercely fought.

There is no doubt that Liverpool was not a lone voice of protest during the turbulent 1980s. There were demonstrations, strikes, occupations, revolts against governmental authorities and even riots in some major British cities during this volatile period. However, after searching historical archives dedicated to this issue it is obvious that the national press often set their sights squarely on Merseyside as the ground-zero for much of the working-class unrest erupting in this period. Perhaps this was done with a prejudicial bias, or maybe there was an element of truth that supported the stereotype of Liverpool being at the barricades of trade union militancy. Nevertheless, the ready mimicry of the 'whinging bolshie Scouser', often sneered at by bourgeois detractors from the Home Counties, seemed an ever-ready stereotype permanently stamped onto the lexis of British popular culture. A perusal of press reports from the time documents factory occupations in Manchester, a number of wildcat strikes in Glasgow, urban unrest in Birmingham and revolts within the Greater London Council. However, for every dispatch reporting such incidents, there appeared many more pieces focusing instead on similar activities occurring in Liverpool.

This raises the question, was there something unique about Liverpool which would stoke more resentment, anger and passion into the fires of popular discontent during these turbulent years? Perhaps it was not just the intensity of resistance alone which marked out Liverpool as 'peculiar'. News accounts made it clear that the region was host to a whole gamut of protest, in which nearly every tactical form of dissent imaginable was utilised by a working class increasingly at odds with the modernity encapsulating a post-industrial existence.

Nevertheless, the enormous impact structural unemployment had on this community was in evidence for many years prior to the onslaught of mass de-industrialisation and the neoliberal settlement of Thatcherism. Indeed, statistics demonstrate that throughout the entire twentieth century Liverpool and the Merseyside region consistently experienced unemployment rates at twice the national level – in good times and in bad. Therefore, we must probe whether it was this protracted and painful familiarity with poverty, degradation and joblessness which propelled the working class of Liverpool into becoming the focal point of resistance to Thatcher's neoliberal policies, or if, indeed, the city was merely a convenient media target, ever ready to live up to the usual, tired stereotypes.

Liverpool has alternate themes from its past besides the persistent dilemma of chronic joblessness. Therefore, before drawing any conclusions about Liverpool's connections with working-class radicalism we must examine the role of competing identities other than that of class alone. For instance, the city's association with pre-war sectarianism between competing working-class tribes, coupled with Liverpool's powerful connections to Catholic Ireland have always marked the city as 'awkward' in comparison to other English provincial centres. In many ways Liverpool was more akin to Belfast or Glasgow than most typically 'English cities'.

What is certain is that by the 1980s it was not just the sheer volume of resistance to Thatcher's policies absorbing much of Liverpool's working class; rather, it was also the growing variety of tactics employed in organising these confrontations. Consequently, it can be said that in no other British city had the struggle against Thatcher's redundancies, closures and cuts taken on so many different hues of resistance as was demonstrated in late twentieth-century Liverpool.

In the following chapters several of these campaigns will be examined in further detail. We shall witness how dejected car workers, suffering the devastation of a plant closure, regrouped and railed against both trade union mandarins and the British establishment through reorganising the local branch of their former trade union as a means of mobilising Liverpool's unemployed. A number of significant movements arose from their efforts in politicising many of the area's redundant workforce, notably the establishment of the Transport and General Workers' Union, 6/612 Branch of the Unemployed.

A further chapter in this work will be dedicated to defining what sparked and sustained the Toxteth riots over the long hot summer of 1981. Questions need to be answered concerning what effect youth unemployment played in stoking the fires of resentment in this civil strife. It is especially poignant when one considers how the pains of joblessness provoked an alienated new generation of working-class youth with no visible structures of support or trade unions to turn to for advice and assistance. Dissecting the overarching factors behind this urban unrest will highlight the roles race and age now had as possible competing identities to class, and how such dynamics possibly altered previous conceptions of working-class consciousness.

Thatcher's backdoor use of local governmental structures as a means to enact some of her most unpopular economic policies will also be queried. It must be asked why it was Liverpool, once again, which defied convention and elected a radical-left Trotskyist controlled council in 1983 in order to counteract her government's agenda. Indeed, this was a council whose *raison d'être* was defying Thatcher's mandates of rate-capping and swingeing cuts on local government. Local government would never be the same in Liverpool after Derek Hatton and his followers took the reins of power. The underlying question remains, what provoked a local council once known more for sectarian divisions and parochial conservatism to become so radically leftist in outlook?

Examining this period of mass unemployment, when so many well-paid, unionised jobs haemorrhaged from the local Merseyside economy, questions arise whether self-interest could corrode and replace what remained of strict working-class solidarity. This point is explored in the case of striking shipyard workers at Cammell Laird Shipyards in Birkenhead, who not only defied their trade union bosses by occupying their worksite, but also battled with a large number of their workmates involving such issues as workplace sectionalism and bitter internal squabbles regarding redundancy pay. Such divisions provoke thoughts of whether individual self-interest had finally trumped solidarity at this point in the labour movement. Indeed, had the forward march of labour finally been halted by this point as Eric Hobsbawm prophesied?[1] Did so many of the cherished working-class values as solidarity and mutualism fade into the past, while people sought wider identities beyond the confines of class?

As Thatcherism blended into the ascent of New Labour – a period often seen as a time when trade union power had been almost entirely neutered – a question from Liverpool's docks asks why, then, would 500 ageing Liverpool dockworkers risk their pensions and seniority all for the sake of not crossing a picket line? What would prompt these 'dinosaurs' from a distant past to unfurl the old banners of trade union militancy, and insist on maintaining ties of solidarity with their striking comrades? Had Liverpool's rebellious dockers remained committed to the old working-class values of solidarity, mutuality, collectivism and political radicalism, while labour bosses elsewhere timidly signed on to the 'new reality'?

With these many questions in mind, it must be emphasised from the beginning that this analysis adopts a theoretical perspective loosely derived from the eminent historian E. P. Thompson and his writings on class and class-consciousness. In contrast to previous economic histories of the period concerning the Industrial Revolution, which had treated 'labour' or the 'working class' in an abstract fashion, as victims acted upon by inexorable economic forces, Thompson famously focused his work on rescuing industrialisation's 'losers', such as handloom weavers or poor stockingers, from 'the enormous condescension of posterity'.

The overarching thesis of Thompson's seminal work, *The Making of the English Working Class*, contested notions of working-class passivity and inserted human agency into the heart of the raw process of industrialisation. Thompson insisted that far from being pliant bystanders subject to the decisions of economic and political elites, the English working class was an active participant in its own 'making'. In an intellectual masterpiece of 'history from below', he recreated the complex occupational and political subcultures of opposition that culminated in a pervasive sense of working-class consciousness by 1832.[2]

Thompson's work has been subject to extensive elaboration, emulation and critique. His critics argued, with varying degrees of justification, that his work focused on radical labour elites at the expense of other plebeian groups who retained loyalty to the monarchy and Church. Critics also point to Thompson's flawed emphasis on class homogeneity and his neglect of ethnic and sectional divisions, gender bias and ethnocentrism, as well as a romantic view of cultural agency that underestimated structural constraints.

Allowing for such criticisms and despite the chronological distance between Thompson's opus and this study, his framework retains significant resonance for the subject of this analysis. If it has become commonplace among labour historians to proffer that the working class was an agent in its own making during industrialisation, it is equally plausible to argue that it displayed similar qualities of active resistance as it was seemingly becoming 'unmade' during the years of de-industrialisation. Thus, in the following chapters, the unemployed docker, the redundant car worker, the jobless youth are not portrayed merely as victims of the Thatcherite transformation of Britain's industrial economy. Indeed, it is their understanding of, and ultimately, their reaction to these ever more deteriorating conditions which lies at the heart of their humanity.

In the spirit of Thompson, an emphasis should be made of how groups of workers on Merseyside creatively responded to the predicaments of unemployment with their own set of strategies and sense of social agency. It must be examined if these people responded to increasing joblessness and growing penury by drawing on pre-existing concepts of justice, equity and solidarity. The same values, of course, which had been instilled in many of them from a long established culture and a history made by their predecessors. Nevertheless, taking account of the critiques of Thompson, this study recognises the need to go beyond the experience of white, male, unionised workers to embrace what women, ethnic minorities and unorganised groups did in their collective response to permanent redundancy, and locate the strategic choices they made within the prevailing material conditions. Indeed, it is not assumed that women were automatically absorbed into the same notion of working-class experience as men. Therefore, the gendering of class-consciousness and how women came to understand the economic changes associated with the neoliberal turn will also be explored within the context of the case studies examined.

A final word must be included regarding the methodology employed in this research. Given that much of this study involves an investigation into contemporary and local events, little historiographical work has been written thus far on a number of the topics addressed. Moreover, some of the developments examined in the chapters that follow left no written records. Therefore, it was decided to embark on an extensive network of oral interviews, often involving many of the principal activists involved in the campaigns examined.

The use of oral testimony in itself presents its own set of problems recognisable to most historians who deal in contemporary topics. Personal biases from the interviewee and indeed the questioner, along with the inaccuracies of interpretation and the often unreliable recollections associated with memory, are a few of the most common problems related to corroborating historical evidence. Critics may point to the subjectivity of oral history, but its use as a source has undeniably added to the wealth of interpreting the past, particularly in 'histories from below', and as a vehicle of expression for those in the past who were 'hidden from history'. Oral history often proves to be a valuable means in recovering agency, which is a principal focus of this study. In addition, this method of enquiry provides an intimacy with the past, as it allows both the interviewee and the historian to participate in the formation of the historical narrative, thus democratising to some extent the interpretation of events studied. Indeed, a number of the quotations herein were so vivid, they spoke for themselves. It somehow did not seem fitting to needlessly step on their words with further interpolations and unrequired explanations from the narrator unless further clarification was necessary.

However, whilst this research relied on a fairly wide use of face-to-face interviews from historical actors, it should not be considered a strict study in oral history, per se. The interviews were employed in order to illuminate areas where other sources were either not available or questionable regarding their factual accuracy. Nevertheless, it is not asserted anywhere in this work that these interviews are intended to be a representative sample.

Time progresses and in the post-2008 market-crash era we now have the proper perspective and distance to reflect on those pivotal final twenty-five years of the twentieth century. Did the English working class really crawl off and die after the loss of the Miners' Strike in 1985? Perhaps the English working class was not killed off by the forces of Thatcher and unfettered global capital, but was merely transformed from an industrial-based collective to a more servile pool of hands – still working class, albeit no longer dressed in blue collars and employed in factories, but now kitted-up in polyester uniform shirts emblazed with garish corporate logos, working long hours in supermarkets, warehouses and call-centres.

The following pages cannot directly answer that question, but this work will seek to understand why Liverpool took such a leading role in the battle against the forces of global capital in the last quarter of the twentieth century, and why this resistance occurred here with such passion. In order to proceed further we must establish what made Liverpool such a magnet for confrontation.

Notes

1 Eric Hobsbawm, 'The Forward March of Labour Halted', *Marxism Today*, September 1978, pp. 279–86.
2 E. P. Thompson, *The Making of the English Working Class* (New York, 1966).

1

Unravelling of the post-war consensus and the peculiarities of Liverpool

No other city portrays the economic malaise and industrial unrest troubling Britain in the last quarter of the twentieth century more poignantly than Liverpool. This city and the surrounding Merseyside region had frequently been prone to labour strife since the dawn of organised labour. However, it was the emergence of Thatcherism and the ascent of neoliberal economics which placed Liverpool at the forefront of national protest against the encroaching tide of unfettered, free-market capitalism, swingeing cuts in public spending, privatisation of public services and the loss of British manufacturing. The spectre of spiralling unemployment was arguably the most pervasive feature which encapsulated the political economy and social fabric of Liverpool in the last three decades of the twentieth century. Consequently, it can be proffered that in this period joblessness and economic deprivation blighted Liverpool more than any other major British conurbation.

A perusal of archival sources chronicling reports from leading national news agencies illustrates this contention. Evidence of industrial unrest, public demonstrations, workplace occupations, civil strife and political protest can be found almost anywhere in Britain throughout the 1980s, but press reports seemingly focus on Liverpool specifically whenever public dissent was vented. Obviously, an empirical study examining the amount of protest occurring in which cities with the highest magnitude would be a difficult if not impossible task. This is especially true when one considers the major body of evidence available for such a study would have to be taken directly from media sources.

A more detailed comparative analysis will be addressed in the forthcoming chapters. Nevertheless, a brief insight from the archives of a leading national broadsheet show that during the same final twenty-five-year period of the twentieth century when Liverpool's unemployed were becoming further politicised and mobilised, an attempt to organise the unemployed in Sheffield was also afoot.[1] Unfortunately the effort in

South Yorkshire failed in this instance, whereas in Liverpool it flourished. Indeed, there were also dispatches of factory occupations and sit-ins in Manchester, Bathgate and Preston during this time.[2] Local council workers in Coventry attempted to close off public services in protest at wage and job cuts, just as had been accomplished in Liverpool.[3] Nevertheless, the industrial action in Coventry did not result in the local council adopting a revolutionary platform of self-induced bankruptcy as had occurred in Liverpool.

Over 50,000 workers marched in Glasgow against rising joblessness, but some press reports made note of a lingering sense of apathy, despite the large turnout. They also painted a picture of suspicion from rank-and-file workers of their leadership who were 'strong on rhetoric' but lacking in details of how they planned to bring back full employment.[4] Amongst these notices there were a number of pieces criticising the unusual degree of worker indifference present during this period, with headlines such as 'Why the unemployed are not in revolt', 'March for jobs against apathy', 'A generation fuelled by apathy' and 'Bitterness, resignation and dwindling hope', to name only a few.

It is interesting, however, that the lion's share of articles focusing on working-class militancy within Liverpool at this time make little mention or hints of a similar sense of resignation and defeat.[5] Indeed, one piece plays into the 'cheeky chappy Scouser' stereotype in a report of how some 1,200 soon-to-be idled workers from Liverpool's Tate & Lyle sugar refinery burst into a rousing rendition of 'We shall not be moved' as a sign of their refusal to accept job losses and the plant's closure.[6] Typically, this overly caricatured portrayal of Liverpool in the national media was more common than not. Therefore, when judging the militancy of the region's workforce, press reports alone do not offer the full insight necessary that such a comparative analysis requires.

Furthermore, there is no doubt that the policies of the Thatcher government and the corresponding de-industrialisation of the British economy had an enormous impact on working class communities in every British city. This analysis would never claim otherwise. However, it will note that Liverpool's unique history made it particularly vulnerable to such changes, and because of this, the working class of Liverpool reacted against this further intensification of capitalism in a particularly vocal and aggressive manner when compared to plebeian elements in other provincial British cities.

The central concern of this book will be an analysis of the range and depth of organised reaction from large segments of Liverpool's working class to the many forced redundancies, factory closures and sweeping government cuts in this era of post-industrial decline. It is centred in a time when the neoliberal economic model and Thatcher's own brand of monetarism were pursued by the British establishment as an elixir for what many saw as a failed experiment in cross-party consensus during the immediate post-war era, culminating in thirty years of a welfare state and Britain's first and only dalliance with social democracy.

Neoliberalism emerges as a challenge to the post-war settlement

The battle lines between the forces of collectivism and the proponents of the free market had been drawn long before the ascension of Margaret Thatcher as leader of the Conservative Party in 1975. By the late 1980s, with the fracturing of the left and the neutering of the trade unions it became obvious that neoliberalism had won that war. The political right's campaign against forces supporting collectivism and social democracy was a long-lasting crusade, and Liverpool often found itself to be in the centre of that conflict.

Nevertheless, the clash between capitalism and socialism, between supporters of the free market versus those who advocated a mixed economy, simmered long before it finally exploded in 1979 with the election of the Tories under Margaret Thatcher. The great ideologies of this struggle were represented through the writings of such economic luminaries as Friedrich Hayek on the right, and John Maynard Keynes representing the centre-left. For the first thirty years of the post-war era, it was Keynes who held the upper hand in both British and American politics.

By 1945, after suffering for over three decades from the horrors of two global wars and the destitution of the Great Depression, even 'conservative' Britain coveted a radical transformation from the past. The inter-war slump taught many within the British establishment that capitalism had its limits, just as they learned through the war about the positive benefits gained through state planning, collectivism and collaborating with labour. After the peace, most British political leaders recognised that a level of consensus was necessary in order for Britain to rebuild itself, even if that included working within a mixed economy. Maintaining efficient levels of production, balance of payments and industrial output were, of course, key factors if a post-war rebuilding programme had any chance of success.

It was without precedent, but there was at this time majority support for a planned commitment to full employment. It was vowed that work for every hand was to be considered as much a priority for the labouring classes, as profit was for capital. Government would take the bold step of intervening against market forces, if necessary, to ensure such full employment. The election of a Labour government in 1945 inaugurated this arrangement. What followed was thirty years of cross-party commitment towards social democracy, the welfare state and a mutual acceptance of the mixed economy. The arrangement that emerged in 1945 not only pledged full employment as a priority, but there were also provisions made for a national health service, limited public ownership of certain key industries and some semblance of centralised economic planning. A promise to reduce the old vestiges of class privilege also took on a new level of importance.

Trade unions were granted an important role within the new post-war plan. Trade union leaders were included in the decision-making process of economic policy, and their input was sought by both Labour and Tory governments. The security of full employment lent greater autonomy to local trade union branches, and ultimately, more shop-floor democracy via the empowerment of shop stewards – the lowest ranking union official, but nevertheless the face of trade unionism on the factory floor.

From 1945 to 1979, both Labour and Conservative governments would introduce legislation periodically, which diverted or removed the will of market forces. Keynesianism became the prevailing orthodoxy of the period. Unlike Marx, Keynes did not advocate an alternative to capitalism. Indeed, for Keynes the problem was not capitalism itself, but simply 'laissez-faire' capitalism. It was his belief that unregulated markets had the potential to destroy capitalism if they were left to the selfish pursuit of profit without any care for the rest of society. Keynes' belief in the need for 'responsible capitalism' was entrenched in his opus *The General Theory of Employment, Interest, and Money*.[7] Most trade union leaders, often having to answer to the concerns of both sitting governments in Westminster and their rank-and-file, were satisfied with the post-war arrangement and found Keynesianism a tolerable form of controlled capitalism.

Friedrich Hayek, however, in his pivotal work *The Road to Serfdom*, posed a counterpoint to this arrangement.[8] Rather than controlling markets, Hayek insisted the market must be unchained and left to the free-flowing natural order of the 'invisible hand'. Hayek maintained that it was government meddling in the money supply which increased inflation and depressed corporate profits. According to Hayek all such diversions distorted the market, leading to a continuous crisis of boom and bust, built largely on fictitious capital.

However, just as many on the British left were wary of the absolute dictums of pure Marxism, opting instead for the mixed, social-democratic approach of Keynes, the political right in the UK preferred Hayek only in half-measures. More important to the shaping of neoliberalism, as it metastasized itself in Britain, were the lessons of the Nobel Prize winning economist Professor Milton Friedman, and his circle of followers from the University of Chicago. It was not until the early 1970s when the work of Friedman came into vogue amongst the British right. And only then did neoliberal economic theory gain a sizable momentum in the UK.

The term neoliberal became synonymous with the teachings proffered by Friedman and his colleagues in Chicago. Like Hayek, Friedman and his associates at the University of Chicago extolled the freedom of the individual, they advocated free trade, demanded deregulated markets, celebrated entrepreneurial pursuits, believed in heightened privatisation of public services and less government involvement in personal space. They rejected collectivism in most forms and scorned 'entitlements' and the fostering of a 'dependency culture'. However, unlike Hayek, Friedman and the Chicago School believed the government needed to maintain a role in regulating the central bank and money supply. The Chicago School argued inflation was far more devastating to capital than unemployment. It, therefore, had to be harnessed at all costs: even if that meant sacrificing struggling industries and well-paid blue-collar jobs. In their view, any government that obligated itself to maintaining full employment was part of the problem, not the solution.

The neoliberal model, while radically libertarian in some respects, still derived much of its strength through a veneration for traditional structures such as a strong military presence and strict maintenance of law and order. Combined with a pragmatic approach towards increasing corporate yield, neoliberal ideology ingratiated itself with conservative movements, searching for ways to adapt to the changing nature of the modern world. It promised greater corporate revenues while simultaneously stoking the fires of traditionalism on one hand and individualism on the other.

Furthermore, committed neoliberals argued that allowing the market free rein, unencumbered by government regulation and human manipulation, was the only way to guarantee the economic freedom necessary that could procure political democracy and civil liberty on a global level. Encouraging words, indeed, to many staunch Cold War warriors and corporate chieftains alike. Thus, it was Friedman, and not necessarily Hayek, who won the heart of Tory politicians on the growing right-wing of the Conservative Party such as Sir Keith Joseph and Margaret Thatcher. Neoliberalism was sold to voters by equating its ideals with such cherished Anglo-American values as liberty, individualism and patriotism.

Historians of the Thatcher era have proffered that neoliberalism evolved in Britain through a series of distinct stages.[9] Originally, the ideas tendered by Hayek served more as an oppositional philosophical argument to Keynesianism and the evolving post-war consensus, rather than as a strict structural system of administrative governance. However, by the early 1970s as economic volatility grew more apparent due to embedded inflation becoming aberrantly paired with mounting unemployment, Keynesian measures proved unresponsive.

The 1973–75 recession officially put an end to the post-war economic boom. It differed from previous economic slumps as it introduced a sense of malaise when most Western economies were lumbered by both chronic levels of high inflation and escalating unemployment. A new word came into the lexicon describing this phenomenon: *stagflation*. Prior to this period, Keynesianism had been a proven means for making capitalism function.

The seeming ineffectiveness of Keynesianism to correct this imbalance was a sign that not only had the days of consensus waned, but that the 'golden age' of British trade unionism was also coming to the end of its thirty-year run. More often than not, trade unions were portrayed by the media and political elites from all parties as the problem behind inflation and not the solution. Industrial action in the form of non-sanctioned, wildcat strikes was the common response to escalating consumer prices. British trade unions had become more decentralised as a result of the commitment to full employment. This devolvement has been cited as one of the main catalysts behind the increase in shop-floor activism.[10]

The 1973–75 recession is attributed to several factors, including: the 1973 Arab Oil Embargo, a crisis in corporate profit accumulation, growing imbalances in global trade, increasing dependence on foreign investment, and most notably the abandonment of the Bretton Woods Agreement, which had previously fixed exchange rates and provided for the institution of the World Bank and the International Monetary Fund (IMF). The most recognisable manifestations of this economic slump were high inflation and the corresponding labour unrest which is often associated with rising prices and lagging wages. Mainstream Keynesian methods that would customarily be applied to correct such instabilities proved futile.

The second stage in the growing evolution toward neoliberalism came in March 1976, when rising inflation and a flagging economy forced a Labour government under James Callaghan to seek a multi-billion pound bail-out from the IMF. The much-needed loan came at a high price, however, as the IMF insisted that the British government cut inflation through a system of mandated austerity, wage controls and an overall tightening of the money supply. While not necessarily pure neoliberalism, per se, a strict application of a proto-monetarism was enacted. Fierce resistance from the trade unions made most of the provisions mandated by the IMF unworkable under a Labour government. The now infamous 'Winter of Discontent' of 1978–79, and subsequent crisis in governance which followed, led to the call for elections in May 1979.

Conventional neoliberalism came to Britain, of course, with the 1979 election of the Conservatives under Margaret Thatcher. The commitment to full employment, which had been a mainstay of the political fabric of Britain for nearly thirty-five years, was dropped in favour of a form of crude monetarism. However, it must be asserted that during the 'age of Thatcher', strict neoliberalism did not reveal itself all at once. Rather, its doctrine slid into view incrementally. It was introduced piecemeal and cunningly at any opportunity when Thatcher smelled weakness on the part of the trade unions or the old left. Nevertheless, Thatcher was restrained in her spread of neoliberal reforms by the weather vane of British public opinion. As committed as she was to relieving the Conservative Party of its paternalistic tendencies, the realities of democracy meant that even the grocer's daughter from Grantham had to adopt calculating patience and plan her revolution one step at a time. She would expunge most of the old, One Nation Tory 'wets' from positions of power, one by one, after she consolidated her power with the landslide Conservative victory in 1983.

Trade unions were seen as an impairment to completing the neoliberal project. Many on the right within the Conservative Party were still seething from the upturn in strike activity throughout the 1970s, and the seeming inability of previous governments, both Labour and Tory, to suppress rampant shop-floor militancy. Thatcher took lessons from Friedman *et al.* regarding trade unions. She not only regarded them infamously as 'the enemy within', but the single largest deterrent to economic recovery.

Trade unions were portrayed as unnecessary obstructions restricting management's right to operate in a system predicated on a free market. Neoliberals painted politicians still committed to full employment as servants to the trade unions and not the politics of liberty. They argued that such an allegiance resulted in a closed-shop economy, whereby unions dictated through strikes, which in turn, led to the escalating wage increases at artificial levels that resulted in the rocketing inflation of the 1970s. Consequently, the closed shop was essentially outlawed under successive Tory governments by way of a series of Employment Acts enacted between 1980 and 1993. The power behind British trade unions in the post-war years was heavily dependent on the state. Once the state distanced itself from trade unionism – or as some would say, was openly hostile towards the unions – most union leaders saw no other option but to retreat and capitulate to the 'new realism' of the times.

Widespread market deregulation and the catastrophic levels of joblessness associated with de-industrialisation during this period did much to sap the strength out of the trade union movement. Some dared to fight back, such as the miners in 1984–85, but most trade union leaders felt defenceless against the harsh penalties incurred if they made any attempt to violate the recently enacted Employment Acts. For the first time, union bosses were made personally financially liable for the actions of their members. Consequently, much of the trade union establishment felt the costs of organised resistance were not worth the venture.

Nevertheless, it is often argued that the success monetarism had in slashing inflation brought life back into the economy of Britain. While old industries such as steel and motor car manufacturing were decimated, financial services, banking, property management and the retail sector boomed. Much of this success, however, was restricted to London and the Home Counties, while the old industrial north of England, Scotland, Ulster and Wales were devastated by the loss of their dependent local industrial base. Many on the right argue that the success of their policies can be illustrated by the fact that Conservative governments were repeatedly elected into office from 1979 until 1997. On the other hand, critics of the neoliberal project pointed to a widening gap of inequality, the loss of basic heavy industries and jobs, the increase in social alienation, the decline in social harmony, as well as the shallow materialism brought forth by its proclivity for seedy consumerism and a misplaced worship of the individual.

Despite these obvious flaws, succeeding Labour governments subscribed to many of Thatcher's neoliberal reforms, making this era when the world was supposedly undergoing 'the end of history' into yet another stage of Britain's break from post-war social democracy.[11] The deconstruction of the welfare state steadily continued with New Labour under the leadership of both Tony Blair and Gordon Brown, proving that neoliberalism had become, and still remains, the orthodoxy of British political economy, despite the rising challenges it is currently facing at a grassroots level.

British trade unionism in the post-war era

The 1970s unleashed the intertwining of two potent forces into the British economy, both of which had a monumental impact on much of Liverpool's working class. The first was the rise and fall of militant trade unionism, particularly through the rapid growth and the eventual emasculation in authority of sectional shop stewards. Coinciding with, and intimately related to, this waning of shop-floor power was the de-industrialisation of the British economy. The decline of manufacturing in the 1980s resulted in the most drastic loss of employment since the Great Depression of the 1930s. This trend had an especially negative impact on those engaged in unskilled and semi-skilled manual employment in the manufacturing sector – the traditional mainstay of the British working class.

The shop steward had emerged as the most influential cog in the machinery of British industrial politics in the immediate post-war era. Most authorities attribute the rise in their influence to the increase in shop-floor bargaining power, brought about through the aid of full employment during the Second World War and the post-war boom.[12] During the post-war years, steady growth in production levels was of paramount importance, and managers found it more expedient to negotiate locally on work conditions and grievances in the face of unofficial sanctions. By the late 1960s, the new-found strength of workplace trade union activism had become a central issue in Britain's domestic politics.

Lord Donovan's Royal Commission on trade unions and employers' associations in 1968 famously suggested there were 'two systems' operating in the arena of British industrial relations.[13] The 'formal system', involving national negotiations on an industry-wide level, was in conflict with a pervasive 'informal system' in the workplace, determined by sectional shop stewards and their immediate supervisors. The resulting upward 'wage drift' was said to have helped fuel inflation and fundamentally undermined government attempts at setting incomes policies. Lord Donovan's commission recommended formalising the informal practices through the voluntary codification of workplace procedures and the extension of plant and company-level bargaining.

Accepting Lord Donovan's diagnosis, successive governments sought to reform industrial relations via legislative means. In 1969, Labour's Secretary of State for Employment, Barbara Castle, introduced and then withdrew her ill-fated White Paper, *In Place of Strife*, in face of union resistance to 'penal clauses' such as 'cooling off' periods and pre-strike ballots.[14] Subsequently, Edward Heath's Conservative government introduced the wide-ranging Industrial Relations Act, 1971, which outlawed unofficial strikes. Faced with a wave of industrial unrest in 1972, the Act soon became a dead letter. The return of a Labour government in 1974 witnessed a more sophisticated attempt at managing the 'union problem' via a neo-corporatist strategy.

Labour's 'Social Contract' offered trade unions enhanced legal rights in exchange for cooperation with wage restraint, a burden that was enforced most stringently and disproportionately on public sector workers. While shop stewards had been initially rooted in the manufacturing industry, notably engineering, car making and shipbuilding, the effects of price inflation, incomes policy and more supportive legislation during the mid-1970s encouraged the growth of shop stewards' power throughout the public sector.

In the face of a decline in real wages, the inherently unstable corporatist bargain of the Social Contract broke down in a wave of public sector strikes during the 'Winter of Discontent' of 1978–79. It is uniformly acknowledged that Margaret Thatcher's withdrawal of the Conservative Party from the post-war consensus of full employment and state intervention in industry to free-market liberalism marked a sea change in British politics and economic policy.[15]

This shift had profound consequences for British workers and their trade unions through the successive implementation of increasingly restrictive legislation directed against union activities. These new legal restraints were coupled with a severe recession and escalating unemployment in the first half of the 1980s. This process culminated in Thatcher's long civil war against Britain's miners. Although coal mines and colliers were largely absent from Merseyside, the outcome of the Miners' Strike of 1984–85 symbolised a major political defeat for organised labour in Britain, including trade unionists in Liverpool, where workers were experiencing levels of joblessness at this time unknown since the 1930s.

Nevertheless, it was not just politics that drove a stake through the heart of trade union militancy. Creeping de-industrialisation had been slowly infiltrating most Western economies since the close of the Second World War. Largely fuelled by intense foreign competition and an ever-increasing demand from company shareholders for larger profits, under-investment in British industry became the norm, as production moved offshore to developing nations where labour costs were a fraction of those in Western economies. The shift in economic policy towards neoliberal objectives directly contributed to the collapse of key sectors in Britain's manufacturing industry and resulted in an epidemic of long-term unemployment. This particularly affected working-class males in traditional manufacturing regions such as the north of England, Clydeside in Scotland and South Wales. The end result of these policies was a mass reduction in blue-collar employment, coupled with a weakening of organised labour and the political left.

The de-industrialisation of many Western nations had been looming in the shadows since the close of the Second World War, and this fact became obvious in the United States and Britain by the mid-1970s. Industrial output in the United Kingdom had increased by approximately 30 per cent per decade since the 1930s, but by the mid-1960s manufacturing production began to show marked annual fluctuations. Industrial production peaked in 1973; from this year onward there was a steady and significant decline. Employment in manufacturing peaked in 1966, but by 1970 it stood at 97 per cent of the 1966 figure. In 1973 British manufacturing employment was 91 per cent of that figure, and by 1979 it was only 84 per cent. Between 1979 and 1982, the numbers employed in manufacturing dropped from 7,197,000 to 5,776,000 – a 20 per cent reduction in three years. In 1984, Britain's manufacturing employment was a mere 67 per cent of the 1966 total.

While UK manufacturing employment had diminished since 1966, the full scale of this decline did not become fully apparent until the late 1970s, as unemployment increased to the point where other sectors of the economy could not absorb the enormous loss in jobs. This period of economic gloom in the industrial heartlands of northern England ran parallel to an emerging boom in the service sector percolating through south-eastern England, particularly in London and the Home Counties. The north–south divide became increasingly apparent as parts of the nation suffered immensely, while other areas felt much less impact from the 1980s recession.

By the late 1970s and early 1980s, many of those affected by plant closures and redundancies understood that unionised, well-compensated manufacturing jobs were gone forever, permanently altering a whole way of life for a large segment of the British population. Observers reflected that even in the darkest days of the Great Depression there was some hope for the future, considering that while the jobs may have disappeared, at least the industry remained. By the 1980s, however, it was clear that both jobs and industries had left permanently.[16]

The rise of Thatcherism brought a change in political priorities. Maintaining low inflation coupled with reduced public spending – particularly for revenues earmarked for social welfare programmes, public housing and education – was deemed more important than job creation. The consequences of Thatcher's election in May 1979 finally ended the cross-party consensus based on Keynesian economic solutions. Thatcher inherited a nation which she saw as bloated, inefficient and suffocating private industry to death with burdensome taxes. One commentator observed:

> If the problem was obvious then so, too, for Mrs. Thatcher and her acolytes, were the solutions. These were based as much upon the petty

> bourgeois experience of the Conservative leader, upon her prejudices and 'feelings', as upon her intellectual sugar-coating by the works of Hayek and Friedman.[17]

As a fierce proponent of the free market, Thatcher believed in survival of the fittest when it came to British business, especially manufacturing. It was her belief that Britain had to compete on the world stage, and if Britain's manufacturing sector could not cope, then it deserved to die.

According to Thatcher, the root of Britain's inability to compete was the low level of worker productivity, which in her opinion was proof that the trade unions had grown far too powerful. The former prime minister wrote in her memoirs:

> In spite of what might seem the more immediate and pressing problems of strikes, price competitiveness, and international recession, the root of Britain's industrial problems was low productivity ... The overmanning resulting from trade union restrictive practices was concealed unemployment; and beyond a certain point – certainly beyond the point we had reached in 1979 – overmanning would bring down businesses and destroy existing jobs, and abort those which otherwise could have flourished. Outdated and old jobs have to go to make the most of new opportunities.[18]

Her policies were implemented during an era when the global marketplace was becoming increasingly competitive. They culminated, some would argue, as the British economy was suffering two of the most severe recessions of the post-war era. Other observers have maintained that her abolition of the exchange controls resulted in a substantial amount of British investment leaving the country. Total net external assets rocketed from £10 billion in 1978 to over £70 billion in 1984. These same commentators also contend her policies only nurtured large, multinational conglomerates, while smaller, less prosperous British concerns were neglected and left to die. They argue that Thatcher sold out British manufacturing so City bankers could make economic windfalls.[19]

Nevertheless, many of these same critics conclude that Thatcherism was a product of Britain's industrial decline, rather than the catalyst for it. Britain's industrial deterioration had been apparent long before Thatcher, but they argue her policies intensified the demise of British manufacturing rather than acting as a vehicle to engender greater productivity.[20]

Liverpool's peculiar labour history

The most prevailing facet of Merseyside's economic history in the post-war era was undoubtedly unemployment. Nevertheless, joblessness did not arrive abruptly on Merseyside at the close of the Second World War. The uniqueness of Liverpool's history and location helped launch dramatic cycles of boom and bust, which left an indelible imprint on the city's character. Two of the more important elements to shape the city's outlook for many years were its ties to the sea, and the hardship wrought from the Irish famine.

Liverpool was first and foremost a port city, a place where goods and people from around the world passed through its docks. This maritime tradition gave a more cosmopolitan character to Liverpool when compared to other provincial British cities. Consequently, it is often said that Liverpudlians see themselves more as citizens of the world rather than as denizens of a nation. A fierce belief coalescing ideas of class equality, democracy and a curiosity about the outside world ingrained itself in the minds of many working-class Liverpudlians.

For generations Liverpool's harbour was the region's principal economic driver. This maritime tradition brought with it employment that was mainly casual in nature. Dockers could only work when ships were berthed, and mariners only sailed when voyages were contracted. This lack of stability translated into long stretches of unemployment and underemployment and were accepted as part of the natural tide of life. It was this dependence on the port which primarily determined the city's economic fortunes.

During the nineteenth century, when other British cities participated in the Industrial Revolution, Liverpool's economy failed to diversify. Even as late as the Second World War, the city echoed the rhythms of eighteenth-century maritime life. At its height, Liverpool's port provided direct employment for perhaps as many as 60,000 people.[21] Besides dock work and seafaring, other major employers included such related trades as those firms specialising in the maintenance and repair of ocean-going vessels, as well as wholesalers and suppliers that catered to the needs of the shipping industry. Liverpool's dependence on transportation and commerce as its primary economic activity remained until after the Second World War when the decline of Empire and the rise in trade with Europe placed Liverpool in a detrimental position, both geographically and economically.

Combined with Liverpool's long attachment to the sea, it is the Irish famine of the mid-nineteenth century which also has been cited as having the greatest impact on creating the city's peculiar character. The city was

Britain's main port of entry for hundreds of thousands of wretchedly poor Irish immigrants. The inheritance of this diaspora remains very much in evidence in the surnames and the faces of Liverpool's modern-day inhabitants. This mass Irish exodus helped carve out a unique identity for Liverpool amongst other British cities. No other British city experienced a level of Irish migration greater than Liverpool, including both Manchester and London. Indeed, by 1851 it is reported that 22 per cent of all people residing in Liverpool were Irish born. The only other British city with levels anywhere near Liverpool was Glasgow, where 18 per cent of its inhabitants reported being of Irish birth.[22]

The sheer number of destitute migrants arriving on its shores in such a relatively short period of time overwhelmed the region's social infrastructure, and this had long-term consequence into the twentieth century. One writer observed:

> The aftermath of the Irish famine brought a set of social problems which have never really disappeared despite the passing of over a hundred years ... Perhaps, had even one generation on Merseyside experienced a genuine, sustained boom in its wealth-creating activities, the legacy of 'social deficit' stretching back to the middle of the last [nineteenth] century could have been broken.[23]

Subsequently, dependence on a maritime economy and the lingering effects of an enormous influx of poor, unskilled and largely illiterate immigrants meant that even during the best of times Liverpool was never a stranger to joblessness and abject poverty.

Accordingly, a case for 'Liverpool exceptionalism' has been brought forward by Professor John Belchem of the University of Liverpool. While this theory has been contested, particularly by historians of Empire, Belchem has made several valid arguments. He carries this notion one step further with arguments of a sense of Liverpool and 'Scouse' separateness from the rest of mainstream British society in two important works: an edited collection, *Merseypride: Essays in Liverpool Exceptionalism*, and his monograph, *Irish, Catholic and Scouse*.[24]

Belchem was one of the earliest proponents of the idea that Liverpool was in many ways different, or more appropriately, 'exceptional', to the rhythms of life as experienced in most other provincial English locales. Whereas previous historians have argued it was Liverpool's ties to the sea and its reliance on the Empire for trade which separated it and gave the city its sense of difference from the other British locales, Belchem mainly relies on the Irish diaspora of the mid-nineteenth century as the principal catalyst which separated Liverpool and Liverpudlians from a strong identity with Britishness.

Belchem introduced the notion that Irish migration was so fundamental to Liverpool that the city took on an almost 'American flavour', like that of a Boston or a New York. He has gone on to argue that while the Irish may have migrated to other English cities, notably Manchester, Liverpool's Irish ghettoised and formed a separate and independent community by virtue of the sheer magnitude of their numbers, thus, in time, challenging the native Lancastrian element, and dwarfing other immigrant groups such as the Welsh or Scots. In contrast to Liverpool, Belchem argues, the Irish element in Manchester underwent 'ethnic fade' and eventually blended into the local population. They had never formed a distinct and rival sectarian community in Manchester, as was the case in Liverpool. It was because Irish Catholics came to Liverpool in such overwhelming numbers that reluctance – some would argue, a refusal – to assimilate into the host culture led to a self-enclosed, self-sufficient Irish Catholic constituency. This sense of dissimilarity, Belchem maintains, eventually spread beyond the Irish Catholic dockland communities of Liverpool's Northend to other working-class areas throughout the city. With this culture came a fierce sense of independence, a lack of deference to the Crown and an overall insistence on questioning the establishment.

Consequently, one can conclude that it was less the immigrant Catholic Irish who assimilated, became Anglicised and eventually succumbed to 'ethnic fade'; rather, it was the native British working class whose attitudes became *Hibernicised* to some degree and, accordingly, along with the docklands Irish, forged a unique 'Scouse' character, so distinct from typical portraits of the northern English working class in general. Therefore, it is this sense of separateness, or some would argue marginalisation, from the larger British identity, Belchem argues, which manifested itself into a notion of Liverpool exceptionalism. Exceptionalism, meaning apart or distinct, but not in any sense superior. The city of Liverpool and its Scouse inhabitants were somehow different from a typical vision of northern working-class existence, not better or worse, merely 'different'.

Belchem's research, while dealing with an earlier period than that of this study, develops further convincing arguments that it was the Irish diaspora following the mid-nineteenth-century famine which gave Liverpool its unique character and its sense of 'us versus the rest' parochialism. He posits that it was the overwhelming shadow of Irish Catholicism that made Liverpool different from Britain's other maritime centres such as Bristol and Southampton. The influx of poor, destitute, Irish Catholic immigrants also altered the city's political culture, creating both right-wing attitudes and a system of 'bossism' constructed upon political patronage. While it fostered a sense of alienation from Britain and 'the British', it also drove an enduring demand for social and economic justice. Belchem's works are valuable in drawing parallels and contrasts between local ethnic insularity and trade union militancy. They also highlight the intense solidarity apparent on Merseyside at certain points during the twentieth century, despite signs that sectarian bigotry persisted at least until the Second World War.

Prior to the Second World War several authors have posited that because of widespread sectarianism and a gerrymandered local electoral process, the Victorian and Edwardian working class in Liverpool could only effectively engage in politics through riot and mob violence rather than peaceful protest. This tendency could also be seen as a foundation stone of what eventually developed in the later twentieth century, as a pervasive local culture that celebrated resistance and trade union radicalism.[25]

Liverpool's penchant for workplace militancy is, of course, well documented. Politically speaking, however, Liverpool's conversion to the Labour cause came remarkably late, compared with other northern cities.[26] This late shift in political allegiances was caused by a local political system riddled with abnormalities that were ingrained into the electoral administrative apparatus. It has been argued that this, coupled with the city's unique demographic patterns, is what blocked Labour's growth locally. Only after many years in the wilderness did Labour finally assume control of Liverpool Town Hall in 1955.

Elements of the historiography attribute Labour's late bloom in Liverpool to religious sectarianism and ethnic differences amongst the local working-class electorate. Previously, it had been generally accepted that deep factions within the local party had retarded Labour's growth on Merseyside. It has also been advanced that a strong right-wing Catholic element was the dominant force in Liverpool's local Labour Party prior to the Second World War, which often put the local organisation at odds with national party leaders. Therefore, the local party was factionalised, pitting the dominant conservative Catholic group against a more moderate socialist, Protestant strand, made up largely of skilled trade unionists, whose base was primarily in the city's Southend wards (see Figure 2 for Liverpool's wards and their boundaries). It should be noted that there was also a small but vocal left-wing element in Walton on the Northend of the city, but they were largely marginalised and mistrusted by the two larger factions because of suspected Trotskyist influence.

Other historians of Liverpool politics attribute Labour's local weakness less to sectarian factors and more to a local electoral system tied to practices of the nineteenth century.[27] They cite local election codes that were peculiar to pre-war Liverpool which gave an unfair advantage to the Tories. This resulted in an entrenched political culture unique to Liverpool, which has a long history of bossism more akin to Mayor Daley's Chicago than Joseph Chamberlain's Birmingham. It was an authoritarian style of governance that permeated Town Hall politics, no matter which party, faction or sect was in power.

This study, while sympathetic to much of the scholarship advanced by Belchem and others who advocate the case for 'Liverpool exceptionalism', is less concerned with the prevailing pre-war ethnic and religious identities amongst Liverpool's working class and seeks deeper motivations more so along associations with class-consciousness. Ethnic and religious identities perhaps provide answers more for a lingering cultural character of the local population than they do in relation to notions of protest in the city's labour history in the late twentieth century. This study sees more evidence for exceptionality in Liverpool's long tortuous relationship with unemployment and poverty than it does with specific geography or sectarianism. The painful years of mass de-industrialisation and the shift to neoliberal economic tendencies on a global stage only made that agony even more traumatic for Liverpool, largely in light of its unique, perhaps 'exceptional', history.

Economic decline in post-war Liverpool and its effect on working-class dissent

In an attempt to invigorate the region's economic climate, Prime Minister Harold Macmillan pushed through a series of initiatives which encouraged Britain's motor car manufacturers to expand their production facilities from the highly industrialised West Midlands into non-traditional locales, such as Merseyside. Some of the larger vehicle and parts manufacturers that relocated 'branch' plants into the area were Standard-Triumph, Dunlop, Massey-Ferguson, Lucas Electronics, and most notably Ford Motor Company, which in 1963 opened its largest European manufacturing facility to date in the Liverpool suburb of Halewood.[28] Expectations were running so high in 1965 that the Lord Mayor proclaimed Liverpool to be the 'Detroit of Great Britain'.[29]

In the 1960s, tens of thousands of manufacturing jobs had come to Merseyside with this new-found boom in car plants. Unfortunately, the car factories and their suppliers' plants opened around the same period when the docks and shipping companies were making large permanent cuts in personnel. To the government's dismay, the new manufacturing facilities did little to expand total employment in Liverpool; rather, they served merely as plasters on the haemorrhaging wound of rising local unemployment.

The motor car industry's presence in the region was relatively brief, as most of these factories were mothballed within ten or fifteen years of their arrival. It was reported that in the Merseyside Special Development Area, 384 factories employing ten or more people closed between 1979 and 1982, resulting in the loss of 25,511 jobs from these plants alone.[30] Since 1973, approximately 92,000 manufacturing jobs have left Merseyside.[31]

Motor car manufacturing did not propel Liverpool forward, as had been anticipated. An equally important feature of motor car manufacturing and its relationship to Merseyside is that because of the industry's historical geography, Liverpool was forever relegated to being merely a branch plant town and never a headquarters city. The city's economy was beholden to a small number of very large absentee employers. In 1979, less than 1 per cent of the city's firms provided nearly 40 per cent of total employment and 57 per cent of manufacturing jobs were in factories employing over 1,000 workers, in contrast to the national average of 29 per cent.[32] These companies made decisions based on their global interests rather than local considerations. In the post-war rush to modernise the local economy, Liverpool had ceded control of its economic destiny. Nevertheless, the car manufacturing industry arguably saved the region from complete economic collapse, when ironically, the rest of the nation was enjoying a prosperous period of nearly full employment.

From its luminous days as Britain's gateway to Empire, to the supposed bountiful years of post-war prosperity and purported full employment, Liverpool struggled with unemployment and underemployment more so than any other British city. Indeed, national statistics clearly demonstrate Liverpool and Merseyside consistently registered double the national average in the statistical rate of unemployment. Pockets of extreme deprivation were also in evidence, particularly in the residential neighbourhoods surrounding the dockland wards. Even as recently as the 1980s, official government statistics illustrate unemployment levels as high as 45 per cent in some of these areas. Within these neighbourhoods ethnic minorities and the young were especially susceptible to high rates of joblessness.[33]

Statistics indicate that by the 1950s post-war prosperity and full employment seemingly bypassed Merseyside. Unemployment levels remained high while they dropped to record lows throughout the rest of the United Kingdom. Liverpool's miles of docks were still an important part of the local economy, but as Britain traded less with its former colonies of Empire and looked more towards Europe, the volume of cargo passing through the portside quays dwindled. Between 1966 and 1994, the number of ships arriving in the Port of Liverpool was halved, while traffic through ports in the south-east of England, such as those at Dover and Felixstowe, increased more than four-fold.[34]

Unfortunately for Liverpool, this drop in trade came at a time when the shipping industry was moving more towards containerised vessels which required far fewer personnel to load, unload and man. The 'container revolution' in shipping further slashed jobs on Merseyside. Containerisation meant ships could be loaded or unloaded in twenty-four hours or less, and this profoundly changed both the jobs of seafaring and stevedoring. It also altered the complexion of the city.

The marginalisation of Liverpool's port not only traumatised the region's economy, it also created a void in the social and political fabric of its society. Liverpool's working-class communities were particularly affected. Obviously, the high levels of long-term unemployment held negative consequences for these neighbourhoods. Anesthetised by the despair of joblessness and lack of opportunity, many residents withdrew from the political process altogether. Consequently, this reduction in civil engagement also reduced their voice in the affairs affecting them most: crime, poverty and urban decay.

Rooted in the casual labour associated with docks and seafaring, and later compounded with the boom and bust cycle of the area's other major industry, motor car manufacturing, this close familiarity with unemployment, underemployment and poverty remained from one generation of Liverpool's working class to the next. The consequence of this acquaintance with joblessness, deprivation and the daily inconsistencies of casual employment resulted in a local working class that developed distinctive defence mechanisms. This was particularly noticeable in the way Liverpool's working class chose to articulate an especially militant form of trade unionism. In adapting to these conditions a lingering sense of grievance germinated on Merseyside, and a working-class culture prizing resistance and fierce independence permeated the social milieu. Therefore, it can be understood how this adherence to independence coupled with a sense of separateness from 'mainland Britain' became pillars of a distinct local identity.

Liverpool's association with radicalism can be traced over an extensive and passionate history; its origins are usually drawn from a selection of circumstances, first of which is the region's ties to a pre-industrial maritime economy, seemingly devoid of the influence and wealth that industrialisation brought to other British cities. Consequently, Liverpool has traditionally suffered higher levels of poverty, joblessness and underemployment, which is often the result of a workforce largely comprised of unskilled labour.

Nevertheless, while the casualism associated with seafaring and stevedoring may have bred poverty, it also fostered within the worker a unique sense of independence and agency. Under a casual system of labour workers could be their own men and choose when they wished to work. Such a level of independence is usually beyond the scope of most labourers employed in manufacturing. Similarly, such liberties were also beyond the pale of understanding to many national trade union bosses who often met fierce resistance from rank-and-file members attached to Merseyside branches.[35]

When manufacturing finally did arrive on Merseyside in the 1950s and 1960s, the industries which prospered were profoundly dependent on unskilled and semi-skilled labour involved in highly repetitive assembly-line processes and under strict supervision. Such rigid production practices frequently resulted in ferocious friction between labour and management. Liverpool was no exception to this norm. Furthermore, the branch plants purposely enticed to locate in Liverpool were particularly vulnerable to heavy-handed management and threats of closure compared to production facilities based abroad in cities home to corporate headquarters.[36]

Despite the popular association of Liverpool with workplace militancy, some counter that this should be regarded as a myth. This position is argued that Liverpool is not especially unique in this respect; rather, it is the nature of the industries which make up the bulk of the local economy – namely, motor car manufacturing and dock transport. Both of which, no matter where they were located, were of a particularly monotonous yet structured nature which made them susceptible to highly volatile work relations with company management. It has been argued that Liverpool was not so terribly unique or 'exceptional' in that regard.[37]

Nevertheless, it cannot be denied that the city has a history all its own. Liverpool's role as a port and maritime centre marked it out as different in many respects to other British cities. Its cosmopolitan population gave it an outward-looking character with its sights focused more on Shanghai and New York, rather than looking inward to Manchester and London. It remains, even today, arguably the least 'British' of the nation's major cities.

Conclusion

We shall see that the working class on Merseyside experimented with and adopted a whole range of responses to mass unemployment. A number of these approaches were attempted elsewhere, but what made Liverpool so unique was that within the brief space of two decades nearly all of the different tactics deployed in other parts of Britain were also used on Merseyside but in greater number, intensity and certainly with more media attention. These actions, it will be argued, grew out of Liverpool's long historical connections to a notional oppositional culture, which itself will be shown was derived mainly from the area's long familiarity with the degradations associated with mass unemployment. The findings from this research suggests that if there was any sense of alienation from the larger British society as a whole, these feelings did not detract from notions of class-consciousness; indeed, as we shall see, it was these very ideas which reinforced a sense of self-awareness with regard to class. Mass unemployment and lack of opportunity were the building blocks of this local identity. It was the refusal to accept such conditions that proved to be as much of a part of the local character as geographical ties to the sea and the history of the Irish famine.

The organised replies by working-class Liverpudlians to the economics of neoliberalism included the use of many tactics. We shall explore only a few of these campaigns in detail. They will include the instigation of non-sanctioned wildcat strikes, a scheme for organising the unemployed within an established trade union branch, the eruption of inner-city rioting largely in response to the lack of economic opportunity, the embracement of radical Trotskyist municipal politics, workplace occupations, and community-based movements resisting redundancy. In addition, there were attempts at workers' cooperatives and alternative plans formulated by workers fighting factory closures on Merseyside at this time. What made Liverpool different from other British cities was the sheer range of initiatives employed during this struggle, the intensity and commitment of their deployment, and the frequency of their concurrence.

Notes

1 *Guardian*, 7 February 1982.
2 *Guardian*, 11 August 1981. See also: *Guardian*, 12 February 1982; *Guardian*, 18 February 1983.
3 *Guardian*, 22 November 1981.
4 *Guardian*, 23 February 1981.
5 *Guardian*, 1 March 1981; *Guardian*, 17 March 1983; *Guardian*, 5 December 1987; *Guardian*, 10 May 1983. Eric Hobsbawm discussed the phenomenon of waning working-class militancy in great detail in his landmark paper, 'The Forward March of Labour Halted', *Marxism Today*, September 1978, pp. 279–86.
6 *Guardian*, 24 January 1981.

7 John Maynard Keynes, *The General Theory of Employment, Interest, and Money* (London, 1936).
8 Friedrich A. Hayek, *The Road to Serfdom* (London, 1944).
9 John McIlroy, 'Britain: How Neo-Liberalism Cut Unions Down to Size', in Gregor Gall, Adrian Wilkinson and Richard Hurd, eds, *The International Handbook of Labour Unions: Responses to Neo-liberalism* (Cheltenham, 2011), p. 82.
10 John McIlroy, 'A Brief History of British Trade Unions and Neoliberalism: From the Earliest Days to the Birth of New Labour', in Gary Daniels and John McIlroy, eds, *Trade Unions in a Neoliberal World: British Trade Unions under New Labour* (Abingdon, 2009), p. 25.
11 The 'end of history' reference is an allusion to Francis Fukuyama's popular monograph from the period, *The End of History and The Last Man*, in which he argued that the fall of state communism and the hegemony of neoliberal economics was leading mankind into an era of international consensus devoid of ideological polemics. See: Francis Fukuyama, *The End of History and The Last Man* (New York, 1992).
12 For accounts on the expanding role of shop stewards see E. Batstone, I. Boraston and E. Frankel, *Shop Stewards in Action* (Oxford, 1977); Arthur Marsh, *Managers and Shop Stewards: Shop Floor Revolution?* (London, 1973); J. F. B. Goodman and T. G. Whittingham, *Shop Stewards in British Industry* (London, 1969); Ralph Darlington, 'Shop Stewards' Leadership, Left-Wing Activism, and Collective Workplace Activism', *Capital & Class*, vol. 26, no.76 (Spring 2002), pp. 95–126; Ralph Darlington, *The Dynamics of Workplace Unionism: Shop Stewards' Organisation in Three Merseyside Plants* (London, 1994).
13 Baron Terence Donovan, *Report of the Royal Commission on Trade Unions and Employers' Associations* (London, 1968).
14 Barbara Castle, *In Place of Strife: A Policy for Industrial Relations* (London, 1969). See Peter Jenkins, *The Battle of Downing Street* (London, 1970).
15 There is an extensive literature on Thatcherism: see, for example, Eric J. Evans, *Thatcher and Thatcherism* (2nd edition, London, 2004); Peter Riddell, *The Thatcher Era and its Legacy* (Oxford, 1991); Margaret Thatcher, *The Downing Street Years* (London, 1993).
16 Tony Dickson and David Judge, *The Politics of Industrial Closure* (London, 1987), p. 100.
17 Dickson and Judge, *The Politics of Industrial Closure*, p. 19.
18 Thatcher, *The Downing Street Years*, pp. 92–3.
19 Dickson and Judge, *The Politics of Industrial Closure*, p. 22.
20 Dickson and Judge, *The Politics of Industrial Closure*, pp. 26–7.
21 Tony Lane, *Liverpool – City of the Sea* (Liverpool, 1997), p. 20.
22 Eric J. Evans, *The Shaping of Modern Britain: Identity, Industry and Empire, 1780–1914* (London, 2011), p. 260.
23 P. E. Lloyd, *Manufacturing Industry in the Inner City: A Case Study of Merseyside*, North West Industry Research Unit, Working Paper Series No. 2, School of Geography (Manchester, 1977), p. 1.

24 John Belchem, *Irish, Catholic and Scouse: The History of the Liverpool-Irish, 1800–1939* (Liverpool, 2007). See also John Belchem, *Merseypride: Essays in Liverpool Exceptionalism* (Liverpool, 2000).
25 John Belchem, ed., *Popular Politics, Riot and Labour: Essays in Liverpool History 1790–1940* (Liverpool, 1992).
26 Sam Davies, *Liverpool Labour* (Keele, 1996). See also: long-time Liverpool Labour MP Eric Heffer's political memoir, *Never a Yes Man: The Life and Politics of an Adopted Liverpudlian* (London, 1991), which reinforces another view of the local political culture in a way that only an outsider's eye can catch.
27 Davies, *Liverpool Labour*.
28 Huw Beynon, *Working for Ford* (Harmondsworth, 1984), p. 75; Roy Church, *The Rise and Decline of the British Motor Industry* (Cambridge, 1995), p. 63.
29 *Liverpool Echo*, 24 September 1965.
30 Dickson and Judge, *The Politics of Industrial Closure*, pp. 27–9.
31 *Liverpool Daily Post*, 2 July 2007.
32 Jon Murden, 'City of Change and Challenge: Liverpool since 1945', in John Belchem, ed., *Liverpool 800: Culture, Character & History* (Liverpool, 2006), p. 435.
33 Please refer to Tables 2.4, 2.9, 2.10, 2.11, 2.12, and Figure 1 of this book. See also Central Policy Unit, *Census Key Statistics in Liverpool Wards: 1971/1981/1991* (Liverpool); Lloyd, *Manufacturing Industry*, p. 2; Lane, *Liverpool*, pp. 126, 134, 138–9.
34 Lane, *Liverpool*, p. 23.
35 Ralph Darlington explored the seeds of workplace radicalism in Liverpool history and its results in: Ralph Darlington, 'Workplace Union Militancy on Merseyside since the 1960s: Extent, Nature, Causes, and Decline', *Historical Studies in Industrial Relations*, vol. 19 (Spring 2005), pp. 123–52.
36 Darlington, 'Workplace Union Militancy', pp. 138–9.
37 Dave Lyddon, 'Strike Statistics and Militancy: A Comment', *Historical Studies in Industrial Relations*, vol. 19 (Spring 2005), pp. 153–70.

2

Employment and unemployment on Merseyside, 1945–98

Throughout the late twentieth century, the presence of mass unemployment was a consistent feature of Merseyside. Indeed, for much of this period the name Liverpool itself became synonymous with joblessness and all the negative images such deprived circumstances suggest. In this chapter, Liverpool's connection to unemployment in the late twentieth century is charted. Prior to analysing economic trends and their relationship to employment and joblessness on Merseyside, we shall address the complexity of collecting and interpreting unemployment statistics in the United Kingdom. Finally, the social consequences of unemployment for individuals and their communities will be discussed in greater depth.

Measuring unemployment

When compared to other Western nations, a standardised system of quantifying joblessness is a relatively new protocol for the United Kingdom. The details of who counted as unemployed and who did not, while generally measured universally throughout Europe, came relatively late to Britain, and only after greater integration within the booming economy of the European Economic Community was it finally considered.

Throughout much of the twentieth century statistics for measuring joblessness in the UK were often a mismatch of figures compiled according to dissimilar criteria, seemingly manipulated more for the sake of political advantage rather than as a record of accurate measurement.[1] A brief example illustrating such politicisation of these statistics can be demonstrated by government policy changes made as late as 1988. Whilst in the midst of a protracted period of high unemployment, the Conservative government announced that the official number of people who would be counted as unemployed would thereafter be measured by 'per cent of entire workforce', as opposed to the smaller set of total respondents enumerated earlier, which had been termed, 'per cent of workers'. Thus, the pool of people considered gainfully employed widened to include the self-employed, HM Forces and non-paid participants in government training schemes. The total number of unemployed became a smaller percentage of an enlarged definition of the employed. Consequently, official national unemployment rates dropped across all categories.[2]

Prior to this redefining of who was unemployed in 1988, another major change in the collection of unemployment data occurred after October 1982, when the government no longer required workers who were made redundant to register with a local labour exchange. After this point laid-off workers applied for job seekers' allowance on a voluntary basis. This legislation also lowered official rates of joblessness since government statistics collected on unemployment at that time were based on the number of people registering for work at local job centres.[3] Fewer people signing on the register meant lower rates of unemployed workers. Altogether, between 1978 and 1992, there were nearly thirty changes redefining who was considered employed or unemployed, which caused much political controversy.[4]

Local statistics detailing the numbers of unemployed in the United Kingdom are also notoriously difficult to interpret for practical reasons. The majority of displaced workers register at a labour exchange nearest their home, rather than in the locality where they worked. Dense urban geography leads to further confusion: official boundaries often change from one census to the next, sometimes perplexing researchers as to where London begins and where it ends. Another potential dilemma is posed by the attribution of suburbs: for example, should one be considered a part of Bradford or is it a suburb of Leeds? From the 1970s, it became increasingly clear that official government unemployment statistics could not be relied on as an absolutely accurate measurement of joblessness. Therefore, they should be considered more as a tool for plotting general trends, rather than a precise measurement.

Further questions remain. For example, which groups of jobless people should be included in the overall calculation? Some of those left out are the short-term unemployed. This category includes those made redundant due to seasonal factors or the casual conditions of their employment, which for Merseyside alone would prove to be a substantial percentage of its workers. This type of employee was removed from the tabulation after 1972. This is regrettable since studies have demonstrated a strong correlation between an increase in short-term unemployment, or 'frictional unemployment', and long-term unemployment or 'structural unemployment'.[5]

Others not counted include recent school leavers and those entering the job market for the first time. This too is unfortunate since youth unemployment is especially detrimental to the fabric of society. Similarly, members of ethnic minority groups of every age – who frequently suffer the highest rates of joblessness – were, until 1970, also omitted as a separate category in the *Department of Employment Gazette*.[6] The disabled are yet another group often considered 'unemployable' and, thus, not calculated into the formula. Finally, the statistics do not take into account those dejected workers who have given up hope of ever finding work and have retreated altogether from searching. Registered workers actively seeking employment are known as the primary unemployed, and they are the only class of worker enumerated in official unemployment statistics. The various categories of jobless people described above are termed the secondary unemployed and, thus, not formally included in the official count of joblessness. Critics counter that if the secondary unemployed were included, a much more reliable picture would emerge of true joblessness in Britain.[7]

Unemployment statistics and economic deprivation on Merseyside since 1945

While official figures detailing unemployment in Britain should not be accepted as a precise measurement, they do illustrate trends and patterns which must be considered in this survey. The City of Liverpool and the Metropolitan County of Merseyside through their history have normally led all other urban areas of Great Britain in rates of unemployment and other indicators of general economic deprivation.

This stagnation can be demonstrated by a series of statistics consistently reflecting such negative trends. From a variety of sources we can construct a multi-dimensional portrait of social conditions in post-war Merseyside. The first piece of evidence is described in Table 2.1. It is a bi-annual tabulation of official unemployment statistics for Merseyside and the United Kingdom from the years 1978 to 1998. Table 2.1 proves Merseyside maintained a post-war pattern of unemployment at rates approximately twice the national average. During the two decades illustrated, the official unemployment rate never dropped below 10 per cent until the very end of the period, even when calculated by using the more wide-ranging definition of the workforce.[8] The rapid acceleration of unemployment in the first half of the 1980s is readily apparent. Between January 1985 and July 1987, the Merseyside rate did not fall below 20 per cent.

Table 2.1 Percentage and numbers of unemployed on Merseyside

Year	Number of unemployed in Merseyside	Per cent unemployed in Merseyside	Per cent unemployed in United Kingdom
January 1978	83,374	11.6	6.4
July 1978	90,165	12.5	6.6
January 1979	83,666	11.5	6.0
July 1979	87,327	12.0	6.0
January 1980	86,491	11.8	6.1
July 1980	102,046	14.1	7.8
January 1981	113,029	15.7	10.1
July 1981	128,688	17.9	11.9
January 1982	134,106	18.7	12.9
July 1982	140,591	19.6	13.4
January 1983	138,548	19.2	13.8
July 1983	134,089	18.5	12.3
January 1984	140,398	19.4	13.4
July 1984	135,936	18.7	12.9
January 1985	141,708	21.3	13.9
July 1985	139,357	21.0	13.4
January 1986	142,696	21.5	14.1
July 1986	139,300	20.6	11.9
January 1987	136,100	20.1	11.9
July 1987	126,039	20.0	10.5
January 1988	119,355	19.3	9.8
July 1988	107,720	17.4	8.2*
January 1989	99,971	16.1	7.4*
July 1989	89,594	14.5	6.2*
January 1990	84,423	14.1–12.6*	6.0*
July 1990	80,446	13.7–12.0*	5.7*
January 1991	86,675	14.7–12.9*	6.9*
July 1991	93,274	16.5–14.5*	8.3*
January 1992	97,784	17.3–15.2*	9.4*
July 1992	98,134	17.2–15.2*	9.8*
January 1993	100,099	17.5–15.5*	10.8*
July 1993	96,469	17.1–15.3*	10.4*
January 1994	95,413	16.9–15.1*	10.3*
July 1994	89,081	15.8–14.1*	9.4*
January 1995	84,789	15.0–13.4*	8.9*
July 1995	80,155	14.6–13.1*	8.3*
January 1996	78,900	14.3–12.9*	8.3*
July 1996	76,578	14.4–12.8*	7.7*
January 1997	69,732	13.1–11.7*	6.8*
July 1997	61,506	11.9–10.7*	5.6*
January 1998	57,206	11.1–10.0*	5.3*
July 1998	53,886	10.7–9.5*	5.0*

Note: Figures marked with an asterisk represent 'per cent of entire workforce' system.
Source: Department of Employment Gazette.

Table 2.2 Unemployment rates for Liverpool and the United Kingdom

Year	Liverpool	United Kingdom
1971	10.6%	4.1%
1981	20.4%	8.6%
1991	21.6%	8.7%
2001	10.6%	5.3%

Source: Central Policy Unit, *Census Key Statistics in Liverpool Wards: 1971/1981/1991* (Liverpool).

Table 2.3 Unemployment percentage rates for England's largest metropolitan counties

Metropolitan county	July 1981	July 1982	July 1983	July 1984	July 1985
Greater London	8.0	9.5	9.5	10.0	10.5
Greater Manchester	13.4	15.1	14.3	14.4	15.4
West Midlands	15.2	17.0	16.2	15.8	16.5
West Yorkshire	12.1	13.4	12.7	12.7	14.0
South Yorkshire	13.7	15.6	15.2	15.9	17.3
Merseyside	17.9	19.6	18.5	18.7	21.0

Source: Department of Employment Gazette.

Table 2.2 contains less detailed data, but by using different sources it corroborates the information in Table 2.1, in relation to joblessness for Liverpool from 1971 to 2001. While it depicts a similar general trend to that indicated in Table 2.1, the rate of unemployment in Liverpool is significantly higher, reaching over 20 per cent in both 1981 and 1991. Table 2.1 and Table 2.2 not only show that Merseyside suffered disproportionately high rates of 'official' unemployment during the recession of the 1980s, but they also illustrate that these levels remained very high throughout the 1990s when the rest of the UK was showing signs of economic recovery.

Nevertheless, it must be stressed that during the early to mid-1980s, when unemployment hit its peak in Britain, Merseyside was in the lead amongst the nation's largest urban centres, as evidenced in Table 2.3. This is also significant because each of these urban areas, with the exception of Greater London, were especially reliant on manufacturing. This data is important in that it clearly proves Merseyside was far worse off when compared to all other major British cities.

Table 2.4 Changes in manufacturing employment and total employment (1981–96)

	Percentage of manufacturing jobs lost or gained	Percentage of total jobs lost or gained
Merseyside	−61	−25
Greater London	−59	−6
Coventry	−54	−10
Bristol	−51	+2
Edinburgh	−49	+10
Clydeside	−47	−9
South Yorkshire	−46	−15
Greater Manchester	−43	−3
Tyneside	−42	−4
Plymouth	−39	−2
West Midlands	−37	−6
Leicester	−35	−4
Doncaster	−33	−9
Nottingham	−33	+12
Stoke-on-Trent	−31	−6
Cardiff	−27	+5
West Yorkshire	−26	+4
Wigan	−23	−3
Hull	−21	+5
Sunderland	+9	+3

Source: Ivan Turok and Nicola Edge, *The Jobs Gap in Britain's Cities: Employment Loss and Labour Market Consequences* (Bristol, 1999), p. 43.

An even clearer illustration of how both the economic recession of the 1980s and late twentieth-century de-industrialisation negatively impacted Liverpool far more than any other British conurbation can easily be evidenced by the information provided in Table 2.4. This table clearly illustrates the differences in the level of negative impact the forces of de-industrialisation and economic recession played on British cities in the last two decades of the twentieth century. Liverpool and the Merseyside region suffered far more than the other British conurbations cited, as Merseyside led both tables in loss of manufacturing jobs and the total employment with an astounding 25 per cent loss in all jobs between 1981 and 1996.

Table 2.4 also establishes that some British cities were able to ride the winds of change and actually increase jobs in the face of a de-industrialising economy. For instance, cities such as Nottingham, Bristol and Leeds (West Yorkshire) obviously managed to diversify their economy and to accommodate a growing service and education

Table 2.5 Population of Merseyside, 1981–2001

1981	1,522,000
1991	1,433,800
2001	1,367,800

Source: Office of National Statistics.

sector. The growth in total employment in the national capital cities of Edinburgh and Cardiff obviously reflect the growth in public sector employment. Manufacturing actually grew in Sunderland because of the expansion of Japanese car makers into British markets. Nevertheless, according to the evidence provided by this table, Liverpool suffered the greatest job loss during this pivotal period in history.

Significant population loss over an extended period is a further indicator that an area has suffered from sustained levels of substantial unemployment. Liverpool was no exception to this rule. The population of Liverpool fell by nearly one-third, from 750,000 in 1961 to approximately 490,000 in 1985. This population decline was the highest of any urban area in England and Wales during this time frame. In the earlier part of this period, much of this out-migration was due to slum clearance programmes, whereby many of the city's older, more impoverished neighbourhoods were razed, and the residents placed in the bourgeoning new satellite towns established on the outskirts of the metropolitan area. This would include exurban post-war developments at such Merseyside locales as Kirkby and Speke, where much of the expanding motor car industry was locating. Between the censuses of 1961 and 1971, there was an out-migration to these exurban settlements of almost 19,000 per annum.[9]

The Metropolitan County of Merseyside came into existence in 1974 following the passage of the Local Government Act, 1972. Statistics covering population and employment for this geographical entity are restricted by that starting date. However, census figures for the Metropolitan County of Merseyside displayed in Table 2.5 illustrate the dramatic loss in population resulting from the 1980s recession. In the two decades after 1981, Merseyside witnessed a population loss of 154,200 people, more than 10 per cent. The table suggests that it was after 1981 when many redundant workers began leaving the Merseyside region altogether. The more prosperous areas in the south-east of England were often the final destination for a majority of these migrants.[10]

Just as the nation experienced the recession of the 1980s rather unevenly, so too, geographically speaking, did Liverpool. A review of the unemployment levels within individual wards of the city illustrates this diversity.

Table 2.6 Ward level and city-wide unemployment rates, 1971–91

Census year	Vauxhall	Everton	Liverpool
1971	16.0%	19.8%	10.6%
1981	36.6%	37.6%	20.4%
1991	45.0%	45.1%	21.6%

Source: Central Policy Unit, *Census Key Statistics in Liverpool Wards: 1971/1981/1991* (Liverpool).

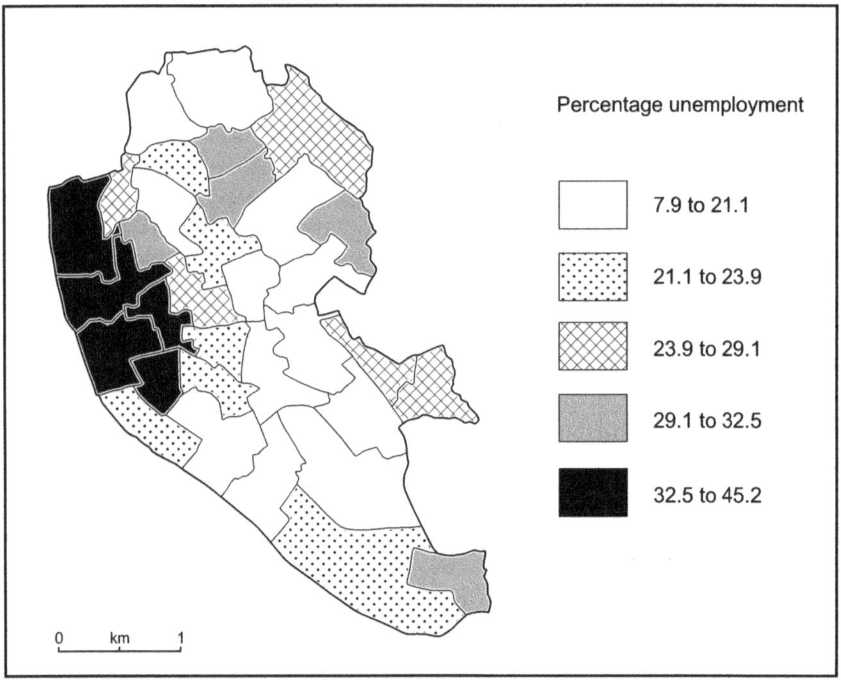

Figure 1 Unemployment in Liverpool electoral wards – 1991

(See Table 2.6 and Figure 1. Figure 2 can be used to plot the individually named wards.) In Liverpool's more middle-class Southend wards, such as Grassendale, Woolton and Church, the unemployment rate in 1991 was less than 15 per cent. However, in the heavily working-class, Northend dockland wards of Everton and Vauxhall it reached over 45 per cent.

This north–south divide in Liverpool was in many ways symbolic of the growing economic disparity within Britain during the 1980s. In the Northend areas of Liverpool, more often dominated by council housing,

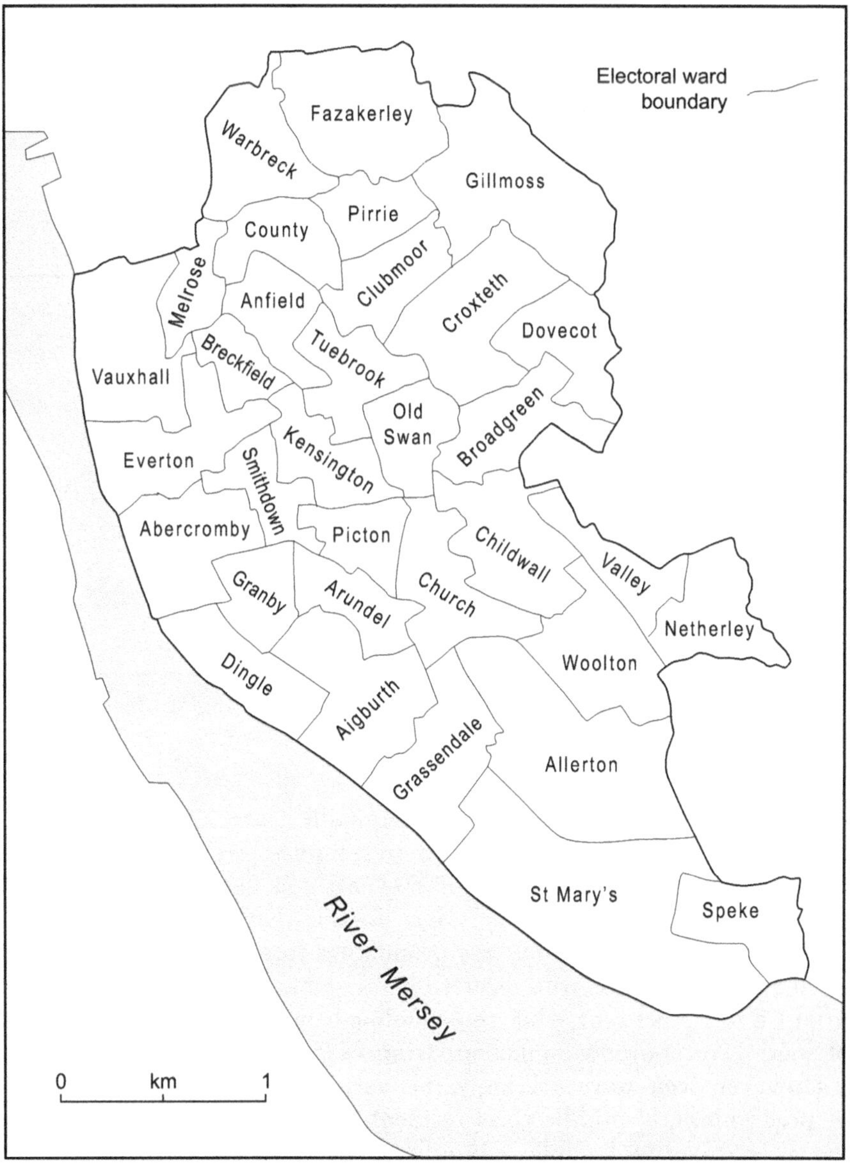

Figure 2 Liverpool electoral wards, 1971/1981/1991

unemployment rates between 1971 and 1981 doubled from 15.5 per cent to 33.7 per cent. Conversely, in the more affluent, owner-occupied housing wards of the Southend, this increase was smaller, illustrating a rise from 4.4 to 8.2 per cent. Car ownership rates for the poorer wards

Table 2.7 Changes in the social economic structure of the city of Liverpool 1961–81

Liverpool					England and Wales			
	Per cent economically active males			Difference 1961 and 1981 proportions	Per cent economically active males			Difference 1961 and 1981 proportions
	1961	1971	1981		1961	1971	1981	
Employers/ managers	7.5	7.7	8.2	+0.7	10.7	12.4	14.1	+3.4
Professionals	2.4	2.9	3.2	+0.8	3.9	5.1	5.1	+1.2
Other non-manual	16.2	17.1	14.7	–1.5	16.7	17.7	16.0	–0.7
Skilled manual	37.2	36.5	33.4	–3.8	39.6	38.9	36.6	–3.0
Semi-skilled manual	18.9	18.8	20.6	+1.7	17.8	15.2	14.9	–2.9
Unskilled manual	15.2	13.6	10.9	–4.3	8.0	7.4	6.3	–1.7
HM Forces/ unemployed	2.7	3.5	9.0	+6.3	3.4	3.3	7.0	+3.6
	100.0	100.0	100.0		100.0	100.0	100.0	

Source: Michael G. Hayes, *Past Trends and Future Prospects: Urban Change in Liverpool, 1961–2001* (Liverpool, 1987).

during this period only inched up marginally from 17.3 to 18.0 per cent. During this same period the more middle-class Southend wards displayed a much larger increase in motor car ownership, with a jump from 55.6 to 61.5 per cent. It is also notable that between 1981 and 1984 the proportion of students originating from the more impoverished Northend wards who received higher education awards, dropped from 1.8 to 1.5 per cent, while those hailing from the more well-off areas of South Liverpool saw an increase from 14.7 to 15.1 per cent.[11]

However, even more strikingly, this data shows the relative scarcity of predominantly middle-class residential districts anywhere within the city of Liverpool. Table 2.7 confirms that a majority of Liverpool's male residents between 1961 and 1981 were manual workers – some 65 per cent in the latter year – with the unskilled or semi-skilled comprising half of such workers; and that the city's percentage of professionals, managers and employers numbered only half the average for the nation as a whole. Manual workers were most vulnerable to the forces of de-industrialisation, particularly those employed in manufacturing.

Table 2.8 Employment changes by sectors and selected industries in city of Liverpool, 1961–85

	Numbers					Per cent change 1961–85	
Sectors	1961	1971	1976	1981	1985	Liverpool	UK
Manufacturing	130,140	110,611	34,504	67,650	47,455	–64	–37
Other production industries	30,140	20,130	14,320	12,768	10,662	–65	–39
Blue-collar services	174,820	129,218	113,293	95,095	87,500	–50	+8
White-collar services	64,750	86,135	90,227	85,680	85,000	+31	+68
Total employment	400,940	346,094	312,344	261,374	230,617	–43	–05
Selected industries							
Food, drink and tobacco	28,080	29,155	24,377	19,489	11,000	–61	–29
Engineering	26,860	21,466	15,227	11,212	8,100	–70	–25
Vehicles (including shipbuilding)	12,880	22,250	23,462	16,491	10,750	–17	–48
Transport and communica tions	65,250	52,531	41,060	33,619	29,000	–56	–20
Distribution	77,240	52,099	43,444	34,065	31,000	–60	+05

Source: Michael G. Hayes, *Past Trends and Future Prospects: Urban Change in Liverpool, 1961–2001* (Liverpool, 1987).

Table 2.8 illustrates a 64 per cent loss in local manufacturing jobs between 1961 and 1985, compared to a fall of 37 per cent nationally. The table demonstrates that engineering, with a 70 per cent decline over these twenty-four years, was especially hard hit by this shift in the economy. The same negative results can be seen for the food, drink and tobacco industries, traditionally associated with raw materials imported through Liverpool's docks. Food, drink and tobacco suffered an employment loss of 61 per cent over the same period.

A 1985 survey of Liverpool's working-age population actively seeking employment bears testament to the changes in the economic order since 1961. Table 2.9 indicates that those listed in the categories actively seeking employment made up 22.6 per cent of Liverpool's working-age population, and those engaged in training combined with the number of people looking for work totalled 25.1 per cent. Consequently, only 53 per cent were employed.

Table 2.9 City of Liverpool population of working age (16–59/64), 1985

	Number	Per cent working age population
Economically active	223,500	75.3
Employed	159,000	53.5
Community programme	3,000	1.0
Youth training scheme	4,500	1.5
Unemployed claimants	57,000	19.2
Economically inactive	73,500	24.7
Involuntarily inactive	10,000	3.4
Voluntarily inactive	31,000	10.4
Permanently sick	12,000	4.0
Full-time education	20,500	6.9
Total working age population	297,000	100.0

Source: Michael G. Hayes, *Past Trends and Future Prospects: Urban Change in Liverpool, 1961–2001* (Liverpool, 1987).

Table 2.10 Duration of unemployment 1973 and 1986 – city of Liverpool and United Kingdom

	January 1973			October 1986		
	City of Liverpool		UK	City of Liverpool		UK
	Number	Per cent	Per cent	Number	Per cent	Per cent
Less than 6 months	16,157	40.5	58.2	16,903	30.4	41.4
6 months–1 year	3,000	22.4	17.7	8,164	14.7	17.1
More than 1 year	14,881	37.1	24.1	30,552	54.9	41.4
1–2 years	–	–	–	8,967	16.1	15.3
2–3 years	–	–	–	5,308	9.5	8.1
3–4 years	–	–	–	4,267	7.7	5.7
4–5 years	–	–	–	3,516	6.3	4.6
>5 years	–	–	–	8,464	15.2	7.7

Source: Michael G. Hayes, *Past Trends and Future Prospects: Urban Change in Liverpool, 1961–2001* (Liverpool, 1987).

As Table 2.10 indicates, many of these displaced workers were unemployed for long periods of time – some indefinitely. In October 1986, approximately 15.2 per cent of Liverpool's unemployed were without work for a period greater than five years. The city's rate of long-term unemployment was nearly double the national average. The ever-present television images of seemingly endless crowds of unemployed people in

Table 2.11 Long-term unemployment in city of Liverpool by age and duration: October 1986

Age group	Unemployed > 1 year Number	Unemployed > 1 year Per cent of age group	Unemployed > 3 years Number	Unemployed > 3 years Per cent of age group	Unemployed > 5 years Number	Unemployed > 5 years Per cent of age group
Under 18	396	12.9	0	0	0	0
18–19	2,145	39.8	148	2.7	0	0
20–24	6,097	49.9	2,866	23.0	750	6.1
25–34	7,972	57.6	4,424	32.0	2,483	7.9
35–44	5,691	65.0	3,459	39.5	2,006	22.9
45–54	5,107	69.0	3,319	44.9	1,976	26.9
55–59/64	3,115	63.5	2,013	42.6	1,249	25.5

Source: Michael G. Hayes, *Past Trends and Future Prospects: Urban Change in Liverpool, 1961–2001* (Liverpool, 1987).

Merseyside's Job Centres and dole queues served as a constant reminder of the permanence of the changes taking place in Britain's economy.

Long-term unemployment seemed especially troublesome for older redundant workers. Table 2.11 highlights the problem of long-term joblessness in October 1986, when unemployment rates in Liverpool were at their highest levels since the Great Depression. This table shows that the chance of redundant workers between the ages of forty-five and fifty-four ever finding work again was slim. Many potential employers were reluctant to invest in training new workers of this age group, fearing a loss on that investment due to approaching retirement. Over 70 per cent of the respondents in that age group were unable to secure employment within the previous year, and close to a quarter of this sample were jobless for five years or longer.

Nevertheless, it was young males between the ages of sixteen and twenty-four who were dealt the severest blows of the 1980s recession. As early as the summer of 1980, Merseyside Job Centres reported there were only forty-nine jobs available for the 13,505 school leavers that year.[12] By October 1986 unemployment for males under twenty-four years of age ranged from 43.8 to 46.6 per cent (see Table 2.12). When compared to national percentages for both male and female unemployment in the 16–24 age group, Liverpool's experiences were especially acute. This was particularly poignant when considering the fact that the city's jobless rate was consistently hovering at twice the UK average.

Table 2.12 City of Liverpool and United Kingdom unemployment claimants by age: October 1986

Age	Males		Females		Total city of Liverpool		UK per cent rate
	Number	Per cent	Number	Per cent	Number	Per cent	
16–19	4,906	46.6	3,552	38.1	8,458	42.5	21
20–24	8,466	43.8	3,753	24.1	12,219	34.9	16.6
25–34	10,755	31.2	3,089	14.4	13,844	24.8	12.5
35–44	7,098	27.7	1,664	9.5	8,762	20.3	7.9
45–54	5,718	24.3	1,679	9.5	7,397	17.9	8.8
55–59	3,102	26.3	1,017	12.3	4,119	20.5	14.1
>60	781	7.5	6	–	787	5.4	5.3
Total	40,826	30.1	14,760	15.7	55,586	24.2	11.7

Source: Michael G. Hayes, *Past Trends and Future Prospects: Urban Change in Liverpool, 1961–2001* (Liverpool, 1987).

In addition to young males, members of ethnic minorities of all ages suffered unemployment at nearly twice the levels of native-born, white Britons. Table 2.13 illustrates national unemployment levels by ethnic origin in 1991; Table 2.14 gives an annual count of nationwide unemployment for both whites and non-whites. Taking into account the desperate economic situation in Liverpool at this time, as well as the national unemployment figures for racial and ethnic minorities, it is probable that Merseyside's non-white population suffered equally severe, if not higher, levels of joblessness as native whites. This is supported by the findings of a study of inner-city Liverpool housing estates with large non-white populations, conducted in the late 1970s. This study found that over 45 per cent of those aged 16–19 were unemployed. It was also discovered that amongst those who were employed, the irregularity of the work available to them made unemployment an everyday feature of life for nearly 90 per cent of the respondents.[13] However, it was not until the 1991 census that respondents were asked to supply their race or ethnic affiliation.

As Table 2.15 demonstrates, Merseyside in 1991 lacked employment opportunities for many members of various racial minority groups.[14] Rates of joblessness of 40 per cent or more in 1991 were considered exceptionally high, as employment increased. Taking into account the concern over dependability regarding previously published 'official' statistics, it can be estimated that rates may have reached 50 per cent or more for this category of worker during the mid-1980s. Many

Table 2.13 National unemployment levels by ethnic origin and gender for 1991

Ethnic group	Results for males		Results for females	
	Economically active	Per cent unemployed	Economically active	Per cent unemployed
White	13,229,723	10.5	9,861,611	6.2
All ethnic minorities	746,346	20.4	531,934	15.6
Indian	228,567	13.4	162,101	12.7
Pakistani and Bangladeshi	130,801	29.5	42,905	3.9
West Indian black	180,764	24.2	166,566	14.4
African black	51,387	29.1	44,459	24.8

Source: Derrick Leslie, Joanne Lindley and Leighton Thomas, 'Decline and Fall: Unemployment among Britain's Non-White Ethnic Communities 1960–1990', *Journal of the Royal Statistical Society*, Series A (Statistics in Society), vol. 164, no. 2 (2001).

Table 2.14 UK annual unemployment rates for both whites and non-whites

	Unemployment percentages for the following groups			
	Males		**Females**	
Year	White	Non-white	White	Non-white
1979	4.4	6.0	5.7	10.8
1981	9.7	17.2	8.7	15.8
1983	12	22	10	19
1984	11.3	22	11.2	21
1985	11.0	22	10.4	19
1986	11.1	21	10.2	20
1987	10.7	18	9.9	16
1988	8.6	14	8.2	13
1989	6.9	13	6.7	11
1990	6.7	11	6.3	11
1991	8.7	16	6.9	13
1992	11	20	7	14
1993	11.7	24	7.2	18
1994	10.6	25	6.9	16
1995	9.4	20	6.3	17
1996	9.1	19	5.9	15
1997	7.6	16	5.4	14
1998	6.3	14.1	4.9	12.6
1999	6.4	13.3	4.7	12.8

Source: Derrick Leslie, Joanne Lindley and Leighton Thomas, 'Decline and Fall: Unemployment among Britain's Non-White Ethnic Communities 1960–1990', *Journal of the Royal Statistical Society*, Series A (Statistics in Society), vol. 164, no. 2 (2001).

Table 2.15 White and non-white economic position on Merseyside – 1991

	All	White		Non-white	
	Number	Number	Per cent	Number	Per cent
Total persons	1,106,839	1,089,414	98.4	17,425	1.6
Economically active males	353,372	347,368		6,004	
Economically active males less than 25 years of age	65,617	64,492		1,125	
Unemployed economically active males	69,065	67,565	19.5*	1,500	25.0*
Unemployed economically active males less than 25 years of age	19,659	19,205	29.8*	454	40.4*
Economically active females	272,041	268,090		3,951	
Economically active females less than 25 years of age	56,264	55,334		930	
Unemployed economically active females	29,492	28,785	10.7*	707	17.9*
Unemployed economically active females less than 25 years of age	11,085	10,813	19.5*	272	29.2*

Note: *Percentage rate is calculated by dividing unemployed economically active by economically active of specific category.
Source: 1991 Census, County Report: Merseyside – Part 1 (London, 1993).

within Merseyside's minority community were angered by the fact that native-born whites seemed oblivious to such statistics and the special concerns affecting their community. High levels of unemployment and lack of opportunity for Liverpool's non-white population remained a constant problem for city leaders.[15]

Social effects of long-term unemployment

The employment data presented above demonstrates Merseyside's perilous economic situation throughout the post-war period. Liverpool's familiarity with joblessness is well documented; however, it must be stressed that de-industrialisation brought forward a new dimension to this experience. The amount of human suffering caused by unemployment and underemployment cannot, of course, be measured by raw statistics. Nevertheless, long-term consequences of factory closures and the resulting poverty can be quantified in a number of ways.

Some of the immediate effects were obvious, as plant closures degenerate into not only loss of jobs in that factory, but come at a cost for everyone in the community as well. Liverpool was no exception to this rule, as so many of its newly founded manufacturing facilities that opened in the 1950s and 1960s were closed permanently during the 1970s and 1980s. The shutdown of these plants, in turn, often meant supplier and parts factories went out of business, causing further job losses. Neighbouring service industries surrounding these factories also found they could no longer do business. Consequently, the death of many shops, pubs and other retail establishments came in response to these large-scale closures. Local government resources were also strained, as less revenue was available to handle services normally provided by city councils and local authorities.

Numerous studies have found that long-term unemployment is debilitating not only to the community at large, but also to the residents as individuals who reside within those areas. Psychological depression is often the end result, as self-respect diminishes and relationships break apart. A sense of gloom and despair frequently takes hold in those affected, prompting a wide range of negative behaviours. Excessive drinking, illicit drug use, dalliances with criminal activities, and a large increase in suicides are just a few examples of the detrimental effects repeatedly cited.[16]

Married men often felt powerless, as they no longer were able to fulfil their traditional role as breadwinner and provider. This was especially pronounced for some men whose wives returned to work, as the economy shifted away from manufacturing and moved towards service industries, dominated by low-paid, part-time, 'traditional' female occupations. The experience of long-term unemployment among young people frequently scarred them for the remainder of their lives. This was particularly true for school leavers who were welcomed into a world with little prospect of a job. In most published studies on the matter, the findings usually point to structural unemployment, more than any other reason cited, as the number one cause for people falling into spiralling cycles of lifelong poverty and government dependency.[17]

The correlation between long-term youth unemployment, drug addiction and crime has been well documented over the years through numerous surveys. In one such study conducted in Liverpool, the researchers' findings were predictable. As is illustrated here from the results of this survey,

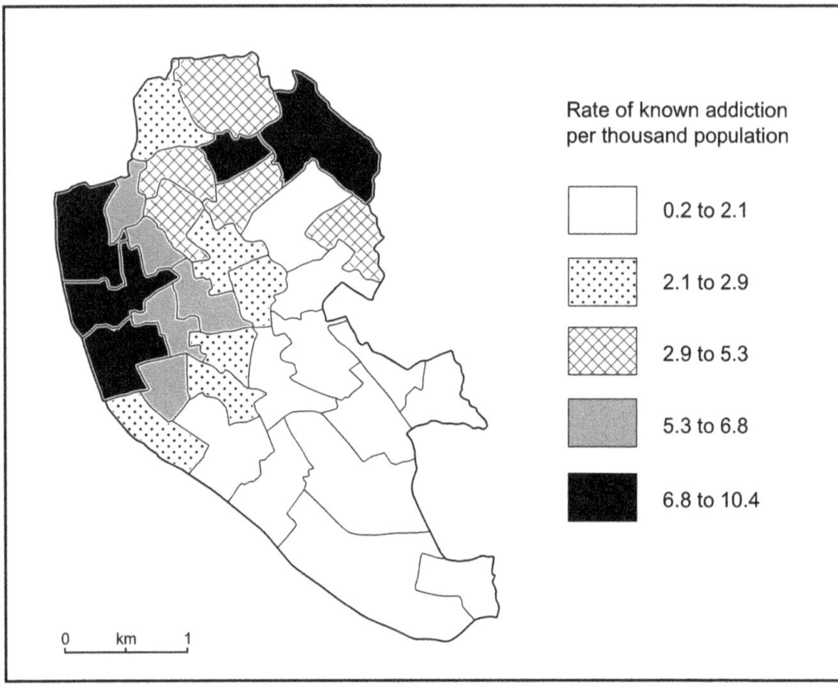

Figure 3 Known drug addiction in Liverpool wards – 1991

a definite relationship was established between the two variables of drug addiction, as marked in Figure 3, and statistics indicating high unemployment as shown earlier in Figure 1. There are obvious correlations, therefore, between Northend Liverpool wards, which suffered the worst levels of joblessness, as represented in Figure 1, and the residential patterns of Liverpool's youth who are registered drug addicts, marked in Figure 3.

Crime almost invariably follows addiction to narcotics, so this might partially explain how it came about that from 1974 to 1986 lawlessness increased in Liverpool by 86 per cent, and why burglaries jumped by a staggering 230 per cent.[18] Theft and violence had become ever-present reminders of the degree of change taking place in the world far outside the confines of certain neighbourhoods. Crime, substance abuse and poverty were the consequences of mass structural unemployment that accompanied these external changes.

Working-class communities were fragmented, and a whole way of life for many of the residents was irrevocably changed forever – and rarely for the better. Unskilled, ill-educated and unprepared to take part in the technologically advanced economy of the twenty-first century, a large percentage of these people would be lost in the cracks of what remained of the welfare state. Even some of the most battle-hardened from Liverpool's closest-knit working-class communities could not cope with such a rapid transformation.

Conclusion

In this chapter it has been demonstrated that Liverpool's economy suffered a rapid de-industrialisation from the mid-1970s onward. It was also shown that no other major British city suffered such severe and sustained levels of unemployment. Liverpool's long, hard experiences with joblessness gives obvious explanation why its workers refused to accept so many of the forced redundancies becoming apparent as the 1980s approached, and why their responses to these losses seemed so intensely personal and so uniquely Liverpudlian in character. Most Liverpudlians responded to such external economic forces through their own unique understanding of poverty, and it was via their own personal agency that decisions were made both individually and collectively to resist, rather than accept such circumstances as their fate.

When the rest of Britain enjoyed a brief but bountiful period of post-war prosperity and full employment, these good times had largely passed Liverpool by. The impression drawn from the literature and field interviews is that Liverpudlians severely resented these inequities, and proved repeatedly that they were prepared to protest such conditions at any cost in the future. This sense of grievance added to a festering feeling of alienation and separateness, often with hints to the city's earlier days during the wretched Irish famine. It is easy to see how these attitudes manifested themselves in a fierce trade union militancy, for which the city later become so well noted. The many personal and immediate recollections of poverty, the sense of objection felt of being robbed of something that was long overdue, as well as a long local tradition of trade union radicalism, support fundamental reasons why Liverpool's workers battled so doggedly to retain their jobs. It is not surprising, then, that at times, even to this day, a passionate sense that they somehow have been wronged can be detected amongst Liverpudlians. This trait becomes particularly noticeable when their mistrust is levelled at establishment figures in Westminster and the City.

During a House of Commons debate, Terry Fields, the left-wing Labour MP for Liverpool Broadgreen, replied to an opponent's questions on the economic conditions in his constituency by saying: 'I have never known anything other than bad housing, high unemployment, and lack of opportunity for Liverpool people.'[19] This sentiment encapsulated perfectly the feelings of so many people from Liverpool's working class, as they pondered where their community was heading, and what to make of the strange new world of the late twentieth century which loomed ahead. In the following chapters an analysis of the range, number and creativity of their responses to this rapidly changing economy will be examined and it is hoped they may provide better insight into how these dramatic transformations came to be understood.

Notes

1 W. R. Garside, *The Measurement of Unemployment: Methods and Sources in Great Britain 1850–1979* (Oxford, 1980), pp. 1–5 and 62–72.
2 See Table 2.1. See also *Department of Employment Gazette*, June 1988.
3 A. E. Green, 'The Likelihood of Becoming and Remaining Unemployed in Great Britain, 1984', *Transactions of the Institute of British Geographers*, New Series, vol. 11, no. 1 (1986), p. 38.
4 A. E. Green, D. W. Owen and C. M. Winnett, 'The Changing Geography of Recession: Analyses of Local Unemployment Time Series', *Transactions of the Institute of British Geographers*, New Series, vol. 19, no. 2 (1994), p. 143.
5 Garside, *Measurement of Unemployment*, pp. 72–80.
6 Derrick Leslie, Joanne Lindley and Leighton Thomas, 'Decline and Fall: Unemployment among Britain's Non-White Ethnic Communities 1960–1990', *Journal of the Royal Statistical Society: Series A (Statistics in Society)*, vol. 164, no. 2 (2001), p. 385.
7 Leslie *et al.*, 'Decline and Fall', p. 385.
8 After June 1988 the total population of UK unemployed is measured by 'per cent of entire workforce', which means groups previously not taken into account, such as the self-employed, HM Forces and participants in work-related government training schemes, are now counted. After January 1990 local area levels include both the original and new measurement systems. Figures marked with an asterisk in Table 2.1 represent 'per cent of entire workforce' system.
9 Michael G. Hayes, *Past Trends and Future Prospects: Urban Change in Liverpool 1961–2001* (Liverpool, 1987), p. 1.
10 Hayes, *Past Trends*, p. 1.
11 Hayes, *Past Trends*, p. 2.
12 Tony Lane, 'Merseyside under the Hammer', *Marxism Today*, February 1981, p. 18.
13 Lane, 'Merseyside under the Hammer', p. 18.
14 The 1991 census counted the following groups as 'Non-White': Black Caribbean, Black African, Black (Other), Indian, Pakistani, Bangladeshi, Chinese, Asian (Other) and Other than White.

15 Lord Gifford QC *et al.*, *Loosen the Shackles: First Report of the Liverpool 8 Inquiry into Race Relations in Liverpool* (London, 1989), pp. 40–58.
16 Richard Smith, '"Gissa Job:" The Experience of Unemployment', *British Medical Journal*, vol. 291 (1985), pp. 1263–6. See also Colin Pritchard, 'Unemployment, Age, Gender and Regional Suicide in England and Wales 1974–90: A Harbinger of Increased Suicide for the 1990s?', *The British Journal of Social Work*, vol. 25, no. 6 (1995), pp. 767, 769–71, 774–6 and 780; Vanessa Rose and Elizabeth Harris, 'From Efficacy to Effectiveness: Case Studies in Unemployment Research', *Journal of Public Health*, vol. 26, no. 3 (2004), p. 297.
17 Smith, '"Gissa Job"', p. 1265. See also Pritchard, 'Unemployment', pp. 771 and 780.
18 Hayes, *Past Trends*, p. 2.
19 Hansard, House of Commons, 21 February 1985, vol. 73, cc. 1323.

3

British Leyland's closure of the Triumph TR7 plant in Speke: 'the shape of things to come'?

The central concern of this chapter is with the mothballing of Standard-Triumph's Plant No. 2 in the southend Liverpool ward of Speke. The reasons for focusing on this incident are not only because Standard-Triumph was the first car maker to expand into Merseyside during the post-war boom, but also because Standard-Triumph's Speke facility was the first of a number of major motor-related manufacturing establishments in the area to permanently close its gates. This plant closure marked the commencement of a wave of factory shutdowns, and the demise of manufacturing in the city. This case study provides a clear example of de-industrialisation in action, and the detrimental effects industrial closure had on local working-class communities as it played out from the 1970s onward.

Examining the plight of Liverpool's car workers recollects a number of the arguments brought forth by Eric Hobsbawm in his pivotal essay, 'The Forward March of Labour Halted?'[1] In this work, Hobsbawm discussed the emergence of workplace sectionalism, and what he argued was a growing lack of solidarity amongst the British working class in the post-war era. He attributed much of this to the expanding demographic diversity in the working class, as well as, amongst other reasons, a shift from a manufacturing-based to a white-collar, service- and public-sector-dominated economy. Hobsbawm contended that sectionalism had corroded any semblance of mutuality and class-consciousness, once prominently displayed by British workers. He postulated that this growing shift towards individualism had manifested itself in a loss of class-consciousness and a growing sense of apathy amongst workers. Such levels of indifference, Hobsbawm declared, led to a weakening of trade union power and eroded many of the gains previously made by the working class.

Hobsbawm's rather pessimistic analysis of diminishing working-class militancy might also easily be offered as an explanation for the inertia preceding the 1978 shutdown of the motor car maker, Standard-Triumph's enormous No. 2 Plant in Speke, Liverpool. Some observers within the labour movement noted that this factory closure in May of 1978 elicited few outward signs of organised resistance from its idled employees or the working-class community on Merseyside as a whole.

In some respect the shutdown of Standard-Triumph Motors mammoth facility in Speke would serve as a sign of what was to come, as it was the first major factory closure on Merseyside during the painful era of late twentieth-century de-industrialisation. A review of the secondary literature relating to this plant closure discloses little evidence that a sense of a collective class-consciousness from its workforce was visible, nor were there any signs the employees exhibited the level of solidarity necessary to sustain an organised opposition to closure. Indeed, unlike other examples of working-class defiance examined in this book, the Standard-Triumph workers appeared on the surface to reveal little of the collective agency found in the other campaigns of resistance documented.

Nevertheless, a more thorough and detailed analysis of the events surrounding this plant closure could revise such initial judgements. This chapter will dig deeper and investigate whether there was, indeed, some degree of resistance to the permanent redundancies accompanying this factory closure. More importantly, it will question whether this closure would serve as a catalyst for a new wave of working-class activism on Merseyside. Indeed, despite any superficial appearances of worker complacency it must be noted that there were signs of trade union militancy amongst many of the former workers made redundant at this facility. We shall see that many of the workers most vocal in their opposition to this plant closure would later go on to serve in the 1980s and beyond as leading figures in advocating rights for the unemployed.

Standard-Triumph Plant No. 2

The Standard-Triumph Motor Company first opened on Merseyside in 1959 with the completion of its Plant 1 facility in Speke. Like nearly every other manufacturing establishment opening branch plants on Merseyside at this time, Standard-Triumph was lured to Liverpool by a series of government incentives. Standard-Triumph was the first motor car assembler to locate on Merseyside to take advantage of such enticements.. However, it should be noted that this factory had not become a fully integrated manufacturing facility until later in its history. It initially served as a feeder plant, producing sub-assemblies which were shipped to the company's larger establishments in the West Midlands. This factory was intended as the first stage of an industrial development; the second phase consisted of constructing a larger, completely integrated assembly facility.

Standard-Triumph Motors merged with Leyland Motors in 1961, and after a series of other smaller mergers, the company later went on to become British Leyland Motor Corporation (BLMC) in 1968. The firm shortened the name to British Leyland, or just BL, as it was often called. These mergers and acquisitions caused long delays in implementing the second phase of the initial plan for its Speke facility – much to the consternation of Harold Wilson's Labour governments of 1964–70. One former employee recalled:

> Standard-Triumph levelled their site at the same time as Fords in the late 50s (1957–58). When Standards went bust they became part of British Motor Holdings which then became British Leyland. Nothing was built on the site for years until local and central government began to give out grant aid etc., and in 1968 [*sic*] the plant was opened.[2]

Nevertheless, by 1969 the Triumph Speke Plant No. 2 was finally built (see Figure 4). Its integrated capabilities were not completely utilised until

Figure 4 Aerial view of British Leyland's Speke facility, 1976

several years later with the introduction of the Triumph Toledo, the first of a number of models assembled entirely on location at the Speke factory.

Despite the increase in jobs, many employees felt there was never a long-term commitment from the company to this factory or to the Merseyside area. The physical structure of Plant 2 appeared flimsy and merely temporary in the eyes of some. A common opinion held by a number of the original employees was: 'It just didn't seem as if they'd come to stay.'[3] One former worker elaborated further: 'The first thing that struck me when I went into the place and started there was the pre-fabricated nature, you know, a thrown-up job.'[4]

This sense of vulnerability was to prove well founded. A former shop steward remembered the short-sightedness of Standard-Triumph management, and how their actions often conveyed a feeling of impermanence during the plant's early days:

> The only reason why they [Standards] built Plant 2 was because the [Harold Wilson's Labour] government pressed them to live up to their end of the original bargain ... They would have preferred to keep everything back in the West Midlands if they could ... after they opened and we were gearing up for the Toledo there was a lot of teething problems because of failures by management, suppliers ... we never had a full week's wages for a full twelve months! They were forever laying you off. They would send you home after only a couple hours work, quite often at 2 or 3 o'clock in the morning ... people were sick and tired of getting sent home at all hours of the night and never getting a full week's pay packet.[5]

Another senior steward also recalled the chaotic nature of the plant, and its disorganised system of internal management:

> It was a very, very odd set-up for a car factory ... You had the better part of 7,000 people working there ... I was at Plant 2, which was Paint, Trim and Assembly. When I first went there [1970] the panels were pressed at Plant 1, which was a mile or so [away], in Woodend Avenue. They pressed them, assembled them ... they'd leave Plant 1 all checked and ready to go, but by the time they were brought over to Plant 2, they'd get damaged and knocked about from being loaded and unloaded off dirty wagons. So we'd have to knock those dents out and degrease them all over again, even before we could strip them down, paint and bond them. [To] top it all off, they weren't even fully assembled in Speke. The shell of the car would be fully built here, but it still would have to be loaded again on wagons and shipped down to Coventry to get their engines and gearboxes put in ... It's no wonder they lost money. This, of course, was before we got the contract for the Triumph Toledo. By then they started assembling cars at that plant from start to finish.[6]

The threat of closure loomed large over the Speke workforce since the factory's inception. Many of the workers often felt Standard-Triumph management treated the Speke facility as an afterthought, and that it would last only as long as the government subsidised its existence. Other observers believed that company officials considered Speke to be merely a peripheral location and never utilised the plant to full capacity. The factory had a production capacity of 100,000 vehicles per year, but it never exceeded 30,000. These figures also symbolised the marginalisation and insecurity sensed by the Merseyside workforce in their brief, turbulent relationship with Standard-Triumph, aka BL.[7]

The 1970s proved a volatile decade for Merseyside's car workers. Due to growing worldwide competition there had been notable under-investment in UK manufacturing. This was attributed mainly to British management's need for rapid returns in profit in order to satisfy anxious shareholders. The manufacturing sector and the motor car industry in particular was especially hard hit by this form of short-termism. This inability to generate increasingly larger dividends and other factors led to fundamental changes in the attitudes of British investors towards home-grown manufacturing. City traders looked abroad, lured by the promise of lower taxes, no trade unions, fewer government regulations and, most importantly, greater profits. Between the years 1974 and 1979, over 650,000 British manufacturing jobs were lost. It was during that same period, private overseas investment grew by more than 30 per cent each year. It is also important to note that war in the Middle East had doubled the price of imported oil by 1974. From the years 1971 to 1981, oil prices rocketed by 1,473 per cent.[8] These factors had devastating effects on British car makers.

In addition, BL experienced serious financial difficulties in the years before 1973. Around the time of the BL merger in 1968, the first signs appeared that foreign competition, particularly from West Germany and Japan, was beginning to encroach upon the British market. The merger did not cure the company's ailments. Quite the contrary, it brought an intensification of many of the deep-seated problems associated with British car manufacturing: under-investment, poor industrial relations, lack of vision, too many models, over-capacity, poor quality and low worker productivity were all cited as the reasons why BL was in the red.[9] In the eyes of businessmen, politicians and the mainstream media, BL typified the 'British disease' of poor industrial relations, largely resulting from a strike-prone workforce and low levels of productivity.[10]

Imported cars accounted for 33 per cent of all British registrations by 1975, which for the first time exceeded BL's share of 31 per cent. Company production dropped from 1.7 million cars in 1973 to 1.26 million in

1975. In that year the company declared losses of £76 million, representing a net loss of between £90 and £160 on every vehicle sold. Harold Wilson's Labour government had to decide whether to let the 'national champion' die a slow and ignominious death – risking mass unemployment and upsetting the balance of trade – or nationalise the company until it could become profitable once again.[11]

In December of 1974 Wilson appointed Sir Don Ryder of the National Enterprise Board to lead an investigation into the economic malaise of Britain's largest automobile manufacturer. Ryder's panel concluded that of the numerous problems plaguing BL, the most serious difficulties were in such matters as the age and inferiority of the capital stock, inadequate product development and poorly integrated management. The committee also highlighted the large number of man-hours lost through labour strife. A powerful shop-steward system, often led by left-wing militant activists, was cited as the main source of this problem, along with a lack of industrial relations expertise on the part of management.[12]

This was the golden age of shop-steward dominance, as one such steward recounted:

> We were unbelievably powerful. I'll give you an example from the paint shop where I was. There was a guy who at one time worked there ... he became a foreman. Normally, that's like a poacher turned into a gamekeeper ... But he was a decent foreman to the lads in that section, I mean he really was OK... Some of these lads after they became foreman turned into right bastards; you saw the real side of them. But he wasn't; he was still a decent human being ... So one day he got sacked. Just like that, the company fired him. Well, we said, 'fuck that'. We called a sectional meeting, and we said we're not having this (laughs). I mean, he was a boss. He wasn't one of us or a member of our union ... Anyway, so we went out, and we got him his job back. I mean that had to be the first time in history where a trade union threatened to go out on strike in order to get a boss his job back! (Laughs)[13]

Meanwhile, many senior union officials were searching for ways to curb the influence of shop stewards. One retired Transport and General Workers' Union (TGWU) officer from the Liverpool office remembered:

> Let me just stress this. Again, it wasn't dissimilar to the organisation that I was party to in Ford's (The Ford facility in neighbouring Halewood, Merseyside). Although we were members of individual unions, the most important meetings and committees, to me, was the joint shop stewards committee. And the official unions didn't like this particularly. And if you ever read anything about the upheavals down at Ford Dagenham, and

> the way they were able to smash the organisation down there was to sack leading shop stewards. That could only have been done with the compliance of the official union because they didn't like the fact that elected labour representatives, convenors and shop stewards – laymen – were able to say to the official unions: 'You, you and you, butt out of this. We'll say when we need you. We'll say when we want you. We run our own show.'[14]

Therefore, national union officials and company management both had a vested interest in curbing the power of shop stewards, and together they sought answers from the Ryder investigation.

The findings of Sir Don Ryder's panel were published in April 1975. The panel's report to the government was officially known as *British Leyland: The Next Decade*, but was generally referred to as the Ryder Report.[15] Amongst its recommendations was the temporary nationalisation of the company, with the hope it could become viable as a private enterprise again by 1981. This would require a £1,264 million initial investment from the government with an additional £260 million in immediate working capital. The alternative was to let the company go out of business, putting hundreds of thousands out of work. It was estimated nearly 13.5 per cent of the working population of Oxford worked for BL, as well as 9.5 per cent of Coventry and 8.9 per cent of Birmingham. BL was Britain's single largest net exporter, whose exports in 1978 alone amounted to £910 million.

Consequently, as of June 1975 the government retained 95 per cent ownership of BL, and the company was placed under the control of the National Enterprise Board (NEB). With nationalisation, many in the workforce enjoyed a new-found sense of permanence. One senior shop steward at Speke referred to that period when he said:

> I think it was more stable after nationalisation. You know, it wasn't a stable job up to that point. You didn't have a steady job there every single day; it just didn't work like that – it was chaos at times. We certainly had more hope for the future when it was nationalised. As it turned out that was a forlorn hope, but we certainly believed it then.[16]

Once the euphoria of nationalisation subsided, employees came back to the realisation that BL was still a commercial enterprise, and its purpose was to generate profit. A former TGWU official reflected on the situation:

> I never saw it in terms of a 'nationalised' plant. To me, they were just an employer. I would have dealt with them like any other employer that came

across the desk. You were there to get the best deal for the lads, and you were there to fight for them if you had to.[17]

Ryder's recommendations called for a more participatory role for labour, but this greater input from labour would only be granted with the price of a reconfiguration of managerial control, whereby less power would be in the hands of shop stewards. The panel also proposed a greater investment from BL into new and developing technology. Lastly, the panel recommended that the many different models of cars produced by BL had to be rationalised. In the open-top sports car market alone, BL offered the Triumph Spitfire, Triumph TR6, Triumph Stag, the MGB and the MG Midget, each competing with one another for market share.

Nevertheless, along with nationalisation came the call for improved productivity. Even before nationalisation in 1975 there had been pressure from BL management to change from the piece-work pay rate scheme to the more Fordist-style measured day-work system, often referred to as MDW. The piece-work system encouraged a strong shop steward presence, as one car worker said: 'With piece-work, management *asked* you whether the timing was right for certain tasks – they *had* to negotiate – whereas with lean production, management told you what the timings were.'[18]

Before MDW was finally implemented at the Speke plant in November 1973, Triumph workers had exercised a great deal of control over work speeds and production levels. Immediately after MDW was introduced, abrupt changes in the attitude of BL management became evident: numerous time studies, faster line speeds and a general feeling by the workers that they were being led by the whip. MDW removed power from the shop steward and put it back into the hands of the foremen. It gave management control over production. Company managers could instil fear in the hearts of their foremen, who in turn would be ruthless in applying greater pressure on workers manning the assembly-line. One author quoted a Speke worker: 'Under these "terror tactics" the foremen would go to great lengths to get the cars through his section. Quality control became a secondary concern.'[19]

Initially, the fixed hourly wage rates proposed under MDW were strenuously resisted by the unions representing BL workers. The Liverpool union branches were especially averse to its demands, since so many of the BL workers at Speke had previous job experience working at the exhausting pace set at the neighbouring Ford facility, or 'hell camp' as some colourfully described Ford.[20] However, some of these attitudes changed after BL management was forced into offering a generous hourly rate in exchange for adopting their much sought after MDW system. One BL worker remembered: 'The unions negotiated a pound an hour ... A pound an hour was a good deal because with the piecework system we weren't getting nowhere near that kind of money.'[21] A Speke steward also recalled:

> Well, I was a bit sceptical at first, but then we got them up to £42 a week, which for us, we were averaging maybe £30 then, and that's a big jump, you know. We put strong arguments up initially against it, but we always knew eventually it was coming in, so in a way that gave us a better bargaining power. I would say it was generally better for the workforce ... The supervision definitely got tighter. Where with piece-work you had arguments over your timings of the job, but if you didn't really want to work harder, collectively, they weren't going to push it.[22]

Indeed, the car workers were well remunerated by this time. One Speke worker explained:

> I mean it was good money. We were probably some of the best paid workers in all Merseyside then. I had a trade before I hired on with Standards – a lot of the lads did. My brother-in-law, for instance, was a bricklayer. We were skilled men, but we were making a lot more money in that factory.[23]

With the introduction of MDW, workers at BL had acquired monetary gains, but this came at the price of a much more disciplined and structured work environment. The pace of the assembly track now determined production levels, and not the acquiescence of the shop stewards (see Figure 5).

Despite muscle-flexing on the part of management, the company still recognised a loose system of mutuality agreements that were put in place at Speke during the years prior to the BL merger. This notion of mutuality meant that both management and the shop stewards had to reach bilateral agreements before any changes in manpower levels, work assignments or line speeds could be implemented.[24] It is important to note that, even after the merger in 1968, these procedures were still faithfully adhered to by BL management. Mutuality agreements were only set in place at certain BL facilities. Neither Ford nor Vauxhall's Merseyside employees enjoyed such protections, no matter how hard their union branches pushed for similar provisions.[25]

By 1975, the Speke factory was the only BL facility to have the mutuality agreement specifically codified into its labour contract. This act came on the heels of the Ryder Report's push for better industrial relations. The official recognition of the mutuality agreement was written into the labour contract and offered by BL management, along with a liberal

Figure 5 Assembly line workers at British Leyland' Speke facility

increase in hourly pay rates, as an inducement for the Speke unions to accept MDW.[26] Eventually, the BL workers at Speke were pleased they managed to acquire these agreements in writing, because as greater pressure was placed on the company to achieve profitability, these once unwritten but universally accepted mutuality agreements were getting tossed aside at BL's other facilities.[27] Consequently, this now officially recognised mutuality agreement at BL's Speke plant was a prized possession by the Merseyside workforce. It was not something they were willing to relinquish at any time in the future.

Today, most observers admit that the MDW was instituted at BL before adequate manpower levels were established and productivity rates could be agreed upon. This, in turn, created heavier workloads for BL employees, which ultimately made for a more combative, less collaborative relationship between BL management and the trade unions. This antagonistic association was especially noticeable at BL's West Midland facilities after their mutuality agreements had been tossed aside by BL management.[28] One former worker at Speke defended their mutuality agreement:

> We didn't want to lose it because it protected your earnings. It also protected you from getting sent home at 2, 3 or even 4 o'clock in the morning [if there was no more work to do that shift] ... And then they would only pay you up till 3 or 4 o'clock and that was it ... Now we were the only plant to have it [in our contract] because we purposely negotiated it in there ... management absolutely hated that we had it in writing.[29]

Nevertheless, what troubled BL management more than the mutuality agreement at Speke was the sagging sales of their vehicles. The company's share of the UK car market fell from 38.1 per cent in 1970 to 18.2 per cent a decade later.[30] Despite this drop in sales at BL, the British consumer maintained a growing appetite for automobiles during this period. The number of vehicles sold in the UK increased from 1,076,900 in 1970 to 1,513,800 in 1980. One author reminded his readers: 'Japanese imports exacerbated rather than created problems for the industry in Britain.'[31] Declining sales meant decreased profits, and many within BL management called for tighter rationalisation policies and greater efficiency from the workforce. Trade unionists countered company allegations of unproductive personnel with accusations of poorly designed and badly engineered products.[32]

Senior managers at BL were far more inclined to blame declining sales on what they felt was an idle and strike-prone workforce rather than inferior products. Company management often fought their corner by citing the findings of government reports highlighting these inefficiencies. One such account stated: 'It takes almost twice as many man-hours to assemble similar cars using the same comparable plant and equipment in Britain as it does on the Continent.'[33]

Low productivity was not caused by high rates of absenteeism and worker idleness, as was often the case in Italy and France; rather, labour disputes were underlined as the core of this problem. The British car industry experienced ten times as many disputes as any other British industry. Labour unrest in the British car industry was also higher than unrest in car manufacturing elsewhere in Europe. In 1974, one study determined that approximately 66 per cent of all production lost in Britain was due to either internal or external industrial disputes.[34] It was noted that poor labour relations wasted valuable time and resources that could have been devoted to more constructive pursuits, such as design and product development. British plant managers interviewed by a government committee claimed almost half of their time was spent dealing with labour disputes, compared to 5 to 10 per cent by their counterparts in West Germany and Belgium.[35] BL's record was cited as being 'amongst the worst in the industry'. Consequently, improvements in controlling the workforce were seen by company management as top priority. The Speke plant in particular was pointed out as the most fractious, and therefore deserving the tightest discipline.[36]

Both the local and national press enhanced this image of the Speke factory as having a long history of labour unrest. One report referred to this facility as the 'strike bound plant at Speke' with its long history of 'pitched battles'.[37] In reality, this reputation was undeserved. Closer examination of the labour record at BL Speke reveals that the plant had not experienced any labour unrest for five years prior to 1978: an excellent record by British motor industry standards and especially impressive for a Merseyside workforce. One national newspaper stated that the Speke facility, prior to the eighteen-week strike in 1977–78, displayed an 'enviable labour relations record'.[38]

This questions the motives of BL management for summarily blaming lagging sales on their 'strike-prone' workforce, when this was clearly not the case. According to the trade unions, the main reasons why BL products were losing competitive edge were under-investment, a history of managerial blunders, as well as badly designed and engineered vehicles.

Clearly, solutions were needed to bring customers back to the BL badge. However, BL managers were also mindful that a strict new set of rationalisation policies had to be adhered to if they were ever going to return the company to the profitable private sector. Following the recommendations of the Ryder Report, BL management decided the company's extensive sports car line was to be consolidated into one. A new, innovative car line would be produced. Thus, the infamous Triumph TR7 was born. The controversial model was to be marketed in Britain and the United States starting in January 1975. Production of the entire vehicle was to be done exclusively at the Speke plant, starting in September 1974. A slick advertising campaign blanketed the American market, where the wedge-like car was touted on television commercials as 'The shape of things to come'.

The TR7 would be linked with Speke forever. Yet despite the massive advertising drive and its catchy new slogan, the model had a far from fashionable look. It was rejected immediately by sports car enthusiasts in both the United States and Britain. BL originally had high hopes of selling at least 80,000 of the hard-top coupés per annum. However, the vehicle's unpopular design and poor reputation for mechanical reliability meant only a fraction of that figure was sold.[39]

In addition to faulty product development costs were also a growing concern. It was becoming more apparent to BL management that if they wanted to compete with Ford Motor Company, they had to start operating like Ford. This not only meant a commitment to the rationalisation policies recommended in the Ryder Report, but a complete change in managerial attitudes. Beginning in the late 1970s there was a growing trend amongst most manufacturing concerns in the UK and the United States that demanded doing 'more with less' from a tighter regulated and disciplined workforce. BL management reasoned that investment in new technology would be futile if their work practices were not overhauled first.

In November 1977, Prime Minister James Callaghan decided BL needed a change in direction if it were to survive; consequently, he hand-picked South African businessman Michael Edwardes as BL's new managing director. Edwardes' strong views on maintaining free markets and his own right-wing political beliefs were more in common with those of the Leader of the Opposition, Margaret Thatcher, than Labour Prime Minister James Callaghan. However, during his five-year tenure as BL's chief executive, Edwardes made it clear he was dedicated to making BL a profitable enterprise once again. His plans included reducing the 1977 workforce by half, intensifying the pace of production, cutting real wages and neutering the power of the trade unions, largely through a system of weeding out militant shop stewards.[40]

If leadership at BL was seen as weak under the previous managing director, Lord Stokes, it changed dramatically after the appointment of the controversial Edwardes. A clear indication of BL's new change in direction can be seen in Edwardes' style of labour relations. Prior to Edwardes coming on board in November 1977, management preferred a 'softly-softly' approach in dealing with the workforce. Negotiations, worker participation and cooperation were often sought before most major decisions were made by corporate management. However, in the weeks and months just prior to Edwardes 'officially' coming on board, the way of doing business at BL started to change noticeably. The Speke workforce began to take notice and was not pleased with what it saw. The new strategy from BL management was to make demands on the trade unions for work practice reform, and when this failed, management would then wrest concessions from the workforce through conflict and confrontations.[41]

This new style of 'macho management', as it was often called in the press, believed in strict shop-floor discipline and greater empowerment of first-line supervisors. Management asserted its right to manage, even if it was done in a belligerent manner. BL executives took every opportunity to remind their workforce that company managers were in charge, not shop stewards. Along with this increase in discipline, BL bosses also demanded greater flexibility and mobility in the deployment of labour. This was accomplished by breaking conventions that were previously adhered to, as in the case of mutuality agreements. Workers were increasingly given more responsibilities, while manpower levels were reduced through rationalisation. All workers were now held strictly accountable for the completion of these added tasks and were disciplined sternly if responsibilities were not met. Petty rules, such as rigid adherence to meal and break times, which before had largely gone unenforced, were now closely monitored. Overtime costs were also minimised. The assembly process was sped up, and machine tools replaced humans wherever substitutions were deemed more economical.[42]

Another important element in this new management style was the introduction of fear as a means of control. Executives throughout the UK utilised growing unemployment as a powerful lever for manipulating workers' behaviour. Threats of factory closures and lay-offs became common, in conjunction with bullying, swearing and shouting.[43] Job security became the ultimate goal for workers in a de-industrialising economy. Workers were made to feel their jobs were vulnerable, and retention of their livelihoods depended on adapting a more compliant and, some would argue, servile attitude. BL, despite being a nationalised company, was not above employing such demeaning rhetoric.[44] One former shop steward described how things began to change at Speke during this new era of 'macho management':

> The supervision there got to be very dictatorial at times. Because we weren't able to get a lot of cars through, a lot of people were standing around with nothing to do. And the foremen would say, 'You can't do this', and 'You can't do that'. And things would lead to disciplinaries [*sic*] and I thought they should have gone back to giving more leeway, like the old days. Because, I mean they could only force them to tidy around their work stations so much. But then they started coming out with more rules about not being allowed to go into another department and not wanting you to roam around the plant. Obviously people began getting into misdemeanours and smoking where they shouldn't have been, etc ... Managers started giving out three-day suspensions for little things, and the lads thought they were being unjustly treated, but on the other hand that built up a lot of comradeship because people were really becoming annoyed with the way things were changing.[45]

Another former shop steward described some of the management team at Speke: 'They were mostly people not from the Liverpool area, here. They were mainly sent up from the Midlands and the South. They didn't want to be up here in Liverpool, and it showed. Some were OK, but many more were just horrible people, the absolute worst.'[46] An example of this new atmosphere came from one steward:

> One day after this meeting certain people were made up as foremen. The company laid in to them what they expected and what-not. Well one lad was made a foreman, and he had a mate from way back who was working the line. So on this one day he goes up to his mate working the line and says, 'Do you want a ciggie [cigarette]?' Well the old friend says, 'yeah'. So the foreman gives him the cigarette, lights it for him, and then he actually suspends him for one day's pay because he was smoking when and where it was against the rules.[47]

Whether such stories are factually correct mean little, as the people telling these tales sincerely believe their validity. Such perceptions of corporate oppression, even if apocryphal, were etched in the minds of the workers and therefore relevant to their having any feelings of trust in management.

It should be emphasised that many of these changes in company policies and attitudes began in the months before Edwardes' arrival as the new managing director of BL, so they cannot all be ascribed to his chairmanship. In many ways, Edwardes was merely a symbol of the alterations in attitudes of modern British management at this time. However, it must be said that many of the former workers interviewed attributed the new 'macho management' style directly to Edwardes, despite the fact that he was not 'officially' in charge of BL until November 1977. Many felt he was wielding influence over the Callaghan government from behind the scenes in the weeks prior to the announcement of his being selected as chairman of BL.

The trade unions mounted some opposition to Edwardes' plans for contraction. A pamphlet published by the BL Combine Committee reminded the public that the Ryder Report gave many viable alternatives to Edwardes' proposals. They also propagated a variety of ideas among their membership, including tighter import controls, improvement of workers' wages and conditions, greater industrial democracy, increasing government investment, an extensive sales campaign, installing the latest technology as standard on all BL vehicles, and utilisation of all existing factory capacity.[48] Many in Westminster were unimpressed with these alternatives. Consequently, Edwardes' cost-cutting agenda was approved by the Labour government.

Michael Edwardes' baptism to industrial conflict at BL occurred on his first 'official' day in post, and as predicted, this confrontation involved the workforce at Speke. The problem arose because of a change in line speeds and worker deployment. This was done abruptly without consulting the shop stewards working that day, which the unions considered a violation of the mutuality agreement. One steward recalled the events clearly:

> It started in the garage area. The garage area was probably the best area to work in because it was cushier. It wasn't subject to strict timings, they worked in little bays, and they didn't have a trim deck or an assembly line. [Management] thought they'd try and tighten up that area, and so they just implemented a new timing system, and within the Protected Earnings Plan [PEP] Document it clearly stated something of that kind of nature had to be negotiated with the OK of the shop stewards and plant convenors, but instead they just imposed it on us. Well, they then also turned up the line speeds, so we all walked out and the strike was on.[49]

The mutuality agreement was sacred in the eyes of most employees at Speke. It signified job control over seemingly trivial routines that had enormous effects on the welfare of individuals. One worker recalled:

> Because of what the issue was over, the strike was absolutely solid. And a credit to the workforce, a seventeen-week strike, and not one man crossed the picket line, so that shows how important the mutuality agreement was to us. Everybody was solid on this. All realised that we had to keep the mutuality agreement because we didn't want to end up like Ford's or Vauxhall where management determined times, everything, you name it ... Many of the lads worked out at Ford's at one point or another, so we knew what a hell camp that place was. We didn't want Leyland's to end up like that place. As bad as the managers could get at Leyland's they were still ten times better than the slave drivers at Ford's.[50]

It was far from complete industrial democracy, but the mutuality agreement was seen by BL workers as a much fairer way of doing business than the production practices used at Ford or Vauxhall. Nevertheless, from Edwardes' perspective, the mutuality agreement was an unnecessary and costly burden. It was Triumph Plant No. 2 in Speke that Edwardes chose as the site for his first battle with the unions.

The British Leyland strike at Speke, 1977–78

On 1 November 1977, shop stewards from Speke's Plant No. 2 called a walkout that would last a total of seventeen long weeks. Some observers had feared the possibility of a prolonged dispute on the very day Edwardes took charge. It was known that the plant's chief car model, the TR7, was not selling. Inaccurate as the accusation was, it was often suggested by the national press that the Speke car workers were 'strike happy' and largely inexperienced in engineering employment. Lastly, there was the constraints of the mutuality agreement that continued at Speke long after it had been eradicated in BL's other plants. Many felt Edwardes and his team would find an excuse to initiate a rebellion in Liverpool. Consequently, the term 'inevitable' has often been employed in the literature on the closure of Speke.[51]

The allegation that this strike was deliberately provoked is a common theme among former employees, many of whom felt their plant was the test case for the new 'Edwardes Plan'. Press reports pick up the question of provocation and present a grim, drawn-out battle. By the end of December 1977, the *Liverpool Daily Post* posed the question:

> And has the two-month strike at the Speke factory which has halted all TR7 and Dolomite production been allowed to linger on by Leyland's management because the company has over-produced its controversial, wedge-shaped sporting two-seater and, as a result couldn't sell anymore? ... Contrary to the popular middle-class conception of shop stewards as 'Communist sympathisers' – both Mick Everett and Dave Thomas [Convenors of the TGWU and Amalgamated Union of Engineering Workers (AUEW) at Speke] claim to be bitter having lost their good industrial relations record in the past two months [of strike activity]. Then on October 31 the Speke management risked their glowing record of five strike-free years and, at a stride, plunged the factory into the longest strike its workers ever known. Doubtless they [BL management] anticipated that the workforce which had been laid off and idle for weeks would rebel and overthrow their shop stewards, demanding the right to work, as their colleagues in the Midlands had done last summer.[52]

Edwardes was perceived to have profited from an attempt at what one former shop steward alleged was 'union busting':

> The company within only a year or two prior to that strike had taken on a lot of new employees because of the shift they added ... there were some green and inexperienced shop stewards. I mean over 70 per cent of that workforce was in their 20s, with young families. So consequently, if you're still out [on strike] after about a week, you get worried then. My view is that [Edwardes] ... had us on his hit list. I'm sure he saw his opportunity. He realised it was a sensitive thing, it being Merseyside, a place traditionally plagued with high unemployment. And so he waited and if he was presented with an opportunity on a plate then he'd play hard. So it never looked like it was going to settle quick ... he knew a good percentage of these people would struggle the longer it went on. A young workforce – it dragged on over the Christmas season and you aren't getting

> paid anything except for your dole ... But to everyone's credit that strike still remained solid.[53]

Some of the participants in this industrial action maintain Edwardes' questionable tactics strengthened the bonds of solidarity amongst the workers. One steward recalled:

> You have to understand we had that entire plant shut and there were no signs of negotiations. Seventeen weeks and no negotiations! You have to realise that's incredible. And yet no one was opposing the strike. You might have the odd wife who'd appear in the local paper shouting about how her husband wants to work, but no one crossed that picket line. Not one person even attempted to cross that picket line.[54]

From all evidence, the strike displayed a strong unity with little sign of sectional divisiveness. Young and old, skilled and semi-skilled, all appeared to agree that the walkout was necessary. Despite the hardships associated with being unemployed for a lengthy period, the rank-and-file seemed to have been unified and committed to their cause. A former shop steward recalled:

> The people by and large were solid. In any dispute there are always people struggling financially. The people then would spend five or six hours on the picket line and then once they got home their Mrs would be on them about the kids 'needing new shoes' or whatever. And the longer the dispute people can eventually get starved back into work. But we were always a solid workplace. You got to realise you're always going to have the maggots in any workplace, but that place was by and large a solid union workplace. And that's pretty good when you consider all those pressures for such a long time as that strike dragged on. And then you throw in the tactic they [management] started using around this time when they were running around saying how they're going to close this place or that place unless you give in, well that frightens some people, so you'll always get the few who want to give up. But in our case the mutuality agreement was important and we were committed to keeping it.[55]

According to the parties involved, the solidarity and mutual support was not just confined to BL workers. They cite how other local trade unionists such as the dockers were eager to lend assistance:

> The dockers were always great supporters. They were always in our corner during that whole thing. We linked up all the time with the dockers

> and they in turn linked up with us. If there was anything they could do for us, they would. They refused to load and offload BL cargo off ships.[56]

Another strike leader recalled that any internal resistance to continuing on with the strike was marginal, claiming that only outside commentators called for the strike to end:

> Most people in general gave us the thumbs up, but a few of the women, the wives of strikers I mean, were getting critical. Both Bishops started sticking their noses in where they shouldn't have, and the same thing could be said for a couple local politicians. A couple of the wives got this little committee together voicing opposition against the strike, but it was mainly motivated by the press, you see. We really were solid as a group despite what the newspapers printed.[57]

Press reports confirm that some sense of rank-and-file solidarity existed. Nevertheless, an anti-strike movement known as a 'wives committee' did exist, although there is no other evidence beyond this press clipping which implies that their number was limited to six members:

> Six Merseyside housewives will travel by minibus for London today in an attempt to get the Prime Minister to intervene in the 12-week unofficial strike at British Leyland's Triumph plant at Speke, Liverpool ... Mrs. Maureen Crook, the housewives' leader, and her supporters plan to hand in a petition at 10 Downing Street signed by hundreds of people.[58]

With over 3,000 workers directly affected by this strike, and only six wives taking a direct role in opposing this action, it did not appear that this 'wives committee' was a representative or popular movement within the Speke workforce. Even on the generous assumption that the 'hundreds' of petitioners consisted entirely of car workers or their families, they remained a small minority of the total numbers involved.

Certainly, this movement calling for a return to work did not have the same significance as similar reactions during car workers' strikes elsewhere, such as in 1974 when hundreds of car workers' family members converged on picket lines at BL's Cowley plant, demonstrating against industrial action there. In that dispute, the wives met the plant manager and demanded he 'dismiss militant trade unionists who, they said, were depriving their husbands of their livelihood'.[59] Clearly, the situation at Speke was different in some respects from the strike in Cowley, yet once again it was a Liverpool workforce that stood out for exhibiting such strong commitment to maintaining solidarity. It should also be noted that press evidence printed at the time of the strike's occurrence corroborate much of the recollections of cohesion reported by the oral interviews taken during this research.

Nevertheless, despite such demonstrations of workforce solidarity, it took nearly fifteen weeks before the strike was officially sanctioned by the two major unions representing the Speke workers. It was not until 10 February 1978 that national union leaders granted official recognition to the conflict. One retired TGWU official offered a possible explanation:

> I was quite disappointed with the manner that dispute was run, because I felt throughout there was forces at play which could have held great influences in the fate of the Speke plant which did not do this. I mean we had at the time a lot of contacts within the car industry in the West Midlands. I always felt the Speke workers were left to their own devices and were virtually abandoned. It was almost if there was a trade-off going on. As I recall, Edwardes was running loose at the time, and he saw it as his task in life to see how many factories he could close down (laughs) ... They had a well-run branch out there [in Speke] and the convenor, Mick Everett, surrounded himself with very capable stewards, so they could have handled almost anything. It did appear, however, at the time the union nationally, and the union in an official capacity, did not exercise as much influence as they could have done ... There were conflicts of interest apparent to me, because of possibly the fact it was a nationalised company under the influence of a Labour Party government. In my view there was a relationship with the Labour Party at the time, and a relationship with that company in the West Midlands that was a bit too cosy.[60]

Indeed, many trade union insiders felt that both Jack Jones, TGWU General Secretary, and Hugh Scanlon, AUEW President, were more committed to the success of the Labour government and the NEB, than they were to the demands of BL workers in Liverpool. It was widely speculated that they gave tacit approval to the new policies imposed by Edwardes at Speke. Many Speke workers felt they were being made sacrificial lambs in order to prop up a broken-down, government-backed BL.[61] One Speke steward developed this point further:

> They wanted that place closed from the top level. I belonged to a small group of people who went under the name of Triumph Workers, and we heard way back in 1976 that James Callaghan had ordered the plant should be closed. Now we were only young people at the time and never really thought the source who told us – who I'm not going to name, but he was from one of the far left political groups, so we didn't take him serious. I mean who would have thought a Labour government would want to

> shut a factory? At the time, we were, like, 'James Callaghan would never order such a thing, don't be daft'. But I know now that it did come directly from James Callaghan. Edwardes was well briefed long before his first day as head of British Leyland. He was a behind-the-scenes consultant to Callaghan and he told him long before he took over he was going to have to close plants and cut jobs drastically. Liverpool would be the first example he was going to make. He [Edwardes] told him [Callaghan] he could provoke a strike by hitting on that [the mutuality agreement], and then don't negotiate, because he knew what we didn't know at the time, that he had intentions of shutting our plant down.[62]

This testimony carries no corroborating evidence, but once again the actual truth may differ greatly from the *perceived* truth, yet it is perceptions that ultimately determine people's responses. Because of these images, whether true or false, many of the rank-and-file felt the national union fell in line with the wishes of the Callaghan government. Frank Banton, a TGWU branch secretary at Speke, was quoted in the *Liverpool Echo*:

> The national unions let us down very badly – particularly the AUEW. But the trouble was the top union men were also members of the National Enterprise Board. They didn't even negotiate any redundancy pay for us. It's a bloody disgrace.[63]

However, because of the eventual union endorsement, strikers became eligible for strike pay, but this proved to be too little, too late. BL ultimately carried through with its threat and announced closure of the Standard-Triumph Plant No. 2 facility in Speke on 15 February 1978. The factory would no longer be in operation after 26 May 1978, and the adjoining Plant No. 1 would also close down permanently in 1979.

The question for workers then was whether to acquiesce to the factory shutdown and the loss of thousands of jobs, or resist closure. The shop stewards felt that the strike had to come to a swift end first, if workers were to return and prepare for a campaign of resistance. The dispute terminated on 24 February 1978. According to *The Times*:

> The 2500 workers at British Leyland's Speke plant in Liverpool, whose strike over production schedules has cost the company $90 million in lost cars, voted overwhelmingly at a mass meeting yesterday to return to work on Monday. It was just eight days after Mr. Michael Edwardes, Leyland's chief executive, announced his plan to axe the factory, and 17 weeks from the start of the stoppage. The workforce now plans to mount a campaign to save their jobs ... Union officials said the company had agreed to reduce the speed of the TR7 sports car assembly lines at Speke

> from 19 cars an hour to 13 and agreed to manning demands for which the unions have been holding out ... It seems that events have overtaken the Speke situation and that many of the proposed changes that led to the strike are no longer necessary. Indeed, they may not have been necessary when the strike began, though no management decision to that effect had been taken. Strike leaders yesterday rejected suggestions that the closure plan had made them more amenable to company policy. They claimed that the concessions on which the settlement was based had all been by management. Mr. David Thomas, chairman of the joint shop stewards' committee, said the speed of what he suggested had been a cave-in by Leyland had angered many workers. Referring to Mr. Edwardes, he said: 'After 17 weeks you get the clown who caused the dispute finally conceding the point'.[64]

The sudden acceptance by BL management of the same issues it had refused to negotiate for months prior to the announcement of closure seemed suspicious to many of the Speke workers. It reinforced the notion that Edwardes had instigated the strike in order to use it as an excuse for closure. BL management blamed the plant's failure squarely on what it described as an 'unproductive' and 'strike-prone' Liverpool labour force.[65] However, Edwardes later admitted:

> The decision was not taken solely because of the factory's industrial relations record. There was massive overcapacity in production facilities throughout the Cars operations and all locations were under review. Closures were clearly essential, but there was a complex web of inter-dependence between many of them, particularly in the Midlands, which was still the heart of the business. It was obviously not cost-effective to transport the many thousands of components needed to build a car – from washers to engines – from Coventry, Birmingham and other locations to Liverpool.[66]

Edwardes was also clear as to why he felt it was necessary to be especially strong-willed about this decision:

> Many managers were simply convinced that the closure could not be delivered; that the Labour government or the unions would make it impossible to implement ... The decision to close the Speke No. 2 assembly factory was the first test of the new Board's resolve.[67]

Closure and resistance

The scarce literature available recording this particular industrial action suggests that if any plans were afoot at resisting closure, they were doomed to failure. This, of course, echoes much of Hobsbawm's assertions that a growing sense of workplace sectionalism, individual self-interest and fragmentation of the working class were evident.[68]

Clearly, sectionalism was an issue to some degree, and it surely cannot be discounted entirely. Citing BL workers in the West Midlands, one author maintains that many there welcomed the Speke closure as a means of strengthening their own job security.[69] Therefore, this begs the question of whether there was evolving at this time a growing 'factory-consciousness' rather than a class-consciousness? There may be a case for this assertion; however, not all the evidence points towards an increasingly sectionalised workforce in post-war Britain.

It was thought by many of BL's employees, scattered across Britain, that Edwardes needed a quick and successful plant closure if he was going to be able to proceed with his future plans of even more extensive downsizing. Because of the lengthy strike, many of these observers saw Speke No. 2 as vulnerable: an obvious choice for testing the waters. If Edwardes could close Speke, he would also terminate BL plants elsewhere.

Despite assumptions that workplace sectionalism and plant rivalries were present, one activist contended that BL workers elsewhere watched the situation in Liverpool attentively and were hoping the Merseyside workforce would put up fierce resistance to closure.[70] A former shop steward at Speke recalls a conversation with Derek Robinson, TGWU convenor at BL's Longbridge plant in Birmingham:

> Derek Robinson – Red Robbo, as he was called, came up and met us after the announcement of closure came down. Anyway, the Mini … was still in high demand then. So he said, 'Look, they can't get enough Minis. They're talking about putting a plant in Belgium to build them. But look, if you lads up here in Liverpool have a good go at them, and resist the closure, we'll hold a walkout in all the other plants in the Midlands to have the thing made up in Liverpool instead. That will mean more work, more overtime and more jobs for you lads'.[71]

In a time of increasing unemployment, this was indeed a generous proposal were it to be realised. It lends a sense of worker solidarity, rather than the sectionalism thought to be so prevalent. Unfortunately, because of what eventually transpired at Speke, this offer could never be tested. In the meantime, the question remained, should the Speke workforce resist closure by any means possible, or should it acquiesce to company demands and take a redundancy payment in exchange for jobs? The initial offers put forward were thought poor, and seen by many workers as inadequate recompense for giving up their livelihood.

Studies have shown worker resistance to redundancies is primarily weakened by promises of large amounts of severance pay.[72] Analysts have also questioned whether tactics such as a factory occupation would be practical in the Speke situation since the TR7 was not selling. These findings also suggest that at least some of the workforce at Speke must have reached similar conclusions as well.[73] Workers opposed to resistance might well have emphasised the lack of commitment from national union leaders in the past. Such reasoning should have been persuasive to a labour force who had just endured a long winter strike, without the assistance of strike-pay and official support from the unions until near the very end of that struggle. Nevertheless, first-hand accounts deny any sense of hesitation at this point. All evidence available indicates the vast majority of the workers were still in favour of defiance of closure at this point.

Although this support for resistance is countered in some secondary accounts of the strike, contemporary newspapers and recollections from participants involved paint a different picture. It was reported in April 1978 that the overwhelming majority of workers remained in favour of resisting closure:

> There now looks a strong possibility following Saturday's mass meeting when 2750 of the total 3000 TR7 assembly workers voted to oppose the closure of their factory on May 26. Merseyside Labour MPs yesterday promised to back Liverpool's TR7 car workers in their struggle to hang on to their jobs. The pledge came as union leaders warned that the whole of Leyland will grind to a halt if the company goes ahead and shuts the factory at Speke as planned.[74]

Other reports affirm solidarity with the Speke cause was widespread throughout BL's operations: 'Senior shop stewards from all British Leyland plants today promised full support of the Speke workers who are resisting closure of the TR7 plant.'[75] For Speke workers, such inter-plant solidarity encouraged opposition to closure.

It should also be noted that a new shift of workers was hired at Speke just two years prior to the closure announcement. These newer employees made up a large percentage of the Plant No. 2 workforce, and since they had completed less than two years of employment, they were not entitled to statutory redundancy payments. Realising this group's influence over their union's policies, Edwardes sweetened his initial offer and now included all the recently hired employees in the severance package. Before this substantial increase in BL's offer, one former shop steward estimated:

> Probably about 30 per cent of the workforce was prepared to resist all the way no matter what was offered. Then another 30 per cent would

> have went that way, so long as they saw that they had a good lead from the unions both locally and nationally, and then they would have been committed [to organised resistance to closure] all the way. Forty per cent would have said no, they wanted the money. What you have to take into account in the two years prior to the closure was we had taken on a lot of people who were laid off from plants in the region that had already closed ... So these people had experiences in having their factory jobs made redundant, yet they still walked into BL and found work. So in their minds they probably figured leave here, pick up a few grand, and then go on to get another job. Even though we pointed out to them at that time there were sixteen out-of-work people chasing every open job in all of Merseyside – and that was still 1978, before things got really bad later! The reality was we [shop stewards] lacked the experience, and we just couldn't get people to come on board.[76]

The year 1978 does play a significant role in understanding the reactions of the Speke workers, as this was before the age of Thatcher. While de-industrialisation and permanent job losses may have been apparent to most economists and academics at the time, this phenomenon had not yet become a clear reality amongst ordinary workers. Many blue-collar workers engaged in manufacturing throughout Britain at that point did not realise the perilous economic future they were facing. The preciousness of a unionised, well-paid job in the manufacturing sector was still something taken for granted by most blue-collar workers in 1978.

Edwardes and his team put forward their 'final offer', and another meeting was called to discuss his proposal. The shop stewards explained their opposition to this offer to the membership before the vote was taken. The new offer carried, on average, an additional £1,000 in redundancy pay per worker, plus an extension of these benefits to the recent hires. The offer was conditional on a guarantee of full cooperation from the workforce, in their not interfering in any way with the shutting down of operations in Speke, and a promise that there would be no interruption in the transfer of company property to Coventry, where BL was re-locating TR7 production. According to one press account:

> At a stormy two-hour meeting today, Triumph car workers voted to accept Leyland's new redundancy package. But the 3000 TR7 assembly workers who face the sack in three weeks were split in the decision to fight the company's closure plans or accept the improved offer of an extra £1000. In the event the voting was only marginally in favour of taking the money. Shop stewards were given a hard time at the meeting. The AUEW convenor at Speke, Mr. David Thomas, told the meeting the shop stewards

> would abide by the decisions of the meeting, but his speech was drowned by boos and cat-calls. He said afterwards the men's decision to take the money was a 'bitter disappointment' to him, and he conceded that the factory would now inevitably close down in three weeks' time ... 60 per cent of the workers said they wanted to take Leyland's new redundancy terms.[77]

Theories on why the majority of the workers, albeit by a slim percentage, voted to take the money in exchange for their jobs takes on another perspective in light of comments from a former shop steward:

> The amount of the wonga [money] on the table kept changing during the negotiations. And then at the last minute they really increased the wonga. Getting back to what I was saying before, there was a large group of people working out there with less than two years, and like I said the wonga was big, and they too now could get some of it with the latest offer. It was big money. You're talking a few thousand pounds, which [thirty-one] years ago, that was a hell of a lot. Now most of the people working out there were young and in their 20s ... So in the end we [the shop stewards advocating resistance] got killed in the rush.[78]

Such considerations must also be seen in the context of the debts many workers would have accumulated during the seventeen payless weeks of the strike. Yet, in the end, what is most remarkable in such circumstances is not that it was only a slim majority who voted to accept the generous payments, but that such a high percentage of the workforce still expressed a desire to resist closure, despite the rather hefty monetary enticement.

Conclusions

Resistance to factory closure requires an enormous amount of resources and will. In addition to these attributes, one analyst of the Speke closure observed, 'for people to fight they have to think that they have at least a chance of winning'.[79] Viable alternatives to counter management's plans are essential. This necessitates union activists becoming well versed in finance, management and accountancy, as well as possessing skills in media and public relations. During the BL closure at Speke, union leaders would have had to counter management's arguments with clear practical solutions if they had any chance in successfully resisting Edwardes' plan. If the call for resistance of the closure at Speke been affirmed by a yes vote, the question remains: did the shop stewards at Speke possess the skills necessary? Were the stewards confident they would receive support from their national officials, as well as from unions in other BL plants?

When one examines the unique situation at Speke, the scales weigh heavily towards acceptance of the redundancy payments over organised resistance. Blocking closure would have meant a burden on these workers that many were not capable of bearing. Yet what remains remarkable is that, despite the large incentives, those who voted in favour of accepting the final offer secured this decision only by a slim margin.

Nevertheless, no matter what happened at Speke, BL management under Michael Edwardes seemed determined to substantially downsize the company through closing factories and cutting jobs. Perhaps then, the best that the trade unions could have hoped to achieve at this stage was negotiating a generous severance package. Against those odds, it is still surprising that the percentage of workers at Speke who voted to resist closure was so remarkably high. Securing large cash settlements in lieu of future employment at BL meant the workers had some influence on their destiny. Edwardes may have held most of the bargaining chips in this situation, but the workers could at least set a high price for their surrender.

A counter-argument to this is that the workers merely sold out their jobs, and this held negative effects on the remainder of their community in the bleak years to come. The corrosive effect of redundancy payments upon working-class solidarity was amply reflected at Speke. But we must also consider that the amount of money, and the way in which it was paid, was done on the workers' terms. The turn of events at Speke may not have displayed the level of working-class militancy, which will be illustrated in forthcoming chapters of this work; nonetheless, the workers at Standard-Triumph had their say in how events were eventually shaped.

Regarding the central theme of this study, it should be noted that this episode at Standard-Triumph in Speke did not end there. Former employees and members of the TGWU's 6/612 Branch, which represented the bulk of the production workers at Speke, called for a public enquiry into the shutdown of this factory. Many were still angry that a campaign of resistance to this closure had not been launched.

They went to the unusual length of commissioning an industrial sociologist, Huw Beynon, to research and author a pamphlet, which warned other workers of the perils of accepting redundancy payments in lieu of resisting industrial closure. In the pamphlet's introduction, TGWU 6/612 Branch Secretary, Frank Banton, warned:

> We have printed the story so that our lessons may be helpful to other workers. Even if it's only to understand that the tinsel on the redundancy 'carrot' soon loses its sparkle. *Nobody* will defend your jobs if you as workers won't fight for them.[80]

By May 1978, BL's shutdown of Speke was, in many ways, 'the shape of things to come'. It represented the first definitive case study of the closure of a major Merseyside factory by a multinational company and illustrated the challenges and limitations that workers faced in combating such actions. We shall see in the following chapters that Merseyside workers, when subsequently faced with redundancies, often did draw significant lessons from the events at Speke. In the following two decades they attempted to fight unemployment through a wide range of imaginative responses and strategies. In the next chapter we shall analyse how the activists of the TGWU 6/612 Branch became the nucleus of much of this activity.

Notes

1 Eric Hobsbawm, 'The Forward March of Labour Halted', *Marxism Today*, September 1978, pp. 279–86.
2 Transcript of an oral interview with trade union official Frank Banton conducted by Michael Carden in: Michael J. Carden, 'Union Democracy and Incorporation: A Case Study of the T.G.W.U. Merseyside Division with Particular Reference to the Dock Industry', unpublished MA dissertation, University of Liverpool, 1996, p. 6.
3 Huw Beynon, *What Happened at Speke* (Liverpool, 1978), p. 15.
4 Beynon, *What Happened at Speke*, p. 15.
5 Interview with Phil Ash.
6 Interview with Tony McQuade.
7 Karel Williams, John Williams and Colin Haslam, *The Breakdown of Austin Rover* (Leamington Spa, 1987), p. 48.
8 Hugo Levie, Denis Gregory and Nick Lorentzen, eds, *Fighting Closures: De-Industrialization and the Trade Unions 1979–1983* (Nottingham, 1984), pp. 31–33.
9 Central Policy Review Staff, *The Future of the British Car Industry* (London, 1975). See also Roy Church, *The Rise and Decline of the British Motor Industry* (Cambridge, 1995), p. 96.
10 David Marsden, Timothy Morris, Paul Willman and Stephan Wood, *The Car Industry: Labour Relations and Industrial Adjustment* (London, 1985), p. 6.
11 Church, *The Rise and Decline*, p. 104.
12 Marsden *et al.*, *Car Industry*, p. 6. See also Beynon, *What Happened at Speke*, p. 8; Austin Rover Online, Facts & Figures, History: www.aronline.co.uk/index.htm?ryderreportf.htm.

13 Interview with Tony McQuade.
14 Interview with Eddie Roberts. See also Joe England, 'Shop Stewards in Transport House: A Comment upon the Incorporation of the Rank and File', *Industrial Relations Journal*, vol. 12, no. 5 (1981), pp. 16–29.
15 Baron Don Ryder, *British Leyland, the Next Decade* (London, 1975).
16 Interview with Kenny Routledge.
17 Interview with Eddie Roberts.
18 Michael Richardson, Paul Stewart and Andrew Danford, 'Labour Struggles in the British Automobile and Aerospace Industries 1950–1982', paper presented to AUTO21 Conference, Workers and Labour Markets in the Global Automotive Industry, McMaster University, Hamilton, Ontario, Canada, 22–23 October 2004.
19 Beynon, *What Happened at Speke*, p. 21.
20 Beynon, *What Happened at Speke*, pp. 16–17.
21 Interview with Phil Ash.
22 Interview with Kenny Routledge.
23 Interview with Tony McQuade.
24 Paul Willman, 'The Reform of Collective Bargaining and Strike Activity in BL Cars, 1976–1982', *Industrial Relations Journal*, vol. 15, no. 2 (June 1984), pp. 8–9.
25 Church, *Rise and Decline*, pp. 66–7.
26 Beynon, *What Happened at Speke*, p. 25.
27 Beynon, *What Happened at Speke*, p. 6.
28 Dave Lyddon, 'The Car Industry, 1945–79: Shop Stewards and Workplace Unionism', in Chris Wrigley, ed., *A History of British Industrial Relations* (Cheltenham, 1996), p. 205.
29 Interview with Phil Ash.
30 Williams *et al.*, *Austin Rover*, Table B2, p. 126.
31 Church, *Rise and Decline*, p. 113.
32 Church, *Rise and Decline*, p. 119.
33 Central Policy Review Staff, *British Car Industry*, p. 79.
34 Central Policy Review Staff, *British Car Industry*, pp. 101–3.
35 Central Policy Review Staff, *British Car Industry*, p. 99.
36 Willman, 'Reform', p. 7.
37 *Liverpool Echo*, 25 May 1978.
38 *The Times*, 16 February 1978. See also Beynon, *What Happened at Speke*, p. 20.
39 Beynon, *What Happened at Speke*, p. 18.
40 Richardson *et al.*, 'Labour Struggles'.
41 Williams *et al.*, *Austin Rover*, p. 6.
42 Marsden *et al.*, *Car Industry*, pp. 98–9.
43 Marsden *et al.*, *Car Industry*, p. 115.
44 Tony Dickson and David Judge, *The Politics of Industrial Closure* (London, 1987), pp. 109–10.
45 Interview with Phil Ash.

46 Interview with Kenny Routledge.
47 Interview with Phil Ash.
48 Leyland Combine Trade Union Committee, *British Leyland, the Edwardes Plan and your Job* (Kidderminster, 1980), p. 11.
49 Interview with Kenny Routledge.
50 Interview with Kenny Routledge.
51 Ron Bean and Peter Stoney, 'Strikes on Merseyside: A Regional Analysis', *Industrial Relations Journal*, vol. 17, no. 1 (March 1986), p. 9–23.
52 *Liverpool Daily Post*, 30 December 1977.
53 Interview with Tony McQuade.
54 Interview with Kenny Routledge.
55 Interview with Tony McQuade.
56 Interview with Tony McQuade.
57 Interview with Phil Ash.
58 *The Times*, 24 January 1978.
59 *The Times*, 23 April 1974.
60 Interview with Eddie Roberts.
61 Beynon, *What Happened at Speke*, p. 29.
62 Interview with Kenny Routledge.
63 *Liverpool Echo*, 25 May 1978.
64 *The Times*, 25 February 1978.
65 Beynon, *What Happened at Speke*, p. 20.
66 Michael Edwardes, *Back from the Brink* (London, 1983), p. 74.
67 Edwardes, *Back from the Brink*, pp. 74–5.
68 Marsden *et al.*, *Car Industry*. See also Dickson and Judge, *Industrial Closure*.
69 Marsden *et al.*, *Car Industry*, p. 154. See also Beynon, *What Happened at Speke*, p. 40.
70 Alan Thornet, *Inside Cowley* (London, 1998), p. 254.
71 Interview with Tony McQuade.
72 Levie *et al.*, *Fighting Closures*, p. 192.
73 Marsden *et al.*, *Car Industry*, p. 154.
74 *Liverpool Daily Post*, 17 April 1978.
75 *Liverpool Echo*, 5 May 1978.
76 Interview with Kenny Routledge.
77 *Liverpool Echo*, Weekend Edition 6/7 May 1978.
78 Interview with Tony McQuade.
79 Beynon, *What Happened at Speke*, p. 39.
80 Beynon, *What Happened at Speke*, p. 1.

4

The TGWU 6/612 Branch of the Unemployed: working-class politicisation and mobilisation

If the 1978 shutdown of Standard-Triumph Motors in Speke signalled the opening volley of industrial closures on Merseyside, it might also have been the spark that stimulated a long litany of imaginative responses to forced redundancies and closures by Liverpool's growing army of unemployed. This chapter analyses several of these initiatives which were often contrived and commanded by a group of redundant Standard-Triumph workers who were made jobless through that specific plant closure. These initiatives included: restructuring their old TGWU 6/612 Branch from organising car workers to being a local trade union branch representing Merseyside's unemployed; initiating a public awareness campaign in the form of the much publicised 'People's March for Jobs' in 1981; establishing the Merseyside Trade Union Community and Unemployed Resource Centre (MTUCURC) in Hardman Street, Liverpool; and instituting the 'One Fund for All' as a campaign fundraising network.

The reawakening of the TGWU 6/612 Branch

When the workers at the Standard-Triumph Plant No. 2 in Speke accepted their redundancy cheques in May 1978, most of the now unemployed workforce never conceived that their involvement with the TGWU's 6/612 Branch would continue. It was assumed the branch would dissolve once the remaining workers at Standard-Triumph Plant No. 1 were dismissed after final closure, scheduled for the following year. Most of these redundant workers had not anticipated the unfamiliar, post-industrial landscape awaiting them beyond the factory gates. As we have seen, this period signalled the beginning of an era when declining opportunities for well-paid manual work was evident throughout Britain, but especially on Merseyside. The newly unemployed also encountered a myriad of difficulties in negotiating the bureaucracy of an overstretched welfare state. As one former TGWU 6/612 official recalled:

> There was a growing problem with signing on – you know, it was becoming more difficult to get your benefits. And what was happening was people were going down, trying to collect their dole or their 'sosh' [social security], and they were getting knocked back because of all the new government policies. Lads and girls who had worked the shop floor were getting in touch with their former shop stewards even after the plant had closed and would say, 'Hey, these bastards aren't paying me my dole' ... So we realised something had to be done. This was around the time when people in Liverpool were organising for welfare rights, so we realised something had to be done for unemployed people. Most of us who were active in the 6/612 came to the conclusion that the unemployed were in just as much, if not more, need of representation than people in work.[1]

The election of the Conservative government in 1979 indicated not only a tighter rein on welfare benefits; it also introduced more stringent trade union legislation. This played a role in changing the focus of the 6/612 Branch. The same TGWU official further explained:

> It was just about this time that Dunlop's, just down the road from us in Speke, announced their closure, so you had at least 3,000 more people out of work there. And the various new laws knocking around at that time said they could lose their severance pay if the Dunlop workers involved themselves in any type of industrial action. So our leader [Bobby Owens] ... came up with the idea we picket that plant for those workers. We picketed that plant for three months. It became known as the community picket. If you think of it, we lost 7,000 jobs at British Leyland, plus the 3,000 at Dunlop, totalling over 10,000 jobs in the Speke area alone – good jobs with good pay, sick benefits and good pension schemes ... Massey-Ferguson, again, closed around this time, 3,000 more jobs gone. Pressed Steel Fisher went, that was 3,000 jobs. Meccano went, that was another three or four thousand jobs. Tate & Lyle went ... So the biggest activists from a lot of these places joined forces with us in the 6/612. Scousers being Scousers, people began calling us the 'Branch of the Unemployed', but that was a misnomer because we always made sure we included and recruited members who were – at least a few people were in work.[2]

By the early 1980s, it was estimated that approximately 90 per cent of the branch were unemployed. Yet branch officials insisted it was important they also represent the employed too:

> We wanted to remain an active trade union because we wanted to get people back in work. It was important for us to have shop stewards in some of these places that might hire again. This way if work comes back we can say, 'Hey, look, we have union members here – paid up union

members, who should have first crack at whatever is available'. We were reasonably successful at finding work for some members too.[3]

This 're-invention' of the branch involved greater politicisation on the part of its membership; consequently, this also lent a renewed awareness of the powerful influence trade unions still had on public policy. According to one contemporary commentator:

> The defiance of a group of unemployed workers in Liverpool could mark the start of a fight back against unemployment by Britain's trade unions. Branch number 6/612 of the Transport and General Workers' Union used to organise workers making the sleek TR7 Triumph sports car in British Leyland's factory on the Speke industrial estate. In 1978 the plant was closed and the workforce consigned to the ranks of the unemployed. The union branch was kept going, initially just for a few months, to tie up loose ends such as pensions and redundancy payments. Then came something totally unexpected, more and more members began attending branch meetings and taking part in union activities. As people struggled to understand how and why they happened to be on the dole, they started asking tough questions and looking hard for answers. A new sense of shared purpose and commitment began to develop. So the union decided to continue branch 6/612 and to include workers from other Merseyside factories that were closing down. Current membership is around 400. Branch secretary Billy Mulholland believes it is vitally important to keep unemployed workers active within the trade union movement. He is opposed to any suggestions of a separate 'unemployed workers' union', which would have no bargaining power and would drift into isolation from the mainstream labour movement. Paradoxically, 6/612 branch is now the liveliest and most forward-looking in the Liverpool area.[4]

According to the original leading figures involved in altering the focus of this branch, they were committed to remaining within the organised trade union movement. Their oral testimony points out that they did not wish to operate as a separate entity, as had been the case of the National Unemployed Workers' Movement (NUWM) during the inter-war period. Branch officials also understood that Liverpool's unemployed needed the resources that only a trade union could provide, otherwise, they could possibly suffer the same isolation which caused the demise of the NUWM.

One former advocate for Liverpool's jobless remembered: 'We argued strongly that on Merseyside the unemployed had to be organised within unions, rather than separately like we did in the 1930s under the leadership of the Communist Party, because we believed that split the movement and led to all kinds of divisions between those in work and those who were out of work.'[5]

The 6/612's leaders also claim they were conscious of the need for political mobilisation regarding unemployment and welfare rights. They assert their awareness of having the backing of a large union, such as the TGWU, meant access to the resources and political influence needed to achieve their goals, as one branch official emphasised:

> What kind of clout would you have without union backing? We wanted to maintain the TGWU ties because they were the dominant and most powerful trade union in Britain at the time, and by a country mile. We saw what happened in the 1930s with the likes of the NUWM, and we weren't going to make those same mistakes. We wanted to keep it a fully integrated branch of a trade union, that just happened to be predominantly made up of unemployed workers that campaigned for the issues concerning the unemployed ... We also knew as long as we had the TGWU backing, the likes of the TUC, which can be somewhat conservative – small c – at times, would have fuck all to say about how we ran things up here.[6]

Along with this desire for local control came testimonies praising vibrant leadership from a number of individuals associated with this branch. Most notable was a young car worker named Bobby Owens: 'Bobby was the man. He was the brains, the architect behind all of this. He thought up the idea of what we did with this branch. He was the one behind the Unemployed Centre in Hardman St., the One Fund for All. You name it, and Bobby was right there.'[7] Bob Braddock, community activist in Liverpool during this period, described Owens as 'One of the founding members and guiding lights' of the struggle.[8] Owens, who is deceased, was quoted in a news account from the period:

> There is a lot of despair about, particularly among young people who have never had a proper job and older men who think they never will get another ... We are opposed to a separate union for the unemployed. Anyone who is unemployed can join the TGWU here. The 6/612 Branch effectively determined the union's national policy toward the unemployed at our conference.[9]

Owens' leadership of the TGWU 6/612 Branch and persuading the old guard

Bobby Owens, the charismatic branch leader, along with his lieutenants, was able to persuade union officials of the importance of radical organisational change during this period of unparalleled unemployment. The evidence suggests he was successful in convincing regional, and later, national union officials, that the trade union movement had a responsibility to integrate with the growing numbers of unemployed workers in Britain.

This agitation for change by the 6/612 Branch activists contributed to a questioning, by many trade unionists, of the TUC's unwillingness to organise the unemployed. Given the apparent permanency of high unemployment, these jobless activists argued that redundant workers should hold the right to retain union membership and their union branches preserved. It was also contended that representing the unemployed would allow those who were employed a means of control over those without work. It was argued that unionising the unemployed could help prevent the jobless from undercutting wage rates and would also limit the potential pool of blackleg labour. Moreover, an appeal was made that the retention of members and branches would maintain numerical strength, and hence, political clout within the labour movement.[10] Eventually, many union officials believed that establishing a link between those in work and the growing numbers of jobless people was essential if any semblance of working-class solidarity was to be sustained.[11]

The records of the TGWU's Biennial Delegate Conference (BDC) in 1981 demonstrate this new desire to retain unemployed members. Several delegates advocated this policy, including one who asked:

> What do we do for the unemployed? It is the old saying again is it not? Organise, educate and agitate – and we have to stand shoulder to shoulder; the employed have to stand shoulder to shoulder with the unemployed in their struggles. That is the duty of every trade union member, and our union has to be in the forefront of that ... We have to retain these members of ours who are placed out of work. When I say 'retained' I mean that they retain their union card, their contact with the branch and the involvement with the branch so that again, the employed are working alongside the unemployed ... We also have to be prepared to accept people who are not in a job, who want to be part of the trade union movement. I believe that unless we do that we leave them open to the far right, the fascists of this world, who are already standing outside school gates trying to recruit kids into that kind of movement.[12]

Deputy General Secretary Alex Kitson assured delegates that the leadership was very much in favour of retaining the unemployed and stated that the union's executive supported this measure:

> We have to carry on organising services for the unemployed. That has been called for from the rostrum, and you can take the assurance that

the General Executive Council (GEC) already have that aboard. There are now over fifty unemployed centres organised by unions and trades councils. We have unemployed member branches and we have to carry on retaining our membership when they leave their jobs.[13]

As one union activist recalled, it was not difficult convincing TGWU officials of the importance of maintaining a link with the unemployed:

What you have to understand here is that the people we had who were active in the 6/612 at that time were in high standing within union circles ... We had people who served on regional committees, national committees. Stan Pemberton for instance, was the president of the union. He was one of the lads we picked up after a bunch of them were sacked at Dunlop's ... he sat on the Executive [General Executive Committee of the TGWU]. He was the Chair of the Executive! Now at this time everyone could see what was going on. Thatcher was coming in, and she was making no bones about what her plans were ... People like Pembo [Stanley Pemberton] and Bobby Owens were the kind of people who were well respected within the organisation. In the 6/612 alone we had big names like Pembo and Bobby, as well as good solid lads like Tony Boyle, Steve Alcock, Kenny Routledge, Phil Ash and Billy Mulholland to name just a few. The national leadership listened when people like this spoke.[14]

One observer described the 6/612 Branch as 'punching above its weight' in the world of trade union politics. However, this same trade unionist also recalled some initial resistance from the TGWU national leadership:

There always was a direct link between the 6/612 Branch and the Regional [TGWU Regional Committee] because Bobby Owens, who would go on to become the Regional Secretary, was a 6/612 member ... Initially, I think the old guard at the top of the trade union movement couldn't see a role for unemployed members, because they probably thought, 'Well, what could we do for these people?' But it took those who had been politicised to convince them that this had to be done. It took some work, but the nice thing about the 6/612 Branch was that it was largely made up of ex-shop stewards, and organisers, and councillors, so they were all political in one way or another. Because of this, they knew a lot about organising. They knew who to ask, they could put the arm on people, they could put pressure on people, and they knew the right channels.[15]

The power that lay activists like Owens wielded derived from their involvement in an internal pressure group within the TGWU, the Merseyside Coordinating Committee (MCC). The MCC was a loose organisation of TGWU shop stewards on Merseyside who sought greater integration between full-time union officials and lay activists. It became a vehicle for stewards to gain knowledge and experience at union organisation and politics. This body also challenged the autonomy many full-time officials previously enjoyed. Starting out as shop stewards and lay activists, many of these newcomers were increasingly working their way into leadership positions within the union hierarchy and were becoming more aware of internal trade union politics. This, in turn, re-invigorated rank-and-file activism, and it also meant the left gained greater confidence about steering the union towards more radical political positions.[16]

Despite its growing influence, the MCC was reluctant to confront the TGWU leadership directly, instead it tended to publicly support official TGWU policies and agendas, while at the same time lobbying for rank-and-file interests. MCC leaders worked within formal TGWU structures, which in turn, legitimised their position with senior union officials. The appointment of Owens in 1985 to the prestigious position of TGWU Regional Secretary – a post invariably reserved for a full-time officer – can be seen as testimony to the influence unemployed activists and shop stewards gained during this period.[17]

While the TGWU was easily persuaded to reconsider its earlier concerns about representing the unemployed, the TUC was more hesitant about adopting this new perspective. In September 1980, at its annual Congress, there was debate between those in favour of the TUC actively representing the unemployed and those who, while sympathetic, wondered whether the unions, and more specifically the TUC, were equipped to handle their particular needs. Clive Jenkins, General Secretary of the Association of Scientific, Technical & Managerial Staffs, moved the official motion that: 'The Trade Union Movement should not abandon members who ceased to be employed, and that the Movement should also concern itself with the problems of young people who have not been able to find employment on leaving school.' Jenkins argued the trade union movement needed to adjust its orientation as the economy underwent drastic changes:

> I suppose that when you start talking about a revolutionary change in your structure and perhaps then in the policies that might flow from it, it is a difficult and touchy time ... This Depression, with a capital 'D', is clearly getting out of control and we have this radical Right group in the Treasury, including the Prime Minister. I believe that they are now causing quite irreparable damage to parts of the economy and also translating irreparable changes into the entire workforce. That means that the workforce will be different and that there will be people who are not in the workforce and who would like to be there.[18]

Jenkins declared that: 'The government wanted to drive a wedge between those who are in work and those who are not. They want to blame the unions for that problem.'[19]

Jenkins' belief that 'Congress was ready for a change' was not shared by all delegates. A National Union of Public Employees representative at the annual meeting doubted whether the unions and TUC could adequately care for the needs of the unemployed. He suggested, instead, that the jobless should seek the services of unemployed advice centres, such as the one recently developed by the Newcastle-upon-Tyne Trades Council. Despite such reservations, a motion was passed that a special conference should be convened to decide whether the TUC should recognise affiliated unions who represent unemployed workers.[20]

Nevertheless, due to increasing pressure from large trade unions, such as the TGWU, the North West Regional TUC held a conference in November 1980 with the purpose of discussing what services the trade union movement could provide for the unemployed. This meeting decided it was 'necessary to keep contact with the unemployed and to retain them in the Movement to combat the isolation and aberration [*sic*: alienation?] that can affect unemployed workers'.[21] The national TUC leadership hesitated to endorse the creation of union branches for the unemployed. Lionel 'Len' Murray, TUC General Secretary, warned delegates at the TUC's special conference:

> For us to extend the principle of combination to non-employed persons or groups would have profound implications. Above all, we should beware of creating expectations that we cannot or are not prepared to meet. That would be to delude ourselves and to betray the unemployed.[22]

Despite such reservations, the conference agreed to retain branches servicing mainly members who had become redundant due to worksite closure, as well as advancing the open recruitment of unemployed individuals. A memo from the TUC central office stated:

> In view of the grave unemployment crisis now affecting every part of the UK, the General Council decided that affiliated unions should do all that they can to retain and recruit more of the unemployed, and to publicise union services available to unemployed members.[23]

This new provision was endorsed at the 1981 annual Congress. One 6/612 Branch official later reflected:

> Initially the TUC were a little bit of a hard sell, but eventually because of the amount of clout that came with having the T&G [TGWU] endorsement

> behind us – I mean that's a better part of two million members – so the TUC were eventually brought on board with a little kicking and screaming, but as time went on they were sold on the idea … the thought of having a bunch of loose cannon Scousers up in Liverpool making a lot of noise about unemployment probably frightened them at first … they eventually came on board once they saw who was backing us.[24]

Indeed, by 1982, the TUC took the unprecedented step of allowing unemployed members to serve as delegates to Congress: 'This move reflects both the recent massive increase in the level of unemployment and the increased efforts by the trade union movement to insure that the unemployed remained within the Movement.'[25]

Testimony from a number of those on the scene at the time relate that Owens, and his associates in charge of the 6/612 Branch, realised that their primary function from this point forward was to politicise and mobilise the unemployed on Merseyside. Day-to-day general business within the branch encompassed an array of left-wing causes. Such support brought the branch leaders into contact with activists from the radical left, many of whom had little prior interaction with working-class culture or the trade union movement. One branch activist recalled a range of political campaigns:

> Some of the things we used to get involved in with that branch would surprise you. For instance, we were heavily committed to the anti-apartheid campaign in South Africa. We wrote letters to political prisoners in Chile. In fact, we managed to get a few political refugees from Chile jobs in British Leyland. The political prisoners in these dictatorships told us our letters of support meant more to them than money. To get a letter from somebody far away in Liverpool was phenomenal to these political prisoners. It meant solidarity with workers from half-way across the world.[26]

These contacts assisted the branch in constructing a network of political alliances. Further evidence of this intense politicisation can be detected at a meeting of the TGWU Merseyside District in 1986, where a resolution from the 6/612 Branch condemned 'the expulsions and the threatened expulsions from the Labour Party of 12 Liverpool Labour Party members' as a 'purge against' the Militant Tendency on Liverpool City Council.[27] The Militant Tendency was a left-wing faction working within the Labour Party at that time, and condemned by the party leadership as Trotskyist. This, of course, raises the question of how much influence the Communist Party of Great Britain had over Owens and his associates in charge of the 6/612 Branch.

Nevertheless, leaders of the 6/612 Branch asserted to their membership the need for their getting involved in these political struggles, as it was necessary in order to build working-class solidarity. A further aspect of such solidarity was the response of the branch to industrial action by fellow trade unionists. According to one activist:

> One of the things we soon developed around our work with organising the unemployed was making sure that we the unemployed workers were always there to support employed workers who were involved in any industrial struggles. We were engaged in quite a lot of activity in picket lines. That way, we could bolster their reserves and help them by supplying people [to support] their strikes.[28]

The perseverance of institutional ties with the TGWU was crucial to the later success enjoyed by the 6/612 Branch. This maintenance of a trade union structure provided the means available to Owens and other 6/612 activists. Without these resources, many of their campaigns directed at politically mobilising the unemployed would have failed. Three of the most successful of these initiatives are analysed in the remainder of this chapter.

The People's March for Jobs

It became clear to those fighting for the rights of the unemployed that they needed political access, media exposure and additional funding. Affiliation with the TGWU had proved fruitful; however, by 1981 these activists realised that a media event of some kind was necessary to publicise the rising, but often highly regionalised, levels of unemployment. For many trade unionists, the government appeared more concerned with curbing the power of the unions than it was with ameliorating growing joblessness and poverty.

Consequently, the leaders of the 6/612 Branch were among the first to put forward an idea of a 'People's March for Jobs', which would commence in Liverpool on May Day in 1981 and terminate at the Houses of Parliament approximately thirty days later. The organisers of this march hoped 'Middle England' could be persuaded of the detrimental social consequences growing joblessness was having on the nation's industrial heartlands. Lending further credence to the argument that Liverpool was the centre of working-class militancy, the Pier Head in Liverpool was chosen as the commencement point for the march.

The organisers were painfully aware that unemployment had sapped the sinews of the trade union movement. If the demonstration was to succeed, it would require a broad coalition of pro-labour and anti-government factions. One 6/612 activist recalled the composition of the march:

> I first heard talk of such a thing [the march] about six months, no, more like a year before it came off ... because the trade unions and the TUC were behind it, that made it official ... There was a mixture of different people representing a range of views on board. You had the regular standard trade union movement, which was quite conservative, really, and they were trying to keep a lid on things. There was the influence of the Communist Party too, which was also still quite prevalent within the trade union movement at that time. There was also a lot of input coming from all sorts of other left-wing organisations ... We had a lot of support from the single issue movements on the Left like the Campaign for Nuclear Disarmament, the Anti-Nazi League, and so on. Plus, we even had big support from the Church ... so more or less this march helped pull people together.[29]

A press report described the participants of the march as 'a mixed bunch: tidy pensioners and outrageous punks, veteran Labour Party members and "Trots," united by anger. They see themselves less as supplicants, like the Jarrow marchers of the 1930s, and more as shock troops leading an assault on an uncaring capital'.[30]

An umbrella of left-wing organisations and movements coalesced within the People's March. Its ostensible purpose was to highlight the plight of the growing numbers of unemployed, but it was also used as a vehicle to discredit the Conservative government. This was a critical difference between the Jarrow march in 1936 and the Liverpool march of 1981. The Liverpool march of 1981 was comprised of more than just the unemployed demanding work, or people calling for changes in welfare benefits; it also served as a rallying point where all the various factions on the left could demonstrate against Thatcher's right-wing policies.[31]

Labour MP Tony Benn spoke before 20,000 well-wishers gathered at the Pier Head on the banks of the River Mersey, and it was there that he told the 300 marchers before their trek southward that: 'The Northwest is the graveyard of British capitalism', and that it was only fitting that the march should begin in Liverpool.[32] He added:

> This is not a protest march of people pleading for jobs from those who have power. This is a march demanding a change in policies and in the

> structure of our society ... What we are campaigning for is the right to work, to re-equip our industries and to produce for need not only for profit, and also to create the jobs that are so badly needed.[33]

In a letter to *The Times*, TGWU official Jack Dromey, Colin Barnett of the National Union of Public Employees (NUPE) and Pete Carter of the Union of Construction, Allied Trades and Technicians (UCATT), differentiated between the hunger marches of the Great Depression and the People's March in 1981. They emphasised two points:

> Jarrow was a potent symbol for the generation that lived through the hungry thirties. The 'people's march' will likewise arouse the consciousness of the nation. But Jarrow is not Liverpool ... Ours is a different army. The young unemployed now descending on London may not have starved. They have never tasted Army life. They have grown up against the background of the post-war consensus of economic policies which have at their heart a commitment to full employment and the welfare state. Now these young people are rejected ... The march's message is one of confidence, not despair ... In that respect the march is political. To achieve change, pressure must be put on Government for policies designed to return to full employment ...What the people's march is not is party political. No organisation will be allowed to take advantage of the march to promote itself ... Second, the march shows that the trade union movement has learnt, sometimes painful, lessons from its past. Fifty years ago much of the official trade union movement closed its ears to the cries of the unemployed. Not now and never again ... We are committed to maintaining [a] broad base and approach. The trade union movement is learning to work with those who don't share all its views.[34]

Addressing the marchers, Richard Holme, president of the Liberal Party, said that every Western country faced unemployment because of structural change and world recession, but Britain was unique: 'The Tory Government was using unemployment as its main economic strategy. The Tories had deliberately increased unemployment to bring down wage demands and to break the spirit of the working people. They had sown the wind and would reap the whirlwind of bitterness, social division and hardship.'[35]

Among the earliest supporters of the march, surprisingly, were the churches on Merseyside. The Roman Catholic Archbishop of Liverpool, the Most Reverend Derek Worlock, gave his blessing to the marchers, and predicted that in consequence, 'He expected to come under attack, but concern for the unemployed was not solely reserved to political extremists'.[36]

Figure 6 Unemployed marchers arriving in London on 30 May 1981

Participants on the march attested to the sense of solidarity it engendered:

> It was nice, because for me – a lad who grew up in Liverpool – I never had any friends who were from outside of Liverpool. Then, because of this march I struck up friendships with people from places like Birmingham and London. I mean it gave me the chance to learn from people who I wouldn't have naturally met. This is particularly true of young people – I mean I was only nineteen at the time ... But that march changed a lot of things for me just because of the mix in attitudes and the mix of accents ... this march was comprised largely of unemployed Liverpool people recruited by the 6/612 Branch, but there were other people involved too... The most solidarity which came out of that march was from people in work, who saw it wasn't our fault that we were unemployed, and that it could be them next.[37]

The marchers travelled the entire 280 miles to London on foot (see Figure 6). The month-long journey proved arduous. Along the way they raised money and sought publicity for the cause. At night they made do with whatever accommodations and food the local community could provide. The sacrifices of the marchers were chronicled by the *Guardian*:

> The 12–20 mile-a-day treks with overnight stays on school and hall floors were no more arduous than the regime for an extended hiking youth hostel holiday – except that no sane hiker would choose to do those distances by road. 'Tarmac doesn't give and something has to, so it's the skin of your feet', recalled Mr. Fred Sullivan, aged 56, a Llanelli marcher. 'I haven't seen such bad feet'. The sight of small processions limping along bypasses and up rural hills, galvanised factories, trades union branches and Labour parties into booking coaches for London as has no other cause.[38]

Some 300 marchers had set off from Liverpool but after they were joined by supporters along the way, their official number rose to 500 by the time they reached London on 30 May. The Prime Minister chose not to meet with their leaders, claiming such a meeting would serve no useful purpose and criticised the march as being 'of little positive use'. She went on to say:

> I can understand the frustration arising from unemployment that causes people to support the march. But action of this kind contributes nothing to the real task that faces us, that of improving our industrial performance so as to create more jobs on a permanent basis.[39]

Michael Foot, Leader of the Opposition, declared her refusal 'mean and miserable'.[40] The Labour MP, David Winnick, vehemently attacked the Prime Minister's decision:

> Why is she so high and mighty that she will not receive the marchers? I know that the Secretary of State for Employment will do so. It is perhaps an indication of the support that the march has received throughout the country that a Cabinet Minister is to receive the organisers. However, I hope the Prime Minister will do so. It is her policies that are largely responsible for the unemployment from which we are now suffering. She is the first to defend those monetarist policies inside and outside the House. Why does she not defend them to the victims of monetarism?[41]

Despite the prime ministerial snub, the march had generated publicity and garnered significant support. As the marchers entered London they attracted enormous crowds of supporters:

> So many people wanted to join the final stage that the tail end of the march left Hyde Park more than 1½ hours after the front had finished the two-mile trek to the [Trafalgar] Square. Police estimated that between 40,000 and 50,000 people walked this last leg, while up to 50,000 more waited for them in Trafalgar Square. The organisers put the figure at 100,000 growing to 150,000 by the time the march ended. There were

> huge cheers for the original marchers ... They were at the head of what became one of the biggest ever TUC-organised demonstrations. Speakers immediately placed it in historical context liking it to the Jarrow March in 1936 and the Peasants March to London in 1381. And whatever the actual numbers involved yesterday, the organisers and Scotland Yard agreed that it was one of the biggest marches London had seen for some time ... TUC General Secretary Mr. Len Murray said it was a 'people's day', while miners leader Mr. Arthur Scargill said it was 'magnificent'. Mr. Alan Fisher, General Secretary of NUPE, warned the Tory Government, 'You can't ignore us now'.[42]

Despite such publicity and support, there was little chance that Thatcher would alter her course. Nevertheless, the march represented a critical moment in convincing trade unions that commitment to the unemployed must become a priority. The prominent role played by the 6/612 Branch in popularising that strategy merits it being placed on the record. Subsequently, the TUC channelled the funds which were raised during the march into new centres established to assist the unemployed. These centres were the legacy of the People's March for Jobs. One marcher reflected on the legacy of this event: 'When the march finished we didn't want to go home and forget about it. We wanted to do something constructive. And the unemployed centres seemed to be the most productive thing we could do.'[43]

The Merseyside Trade Union Community and Unemployed Resource Centre

In the months following the 1981 People's March for Jobs, 6/612 leaders and local community activists secured a building to serve as a base of their operations. It was located in Hardman Street, central Liverpool. With financial assistance from the Labour-run Merseyside County Council and the trade unions, the MTUCURC opened its doors in November 1983. It was not the first such centre in Britain, but it was by far the largest and most politically active. Over time, thirteen smaller, satellite centres opened on Merseyside, but the Hardman Street facility was the most prominent.

However, it must be noted that even prior to the People's March in 1981, the idea of setting up centres for the unemployed had been adopted at the TUC's 1980 Congress. TUC General Secretary Len Murray subsequently wrote: 'There should be an action programme for the development of unemployed workers' centres throughout the country.'[44] There had previously been debate as to how these new centres were to be funded, and what their precise role within the trade union movement would include. Many on the left-wing of trade union politics felt the centres should be under local control. They saw potential in these buildings as a base of operations that would be ideally suited for campaigning and politically mobilising the unemployed. The evidence suggests that Owens and other 6/612 activists strenuously advocated this approach. The former coordinator of MTUCURC, Kevin Coyne, recalled this was the prevailing philosophy:

> The Unemployed Centre in Liverpool was founded on the basis that unemployment was a creation of political action and therefore only a political solution could solve it. Consequently, Bobby [Owens] and a lot of the staff at the centre, including myself, felt that we had to pursue a policy of campaigning by way of mobilising politically.[45]

Opponents of this approach, including many within the TUC hierarchy, felt the purpose of unemployed centres was essentially to get jobless people back to work and assisting them with welfare rights. One founding member of the Hardman Street centre recalled the initial reaction of the TUC leadership: ‘They didn’t particularly like us at the time, but we ensured we would never do anything that would split us from it … We learned a lot from what happened in the 1930s and the National Unemployed Workers’ Union [*sic*]. We read all the books, and we were determined that we would not split with the trade union movement.’[46]

By way of compromise, the TUC had decided at its 1980 Congress to adopt a two-pronged approach: first, the unemployed were allowed to be union members, and second, the centres would be utilised by the unions, not only as places of recruitment, but also as buildings which provided services for the unemployed in the forms of welfare advice, recreation and job training. The language of the resolution was purposely flexible so that any unemployed centre could elect to chart its own philosophical direction. The question remained whether, if a centre chose to follow a more political or campaigning path, it could also receive funding from central government via the Manpower Services Commission (MSC).[47]

By way of clarification, the TUC circulated guidelines in January of 1981:

> 4. The key factor in the guidelines is that they lay down procedures for obtaining funds from public sources through a major involvement of local authorities and also the Manpower Services Commission (MSC). It may be possible for individual centres to obtain the necessary finance from the

> trade union movement, but realistically – in view of the scale of resources required for a programme of any significance – outside funds are essential.
>
> 5. The guidelines therefore seek to strike a balance between the need for centres to be effective from the Movement's point of view, and the need for public funds and accountability. This was clearly understood and endorsed by the representatives of TUC Regional Councils, on whom the major organisational effort will rest.[48]

For those on the left, the most controversial aspect of these guidelines was the encouragement by the TUC for centres to accept MSC funding. Established in 1973, the MSC was an experiment in corporatism by Edward Heath's Conservative government. Corporatism, of course, in the sense that the trade unions, private industry and the government join forces as equal partners, and together they manage a project. And being a test in corporatism, the MSC functioned as a tripartite public body under the auspices of the Department of Employment, with representatives from business, unions and local authorities.

Initially designed to coordinate employment and job training throughout the United Kingdom, the MSC later mutated in the Thatcher era to what some on the left perceived to be more a tool for her economic policies. To support this stance, they cited the restrictions placed on political activities in the MSC-funded centres. MSC money and guidance came at a price. The MSC agreed to help finance the TUC-sponsored unemployed centres on condition that these facilities would not be turned into focal points of political mobilisation. These restrictions included banning the sponsorship of marches, involvement with industrial disputes and any demonstrations against government policies. However, the TUC made clear that those centres that chose not to accept MSC funding were free to pursue whatever political agenda they wished.[49]

It must be remembered that it was during this period many unions were losing members and experiencing increased financial difficulties. Thus, many of the TUC hierarchy welcomed the MSC's financial assistance, particularly given its continued role in the governance of the Commission. TUC officials argued that the MSC could provide not only funding, but also skills training and employment opportunities. Nevertheless, the MSC's strict guidelines over unemployed centres' activities, and the obligation of the TUC to police these regulations, suggested to militants that the government was utilising this organisational relationship to control the unemployed far more than assisting them. Given such suspicions, and in order to circumvent MSC funding, many unemployed centres approached local authorities for financial backing – particularly Labour-controlled city and county councils.

The TUC's reliance on MSC funding became the subject of debate within the trade union movement, symbolic of the struggle between the right and the left. The right-wing wanted accountability from the centres, and the acceptance of MSC funding meant the TUC could guarantee that control. The 6/612 Branch leadership were very much on the left, and accordingly, they wanted to see greater encouragement from the TUC regarding campaigning and the political mobilisation of the unemployed. The left's frustration with some union leaders over their perceived reluctance to use the unemployed centres for political means can be seen as early as 1981, when John Nettleton, a 6/612 Branch member and a Region 6 delegate to the TGWU BDC, declared:

> They [unemployed centres] are not just where you go for a cup of tea and a biscuit. We have set up education classes in Merseyside for the unemployed, where 85 people are showing up. We are doing courses in social security benefits. We are also educating the lads politically – and this is something that has to go to every region. Again, in Region 6, we have a very good policy on unemployed people, and that policy should be adopted by every region.[50]

Further evidence of this controversy concerning the role of the centres is disclosed in the minutes of a 1981 conference held by the North West Regional Council of the TUC, reproduced in Box 1.

Vague as the TUC guidelines on this subject appeared to some, most interpreted them to mean that without recourse to MSC funding, an unemployed centre was free to politicise and campaign as much as it saw fit. This was the basis on which the founders of the MTUCURC operated, and how the TGWU 6/612 Branch managed to go on to become a major influence throughout the Merseyside trade union community. Bob Braddock, former manager of the Hardman Street Centre, recalled its origins:

> Part of the impetus for the centre came out of the People's March for Jobs in 1981, because it was largely organised by the 6/612 Branch. When people came back from that march there was a feeling that something had to be done. We weren't the first unemployed centre in the country when we opened our doors in 1983, but we were the biggest, and we were certainly the most politically active unemployed centre not only on Merseyside, but probably the entire country. At one stage we had fifty-four paid employees working out of that centre.[51]

The building itself was unique because its enormous size meant there seemed to be endless possibilities for development. Braddock recalled

Box 1 Report of Second Consultative Conference on Services to the Unemployed at the Basement Theatre, Manchester: 28 February, 1981.

The conference was attended by 53 Delegates representing 9 Trade Unions, 4 C.A.T.C.'s and 23 Trades Councils. Bro. D. Farrar Chairman of the North West Regional Trade Union Council (NWRTUC) was at the Chair and opened the Conference.

Bro. C.M. Barnett, Secretary of the NWRTUC introduced the main item of discussion which was the TUC's Guidelines for the establishment and running of Unemployed Workers Centres. The TUC's approach, he argued, reflected the necessity to ensure that the Unemployed Workers Centres promoted by the Trade Union Movement, were accountable to the Movement ... On funding, Bro. Barnett reported that following discussions with the MSC, he was satisfied that finance would be available for soundly based projects.

Sis. Carter, Salford T.C. sought clarification on the purposes of the Unemployed Workers Centres.

Bro. Barnett responded by briefly stating the main aims of the Unemployed Workers Centres, as follows – firstly to give practical advice to unemployed workers, secondly to provide educational and social opportunities and thirdly to seek to maintain links between employed and unemployed workers.

Bro. Spooner (M.A.N.T.U.C.), argued that the Guidelines were unsatisfactory because – (a) they made no provisions for representation of the unemployed on Management Committees, (b) there appeared to be no campaigning role for the Centres envisaged in the document, (c) he also thought there may be conflict between MSC funded centre workers and young people with problems with Y.O.P. for example.

Bro. McClaren (Blackpool Trades Council) argued that the Guidelines had effectively had effectively interrupted the progress which had been made. Blackpool had again approached the local Corporation and has raised the matter with the MSC but he felt the Guidelines were causing difficulties.

Bro. Owens (T & GWU) – [Bobby Owens, 6/612] thought that the main aim should be to establish a network of Centres under the auspices of the Trade Union Movement. He also stressed the importance of Unions seriously looking at the retention of Unemployed Workers. On funding, he argued that the Guidelines left a lot to chance and he argued that the Movement nationally had to take more financial responsibility.

Source: MRC, MSS.292D/135.58/1, Meeting minutes from a conference by the North West Regional Council of the Trades Union Congress held in Manchester on 28 February 1981.

that there was more than enough room on the site to house a reception hall, as well as numerous meeting rooms and offices, which could bring in much-needed revenue:

> It was 48,000 square feet. It used to be Police Headquarters at one time many years ago. So with all that room we came up with the idea of putting a bar in there, where hopefully, we could make some money and not have to go begging for donations. For a while it was a success ...

> We had a profitable bar within the centre called *The Flying Picket*. It was so named in honour of the Great Miners' Strike which was going on when we opened the bar. It became a big labour movement bar and we had an enormous meeting room upstairs which we also rented out to the various trade unions for their meetings. So the centre became the headquarters and offices of a number of local trade union branches. At one stage the bar was contributing about £80,000 a year to the centre through revenues and rents, so it was a big help for a while, but it fell off once more bars started to move into that neighbourhood. There was a thirty-fold increase in the number of drinking establishments in that area alone during this period.[52]

For some time, however, *The Flying Picket* became one of the more popular drinking establishments in Merseyside. Braddock, its licensee, recalled that the venue was important in attracting young people:

> We were very interested in getting young people involved, so we set up music facilities and a concert venue called *Upstairs at the Picket*. It was very good because we attracted some very famous names. We also had a recording studio donated by Pete Townshend of The Who, which we used as a place for young unemployed people to help get their bands into the music business.[53]

One of the former MTUCURC staff remembered that the media attention attracted celebrity interest in the work being done at the centre:

> At the recording studio in the centre in Hardman Street we were given loads of good quality equipment from people like Elvis Costello, Pete Townshend, Yoko Ono who gave money, and Paul McCartney gave us loads of instruments. There really was just a lot of groundswell of support from the pop industry in general.[54]

A contemporary press account highlighted the influence of *The Flying Picket*, the upstairs music venue, the recording studio and the effects these venues had on the young unemployed of Merseyside:

> Danny Tarbuck, a veteran of the Liverpool music scene at 24, is supervising the re-equipping of a sound studio. 'In Liverpool there's plenty of unemployed musicians and bands all waiting for this studio to be finished', he said. 'This is my life; what I've always done for the past seven or eight years, but I'm afraid there's not been many wage packets in that. Now I've got a wage; now I'm living'.[55]

One activist in the unemployed movement recalled the amount of influence the Hardman Street centre had in shaping popular culture in the city:

> The link to culture was important to the centre. Liverpool became a focal point once again for music. There was a little Merseybeat revival around that time, with the likes of Echo and the Bunnymen, Frankie Goes to Hollywood, etc., a lot of bands were emerging out of Liverpool because there was a lot of unemployed lads strumming guitars singing songs about unemployment and whatever. Bands like The La's and Cast and so forth, well they all had their origins in that music studio we had set up in the centre in Hardman Street.[56]

A newspaper account taken from 1987, a time when unemployment on Merseyside was at one of its highest levels, summarised the centre's impressive range of activities:

> But it is in its wider catering for the young and the long-term jobless that the six-year-old centre excels ... The centre has its own pub, *The Flying Picket*, a theatre and cinema used by touring groups and backed by local playwrights; a multi-purpose gymnasium; a visual arts unit; commercial printing plant with computer setting; children's centre; and canteen. It is home for many politically related groups, such as unions, Labour Party, and Trades Council, and provides work for 38 people. Its employment resource group has seen 10 workers' co-operatives successfully launched, while the women's technology scheme gives a basic one-year course in new technology to women over 25. EEC funded, the course has a comparatively high placement rate into industry, while many of the previously untrained women go on to higher courses. In addition to the centre's own courses, other organisations use the 17 teaching rooms and conference rooms for teaching activities. They are backed by an excellent library of 7,000 books, where the speciality is social and union history. Most of the functions are cost effective within a tightly monitored budget. But, aware of the need to avoid media charges of 'politics on the rates', Merseyside and the other centres recognise the need for financial independence, particularly through involving the community in using their resources. 'The employed and the unemployed must be organised together, particularly through their unions', says Mr. Coyne [MTUCURC Coordinator]. 'In the Sixties the unions had neglected community aspects as not their responsibility. But we have to be unashamedly political because politics created unemployment and only politics will solve it', he says. 'It wasn't tea and sympathy that was needed, but active campaigning, including support for new job initiatives. That could come from a more national coordinating role for campaigns through the TUC's employment and organising committee', he feels.[57]

Arguably, the centre's greatest success was the way it combined political activity with the provision of services. Despite its record on political agitation, its former coordinator insisted that assistance to the jobless was not neglected:

> People shouldn't have this view that the centre was some make-work project where you had a bunch of unemployed people sitting around carving up pieces of wood – that it was a scruffy place. It wasn't. It was a state-of-the-art facility which provided excellent job training and educational programmes. For instance, there are three people now who are senior editors with the BBC [British Broadcasting Corporation] who started off doing photography in that centre ... [they] started taking photos at demos and they learned their craft at that centre through fellow unemployed people. They got all their training there, and it was through this training they went on to become cameramen at the BBC and today they're senior editors ... We also had the Women's Technology Centre in Hardman Street. Don't forget this is the end of the 1970s and early 1980s and computer technology was just beginning, but unemployment was high and women were often excluded from the job market ... So, yes, I guess we were providing a service, but we did it with a message.[58]

Despite the centre's success, its staff became increasingly concerned with the financial burden of its campaigning initiatives. Unlike many of the TUC-sponsored unemployed centres elsewhere, MTUCURC resolutely refused to accept MSC assistance, so long as the restrictions on campaigning remained, as Braddock explained:

> We were very adamant about not taking money from the MSC; because there were all sorts of compromises we would have had to give into ... I mean we were a campaigning organisation ... when the miners went out on strike we were in the forefront of organising local support here in town. Now, I mean that's something a trade union would do, but it certainly wouldn't be something a government-sponsored entity would be doing. What made our centre in Hardman Street so unique was the fact we were the biggest. We offered a far wider range of activities at that centre ... Our argument was the service we were doing was political in nature, so we had to be political ... because of the nature and structure of our organisation we were still able to keep up the fight ... So somebody had to have the balls to fight [Thatcher]. We had no other choice but to be political.[59]

Unfortunately for local labour activists, as time went on the centre was more often in the red than the black, and the revenue streams it established through such venues as *The Flying Picket* were no longer sufficient. Thatcher's abolition of the Labour-dominated Merseyside County Council in 1986, which had donated up to £390,000 per year, removed the centre's largest source of revenue. Trade union funding was diminishing too since many unions by this point were experiencing their most difficult financial period in post-war history. Braddock summarised the situation: 'We were broke, and something had to be done.'[60]

The One Fund for All

The leaders of the 6/612 Branch and their activists were in a constant search for funding in order to finance the various campaigning initiatives. The financial overhead at their base, the MTUCURC, was increasing, and the building itself was old and often in need of repairs. Braddock explained the dilemma: 'Union membership fell from its peak at over 13 million to just a little over 6 million in a relatively short period of time ... Because the trade unions just didn't have that kind of strength anymore we had to find the money from somewhere else.'[61]

The centre's principal financial backer, Merseyside County Council, had been abolished by the Thatcher government in 1986. Control of the only other relevant local authority, Liverpool City Council, had swung from Labour to the Liberal Democrats following the budget debacle and subsequent fall of the Militant Tendency-led Labour Party caucus in the early 1980s. A centre official described the relationship with the new ruling group: 'They were not exactly on friendly terms with us or the centre.'[62]

By 1986, the centre was in urgent need of a new revenue stream. The answer came through a fundraising scheme initiated three years previous by members of the 6/612 Branch. Basically, the scheme was founded on regular contributions made by trade unionists in work, which, in turn, supported activities for the unemployed. The centre's Board of Directors decided the 'One Fund for All' (OFFA) programme should be expanded, and used, in conjunction with TUC approval, as the primary funding stream for the MTUCURC. It was also to be operated as a source of income for the smaller unemployed centres throughout Merseyside too. One activist described the fund's origins:

> Rather than stand at factory gates with cap in hand looking for donations, which is usually the normal procedure for working-class endeavours, they decided to approach shop stewards first, and then company officials, if they could approach their workforces at a convenient time, and ask if they'd consider joining this idea they had for a fund to raise money for the various unemployed centres in the area. They were assured it was regulated and supervised by the TUC, and because it was generally felt that a lot of good work and services were being provided by these centres the One Fund for All took off. It proved to be such a success that other areas of the country began adopting it as well.[63]

One founding member and trustee of OFFA reported: 'At its height, I think the fund was raising about three quarters of a million pounds a year.'[64] Another active associate of the Merseyside OFFA suggested a lower figure: 'At one stage we were collecting a quarter million pounds a year. It all went to the centres, and at one stage the Hardman Street Unemployed Centre alone was getting as much as £70,000 pounds a year from the fund.'[65] A national newspaper described the fund's operations:

> It is a common fund into which employed workers agree to pay anything from 10p a week to £10 a month from their wages. Many firms deduct the contributions at source. Last year £120,000 was raised by OFFA, and it is hoped this year to reach £500,000 towards the cost of the 16 centres throughout Merseyside. With other resources the major centre could be made self-supporting. Independence will enable them to maintain their many active campaigns on behalf of the unemployed.[66]

A centre activist explained the amount of empowerment this fundraising scheme had on the Merseyside anti-unemployment campaign:

> We were the only area of the country where a One Fund for All really worked and attracted money. At its height it was raising almost a half million pounds. That was all done by way of 'check-off', taken directly out of a worker's wages ... The interesting thing is that was our call to the trade unions. We said 'Don't give branch money ... send a message that it should be individuals who are giving something like 10p or whatever out of their wages'. But much more importantly when you think that you now have thousands and thousands of individual trade unionists who were buying into it rather than just the branches, so you have ownership. It made members feel more a part of the movement ... That's extraordinarily significant in that sense. But then again you must remember that one in four families in Merseyside in those days was directly affected by unemployment.[67]

OFFA symbolised the value placed on politicisation by the leadership of the 6/612 Branch. It often struggled financially to maintain the campaigning dimension of its cause, but the branch cadre conceived the fund as the route to independence it wished to maintain. It provided the means to politicise Liverpool's unemployed.

Conclusion

The powerful sense of purpose demonstrated by a group of young and relatively inexperienced, unemployed car workers in Liverpool is illustrated by the range of political initiatives examined in this chapter. Arguably, their legacy remains evident. The TGWU's 6/612 Branch still exists as a viable union body today, although now it is part of the Unite union; its focus remains centred largely on the needs of the unemployed. The MTUCURC has moved from its original Hardman Street location to a smaller facility in Mount Pleasant Avenue, Liverpool. It has changed its name to the People's Centre, after the board of directors decided their cause needed to reach out to the wider Merseyside community. Due to growing poverty in and around Merseyside, it was felt the centre could no longer merely represent the trade unionists and the unemployed alone. Nevertheless, the unions retain significant influence, and according to the current director: 'The needs of the unemployed still take precedence.'[68] Finally, OFFA continues as a recognised charity and maintains links with Merseyside unemployed centres. A number of the original campaigning institutions organised by the 6/612 Branch may have changed their name or altered their direction over the years, but the original object of assisting Merseyside's unemployed has been maintained.

The evidence surveyed in this chapter suggests that working-class solidarity was enhanced by the agency of these activists, even if we restrict that claim to the years prior to when several 6/612 leaders became professional union officials. This evidence includes the widespread support for the People's March for Jobs in 1981. The grassroots nature of this event along with the reorganisation of the TGWU 6/612 Branch, and the insistence on a politically orientated resource centre for the unemployed, demonstrates that this was a movement from below, not one imposed on Merseyside's working class by government officials and trade union elites.

Conversely, it can be argued that while the leaders of the TGWU 6/612 Branch, such as Owens, entered union politics as outsiders and agents of change, many of these same anti-capitalists and rebels subsequently became managers of an enterprise employing fifty-four workers. Owens and a number of the other 6/612 activists went on to become a part of the full-time trade union establishment and bureaucracy they originally criticised and sought to transform. Whether the initiatives of the 6/612 Branch genuinely inspired a sense of working-class solidarity, or merely furthered the careers of talented campaigners is a legitimate question, albeit one not necessarily susceptible to an 'either/or' answer.

Nevertheless, it can be argued that their involvement in the many vibrant, multi-faceted campaigns against joblessness on Merseyside proved worker militancy had not expired. If today their legacy seems vestigial and faded, their achievements were real during the 1980s. A former TGWU 6/612 member summarised that volatile period in Liverpool's history:

> There was a kind of community spirit that went right on through until after the destruction of the miners' strike. So that immediate period – those five years [1980–85] or so – brought so many of us together in solidarity. It was quite an optimistic fighting time. And I suppose the fight hung-over for a while longer in most people, but you can see it was fading by about 1990 as the politics of the fight dissipated and people started going their own separate ways.[69]

Yet while the redundant may have considered themselves fortunate to have a trade union such as the 6/612 Branch looking out for their best interests, a question arises as to what support structures were available to the youth who had not yet made the first step on the work ladder? In addition to recent school leavers, what institutions were intact which advocated economic justice for ethnic minorities, many of whom never had the political clout or friends in strategic positions within trade union hierarchies? Who could they lean on in times of trouble? The next chapter will explore these questions in detail.

Notes

1 Interview with Tony McQuade.
2 Interview with Tony McQuade.
3 Interview with Tony McQuade.
4 Ken Ferguson, 'Jobless Unionists Fight Unemployment', *New Internationalist*, no. 117, (November 1982): www.newint.org/issue117/jobless.htm.
5 Interview with Kevin Coyne.
6 Interview with Tony McQuade.
7 Interview with Tony McQuade.
8 Interview with Bob Braddock.
9 *Guardian*, 21 October 1981.
10 Allen Barker, Paul Lewis and Michael McCann, 'Trade Unions and the Organisation of the Unemployed', *British Journal of Industrial Relations*, vol. 22, no. 3 (1984), pp. 392–3.
11 Barker *et al.*, 'Trade Unions', pp. 393–4.
12 Unite the Union Archives Office – Holborn, London, Ref. No. MSS.126/TG/1887/29. Transcribed minutes and record of proceedings of the Transport and General Workers' Union Twenty-Ninth Biennial Delegate Conference, Brighton Centre, Brighton, Sussex UK on Wednesday 24 June 1981. Minute No. 46 – Industrial-Employment Policies-Unemployment, pp. 46–7.
13 Unite, MSS.126/TG/1887/29 minutes and record, 24 June 1981, p. 50.
14 Interview with Tony McQuade.
15 Interview with Bob Towers.

16 Michael J. Carden, 'Union Democracy and Incorporation: A Case Study of the T.G.W.U. Merseyside Division with Particular Reference to the Dock Industry', unpublished MA dissertation, University of Liverpool, 1996, pp. 179–80.
17 Carden, 'Union Democracy', pp. 179–80.
18 Modern Records Centre, University of Warwick (MRC), MSS.292/1980, *Report of 112th Annual Trades Union Congress*, Brighton Centre, Brighton, September 1st to 5th 1980, (Enfield, 1980), p. 382.
19 *Report of 112th Annual Trades Union Congress*, p. 383.
20 *Report of 112th Annual Trades Union Congress*, p. 382.
21 MRC, MSS.292D/135.58/1, *Report of Consultative Conference on 'Services to the Unemployed'*, North West Regional Council of the TUC, 20 December 1980.
22 MRC, MSS.292/90/4, TUC Consultative Conference: Services for the Unemployed, Opening Speech by Lionel Murray, TUC General Secretary, 4 November 1980.
23 MRC, MSS.292D/135.56, Lionel Murray, General Secretary, Trades Union Congress, 12 December 1980, Circular No. 85 (1980–81).
24 Interview with Tony McQuade.
25 MRC, MSS.292D/10.13/2, Lionel Murray, General Secretary, and Brendan Barber, Press Officer, Trades Union Congress, London, UK, 26 May 1982: Press Release.
26 Interview with Tony McQuade.
27 MRC, MSS.126/TG/59/11, 'Minutes of the Merseyside Transport and General Worker's Composite District Committee Meeting', 10 July 1986.
28 Interview with Greg Coyne.
29 Interview with Bob Towers.
30 *Observer*, 3 May 1981.
31 Paul Bagguley, *From Protest to Acquiescence: Political Movements of the Unemployed* (London, 1991), p. 115.
32 *Guardian*, 2 May 1981.
33 *Liverpool Echo*, 1 May 1981.
34 *The Times*, 5 May 1981.
35 *The Times*, 1 June 1981.
36 *Liverpool Echo*, 1 May 1981.
37 Interview with Bob Towers.
38 *Guardian*, 3 June 1981.
39 *Guardian*, 20 May 1981.
40 *Guardian*, 22 May 1981.
41 Hansard, House of Commons, 22 May 1981, vol. 5, cc. 591.
42 *Liverpool Daily Post*, 1 June 1981.
43 Interview with Bob Towers.
44 MRC, MSS. 292D/135.56, Lionel Murray, General Secretary, Trades Union Congress, 12 December 1980, Circular No. 85 (1980–81).
45 Interview with Kevin Coyne.

46 Interview with Kevin Coyne.
47 Keith Forrester and Kevin Ward, 'Organising the Unemployed? The TUC and the Unemployed Workers Centres', *Industrial Relations Journal*, vol. 17, no. 1 (1986), p. 48.
48 MRC, MSS.393D/135.58/1, Employment Policy and Organisation Committee of the Trades' Union Congress, 21 January 1981, EPOC 5/3, Private and Confidential Memorandum – Services for the Unemployed.
49 Barker *et al.*, 'Trade Unions', p. 401.
50 Unite Archives, MSS.126/TG/1887/29 Transcribed minutes and record of proceedings of the Transport and General Workers' Union Twenty-Ninth Biennial Delegate Conference, Brighton Centre, Brighton, Sussex UK on Afternoon Wednesday 24 June 1981. Minute No. 46 – Industrial-Employment Policies-Unemployment, pp. 52–3.
51 Interview with Bob Braddock.
52 Interview with Bob Braddock.
53 Interview with Bob Braddock.
54 Interview with Gill Monglione.
55 *Guardian*, 3 February 1992.
56 Interview with Bob Towers.
57 *Guardian*, 11 March 1987.
58 Interview with Kevin Coyne.
59 Interview with Bob Braddock.
60 Interview with Bob Braddock.
61 Interview with Bob Braddock.
62 Interview with Bob Braddock.
63 Interview with Jack Spriggs.
64 Interview with Tony McQuade. Unfortunately OFFA financial records prior to 13 March 2004 are no longer available.
65 Interview with Bob Braddock.
66 *Guardian*, 11 March 1987.
67 Interview with Kevin Coyne.
68 Interview with Bob Braddock.
69 Interview with Greg Coyne.

5

The Toxteth riots, 1981: unemployed youth take to the streets

Large scale urban riots engulfed Liverpool's Toxteth neighbourhood in early July 1981, lasting over nine days, only to erupt again later that month. This episode of civil unrest caused injuries to 468 police officers, the arrest of over 500 people, and more than 100 vehicles were set on fire. There was damage to both private and public property deemed so severe that some seventy buildings had to be demolished. The culmination of widespread damage and looting not only cost an estimated £8 million, but it also took at least one life as a young man was crushed to death by a police vehicle. The Toxteth riots marked the first time police on the British mainland used CS gas to disperse crowds.[1]

It will be remembered that in the summer of 1981 rioting had scorched through many of Britain's inner cities, including Brixton and Southall in London, Birmingham's Handsworth area, Chapeltown in Leeds, Moss Side in Manchester, and a major disturbance occurred the previous year in St. Paul's, Bristol. Studies have revealed that the outbreak of each riot had a set of highly individualised circumstances, including racial tension and divisions between various ethnic groups, poor police and community relations, criminal opportunism and rising rates of structural unemployment afflicting working-class youth.[2]

Nevertheless, any attempt to ascribe a single and direct cause to what occurred in Toxteth over the summer of 1981 would be overly simplistic. Clearly, a variety of combustible elements collided to produce some of the worst riots Britain had experienced in the twentieth century. Previous studies tender a variety of explanations: racial tensions, over-aggressive policing, selective law enforcement, criminal opportunism and political neglect.

However, the presence of growing joblessness, particularly amongst the youth and all age groups representing ethnic minority backgrounds, and the lack of hope such conditions often produce, must be taken into consideration when searching for reasons why such disturbances erupt and continue to ferment for weeks, even months afterward, as was the case in Toxteth. While it is probable that all of the previously mentioned factors played some role in igniting the unrest in Toxteth, this chapter will question whether the overarching condition which encouraged the eruption and sustainment of such colossal strife was joblessness. It will reflect whether a direct correlation existed between unemployment – in particular, youth unemployment – and if a growing sense of antagonism towards the state was felt by many of Britain's growing army of unemployed youth.

Admittedly, the origins for this disturbance are multi-layered. Nevertheless, it can be argued that many unemployed working-class youths at this time, from all ethnic backgrounds, shared an intense and growing sense of alienation from larger British society. Therefore, it must be questioned if feelings of marginalisation exploded into what could have been seen as the only legitimate means for expressing such angst: taking to the streets and engaging in direct confrontation with representations of state authority, namely, the police.

There was only one government inquiry into possible causes of the urban unrest spreading across Britain that year. Lord Scarman's report on the riot in Brixton in April 1981 was largely completed by the time Toxteth had erupted.[3] Nevertheless, he added a few final pages to highlight the situations erupting in Toxteth and Moss Side in Manchester just prior to the report's publication. Scarman stated unequivocally that Liverpool's unrest, unlike Brixton's, was mainly caused by economic deprivation rather than racial tension. He compared the situation in Toxteth with the 1981 riots in Handsworth, Birmingham, where police and community relations were judged to be exemplary. This suggested that the riots could not entirely be explained by over-aggressive policing. Many Afro-Caribbean Britons residing in the Liverpool 8 – Toxteth area would, of course, disagree with Scarman's comparisons.[4]

Merseyside Police's Chief Constable, Kenneth Oxford, suggested the underlying cause was neither economic nor racial in origin; rather, it was an exploitation of the chaos by local criminal elements.[5] Nevertheless, some observers argued that there had to be more than mere criminal opportunism in order for so many people with no criminal histories to react with such ferocity.

In contrast, Lord Gifford subsequently published an unofficial report on the roots of the Toxteth riots in which he noted the 'destructive effects' of Margaret Thatcher's economic policies. Lord Gifford and his panel concluded that a major factor contributing to this disturbance was the economic marginalisation of, not only the Afro-Caribbean community in Toxteth, but the working-class population of Merseyside more widely. Lord Gifford's report insisted that initiatives introduced after the riots by Secretary of State for the Environment, Michael Heseltine, did little to alleviate this economic deprivation.[6]

The Toxteth riots

The flash point of the violence in Toxteth that summer can be traced to one incident on the evening of Friday, 3 July 1981. As Merseyside police officers were effecting the arrest of a suspect in possession of a stolen motorcycle in Selborne Street, Toxteth, Liverpool 8, the officers were suddenly attacked by someone identified as the suspect's brother, Leroy Alphonse Cooper. During the altercation, the suspect managed to escape and Leroy was arrested. It was this relatively minor scuffle between the police and two local residents that started one of the worst urban riots in twentieth-century Britain.[7] The police officer who attempted to make that arrest recalled:

> Prior to the riots I worked and lived in that area, so I had a pretty good idea how the place worked. At that time I was working in a unit called the Operational Support Division or OSD for short. Normally we worked three or four of us in a vehicle, but that night it was just Sergeant Jerry Evans [no relation to interviewee] and I. Prior to this, we were actually banned from working in that area, because even then there was tension in the city, and we had a reputation for getting involved with things and making a lot of arrests ... Because of all the pressures bubbling at the time, we were told: 'Don't go into that area. We don't want arrests being made unnecessarily, because it could blow'. Well, during that night I heard a radio call go out from an unmarked [police] traffic car that was pursuing a motorcycle in and around parts of Liverpool 8 ... I then heard the bike had come to a halt or crashed on Selborne Street, near the corner of Granby Street ... Well, then we heard a call go out from that location of a 'Con Requires', which is code for a Constable Requires Assistance ... As soon as we got there the plain clothes traffic officer began to put his arrest – the male on the motorcycle, into our van. I later found out that [the suspect] was Leroy Cooper's brother ... Once he put him inside the back of our van; one of the officers asked me how to lock the latch. Well, I actually unlocked it [accidently]. And out bolted the [suspect] and he was gone. That was my mistake. Leroy then turned up ... My Sergeant got out and tried to retrieve him [the suspect], but Leroy punched him [the Sergeant] on the nose and broke his nose – you could actually see it was broken because his nose moved over to one side of his face. It was then that a big crowd circled around – very loud – and now there were a lot of people ... I reached out and arrested Leroy Cooper – had a tussle with him – in fact it was a fight. He bit my ear ... I remember ending up

> on the ground. He kept trying to wrestle away, but I kept hold of him the entire time I was on the ground. Meanwhile I was getting kicked by the crowd – and I mean kicked badly. And then there was a parting of the crowd, as this male then stood above me with a brick in his hand, which he then threw in my face. That split my head open, but I still kept hold of Leroy, and people were still kicking me. Then for some reason he just gave up, and we managed to get him in the van and out of there. I don't know how, but we did.[8]

An alternative view of the events in Selborne Street emerged from members of Toxteth's Afro-Caribbean community in the following press report:

> The incident which started the weekend of violence is already in dispute ... Walter Brown, chairman of the Merseyside Community Relations Council, says however: 'I was there at the time they tried to arrest the youth. We say there was excessive police over-manning, in that they had eight police cars there to arrest one youth. The whole community was angry. It was not just the young people. It was the adults. They were very, very angry at the way the youth was treated by police'.[9]

These comments certainly highlight the seeming lack of understanding between police and the local community. They give a distinct impression that many ethnic minorities in Toxteth felt the police were not there to serve and protect, but to abuse and harass.

The anger levelled at the police that evening did not end with Cooper's arrest. Sensing trouble was imminent, Chief Constable Oxford deployed extra police patrols to the Toxteth area the following day. Towards evening, the police suddenly found themselves under siege by a growing, angry mob. A police sergeant on the scene recalled:

> Myself, and the other Section Sergeant, Roy Bailey, were told to take both our sections and go down to Upper Parliament Street and patrol between Grove and Catherine Streets, which is only about 200 yards of road. There was definitely something in the air that evening. I don't know, but it was like electricity ... we could see a gang of about 20 blacks, and we noticed they were all carrying something in their hands ... Well, I had to suddenly pull [Bailey] out of the way as a rock flew straight past him. So we then turned and ran around the block to Upper Parliament Street where our men were posted ... The locals set up barricades all the way across Upper Parliament Street ... Chief Superintendent of C Division, a man named Joe Squires, he was there with other sections of men patrolling the opposite side of Upper Parliament Street. So he ordered all us to get in a formation and take our batons out. As he said, 'They can only carry two missiles,

Figure 7 Streets alight during the riots in Toxteth, summer 1981

> one in each hand. We'll wait for them to throw the second one, and then we'll charge them'. So we waited, and after they threw the second round we charged after them. They then ran off and scurried into their little holes. We walked up, took all the barricades down, and as far as we were concerned that was it ... [Later] when we went back to Upper Parliament Street there were lines of police already there in riot shields. So we spent the remainder of that night right up till the next morning behind these riot shields. There wasn't anybody who seemed to have any idea of what to do except stand behind riot shields. And so we were getting bombarded with iron railings, petrol bombs, stones – there just didn't seemed to be anyone in charge.[10]

Other reports from that evening portray growing chaos and a breakdown in law and order, describing the streets of Toxteth as reminiscent of the '1941 Liverpool blitz' (see Figures 7 and 8).[11] *The Times* placed much of the blame on the Merseyside constabulary: 'The police lost control of a large area of the multi-racial suburb. Only 800 officers from four North Western forces were deployed, too few men to deal with the violence.'[12] One police officer recalled the lack of direction: 'I was detached from my [group] near Lodge Lane. A lot of us became detached. There was no organisation. There were no orders given. There was really nobody there even to supervise.'[13] The Police Federation, a quasi-trade union for British police officers, registered discontent about

Figure 8 Street carnage during Toxteth riots, summer 1981

the lack of equipment and riot training. There were numerous reports of constables being forced to use bin lids as riot shields and motorcycle helmets for protective headgear.[14]

As Saturday night turned to Sunday morning, fire and ambulance personnel were repeatedly under attack. The police were stretched to the point that it had become tactically pointless to make further arrests: 'By Sunday, we just didn't bother making arrests any more.'[15] Calls for assistance in other areas of the city went largely unanswered as the region's emergency services were almost exclusively engaged in Toxteth.[16]

Looting increased by Sunday evening, as shops along Lodge Lane were beyond the reach of the police and unprotected. Media reports claimed organised gangs from throughout Merseyside took part in the pillaging.[17] A detective recalled the deteriorating situation in a letter he wrote to his mother:

> On Sunday evening, I again went on duty at 11.00 p.m. having heard on the radio before leaving home that a large number of youths had broken into the dairy premises at the top of Upper Parliament Street and had driven six milk floats out into the roadway and down Upper Parliament Street shortly after 9.00 p.m. to act as barricades. The fighting and the destruction that night was to be far more worse than anything previous, although extra police had been brought in from a number of other forces

> ... We were being constantly informed by members of the public who were calling in at the police station that a large number of shops and other premises on Lodge Lane, which is a main shopping road which leads off from the top of Upper Parliament Street, were being attacked by looters. There were no police officers to send to protect their premises. One can imagine the frustration. Never in the history of the city had a situation like this ever prevailed.[18]

A press report provided a similarly vivid account:

> Police in Toxteth, Liverpool were overwhelmed by about 200 rioters late last night in one of the most serious incidents of public disorder in mainland Britain. Hundreds of youths, most of them white, broke through a dense cordon of police riot shields on the second successive night of violence. There were hand-to-hand battles, like a medieval affray. Scaffolding pipes were used like lances to break through the police lines, and within about five minutes of the biggest charge of the night the police were forced to retreat a long distance down Upper Parliament Street ... Police eventually withdrew entirely from the mile-long main artery road of Toxteth and left it in the hands of rioters and looters ... A National Westminster Bank was gutted. In the main assault in Upper Parliament Street, rioters were in command, brandishing riot shields and helmets, left by police. Youths were driving milk floats up and down the street. Horns blared from stolen cars ... A fire hose which the police had been using on them was turned against the police by the victorious rioters. Buildings on fire crackled and spat sparks over a scene that resembled Belfast. A cement mixer was used as a battering ram, but the line of police held until eventually the rioters, using all kinds of weapons, including pipes like clubs, broke through. Officers fell back with head and body wounds. A fire brigade spokesman said they had been unable to get through to the burning buildings because their vehicles had been attacked and windscreens shattered by rioters ... The Princes Park Geriatric Hospital had to be evacuated after a night club next door was set ablaze; ambulancemen moved 96 patients to safety. David Alton, Liberal MP for Liverpool Edge Hill said that he was appalled by the savagery that he had witnessed, adding: 'Police have abandoned part of Liverpool to a mob'.[19]

Several local landmarks went up in flames, including the Rialto Theatre and Ballroom, a long established entertainment venue, which had once showcased acts such as the Beatles, Gerry and the Pacemakers and the Searchers. The club's grand ambience and regular review of top acts attracted a clientele drawn largely from outside of the neighbourhood, with ticket prices beyond the means of many local Toxteth residents. Also levelled was the exclusive Racquet Club – a symbol of Liverpool old-moneyed establishment.[20] Growing anxiety was evident among the local authorities that the chaos would spread to other working-class areas.

As the police presence grew, so too did the number of rioters, who were increasingly drawn from outside of the Liverpool 8 area. It was also evident that the riots were spreading to other areas of Merseyside. In the almost exclusively white working-class districts of Kirkby, Croxteth, Everton, Speke, Garston and Kensington, there were numerous reports of clashes between unemployed white youths and Merseyside Police. There were also incidents of vandalism, assault and looting in these impoverished areas, albeit not on the same scale and intensity as had taken place in Toxteth.[21]

While the first three days of rioting were the most ferocious, much of the unrest persisted for nine days after the initial widespread outbreak on 4 July 1981. Moreover, intermittent incidents of street violence continued well into the autumn of that year. The first three days, however, set the stage. Home Secretary William Whitelaw analysed their characteristics:

> Liverpool 8 has long suffered a range of social, economic and high crime problems. The three days of violence reflect the complexity of the situation. The first night consisted largely of black youths, children of many generations of Liverpool people, erupting against the police. The second saw a concerted attack on the police by white and black youngsters. The third witnessed a predominantly white crowd of looters exploiting the earlier disturbances, while local black leaders played a major part in keeping their young people off the streets.[22]

Rioting intensified again in Toxteth before the wedding of Prince Charles and Lady Diana on 29 July 1981, guaranteeing further media attention. Taxi drivers treated Toxteth as a 'no-go' area after several of them were set upon and attacked by angry mobs.[23] Nevertheless, Chief Constable Oxford agreed to a reversal in policy and implemented a more low-key approach to policing. It was a strategy criticised by many of his officers who predicted that treating the Toxteth area as a 'no-go' area for police would turn the neighbourhood into a sanctuary for criminal elements.

It was during this second round of violence in the late evening of 28 July 1981 that the riots' only fatality occurred. David Moore, a disabled man aged twenty-two, who by all accounts was not a participant in the mêlée between rioters and police, was struck and killed by a police vehicle engaged in 'mobile pursuit'.[24] An eyewitness stated:

> I saw a mob attack a police van across the wasteland opposite my house. The van then charged them hell for leather with its headlights full on. The

> lads were in front of the van and most of them got out of the way, but then I saw this lad. I screamed and covered my eyes. The driver must have known he had hit him but he just drove away.[25]

After news of the death spread, the ensuing riots were the worst in the city since the major disturbances earlier in the month. At its height, just before 2 a.m., on 29 July, hundreds of youths fought a pitched battle with police.[26] The beleaguered Chief Constable defended his decision to employ such manoeuvres against charges that the police were 'out of control': 'We are dealing with large gangs of people hell-bent on breaking the law ... our basic tactic of driving towards them has proved effective. I would much rather use this form of dispersal than CS gas.'[27]

The riots were becoming as divisive politically, at both local and national levels, as they were socially. During an emergency meeting of Liverpool City Council on 10 July 1981, the members of the Council could not even reach agreement on the previous month's minutes.[28] Such internal divisions would intensify in subsequent years, but Council Leader, Sir Trevor Jones, begged councillors to focus on the problem at hand: 'This is the most catastrophic event which has happened here since the Blitz. Today, of all days, let's not argue and make mean, cheap, party political points. Let's rise above it.'[29] Despite this plea, the Council split along party lines. A motion introduced by Labour leader John Hamilton, demanded the Council officially recognise that unemployment and economic deprivation, largely caused by the policies of the Tory government, were the overriding reasons for the unrest in Toxteth. Conservative and Liberal members declined to support this motion.

Margaret Thatcher finally arrived in Liverpool on 13 July 1981, greeted by approximately 1,000 jeering demonstrators. During her five-and-a-half-hour visit she met with police, political and civic leaders, and undertook a ninety-minute tour of the worst affected areas of Toxteth. Although she listened attentively to the various parties, she insisted her government's policies would eventually 'put [Toxteth residents] on a much better footing'.[30]

Aftermath

The aftermath of the disturbances give a better indication of their origins than the events themselves. The ensuing political struggle demonstrated both growing polarisation between the two major parties in Westminster, as well as fissures within the Conservative government. Thatcher had clear views on the riots that summer and held steadfastly to her explanation of the Toxteth conflict in particular. Despite evidence from both the Scarman and Gifford inquiries, she rejected assertions that growing unemployment and deteriorating economic conditions played any role:

> The riots, of course, were a godsend to the Labour Opposition and the Government's critics in general. Here was the long-awaited evidence that our economic policy was causing social breakdown and violence. In the Commons and elsewhere I found myself countering the argument that the riots had been caused by unemployment. Behind their hands, some Conservatives echoed this criticism, complaining that the social fabric was being torn apart by the doctrinaire monetarism we had espoused. This rather overlooked the fact that riots, football hooliganism and crime generally had been on the increase since the 1960s, most of the time under the very economic policies that our critics were urging us to adopt.[31]

Her inspection of Toxteth led her to conclude that the unrest was not the result of economic deprivation, but rather of a weakening of the moral fibre of British society:

> I observed that for all that was said about deprivation, the housing there was by no means the worst in the city. I had been told that some of the young people involved got into trouble through boredom and not having enough to do. But you had only to look at the grounds around those houses with the grass untended, some of it almost waist high, and the litter to see that this was a false analysis. They had plenty of constructive things to do if they wanted ... What was clearly lacking was a sense of pride and personal responsibility.[32]

While her supporters found this appraisal refreshingly blunt, critics judged it rudely patronising: 'Mrs. Thatcher's repeated comments during this period seemed to imply that anyone who suggested a cause for the riots was in some way seeking to excuse them.'[33]

The Prime Minister's views contrasted sharply with the findings of both Lord Scarman in 1981 and Lord Gifford in 1989. Scarman was firm in his conclusion that the Liverpool riots were a consequence of prolonged high unemployment:

> In Toxteth: many of the features of deprivation and decay which characterise Brixton are there repeated ... Unemployment again appears to have particularly affected young people, and within that group, young black people. Street crime is relatively high: in 1980, of the 995 recorded offences of robbery committed within the Merseyside area, over 20% were committed in one of the two police divisions which cover the Toxteth

> area. According to the Chief Constable of Merseyside, the area has historically been one which is difficult to police. Relations between the police and the black community in Toxteth, as was made plain to me when I visited Liverpool, are in a state of crisis ... The element of a deprived area, unemployment and hostility between a high proportion of the youth of the local community and the police seem well established.[34]

Eight years later Lord Gifford's panel drew similar conclusions. While not denying institutionalised racism was a problem, they felt unemployment added a further dimension to this issue.[35]

Despite her own views, Thatcher realised the need to propitiate the 'wets' in her ranks, and to appear that she would address such traumatic events. She appointed her political rival within the Conservative Party, Michael Heseltine, to the unofficial role of 'Minister of Merseyside'. By her own admission, her relations with Heseltine 'had never been easy'.[36] Despite such animosities, Heseltine was charged with conducting an inquiry into the economic situation in Liverpool. Heseltine said of his new responsibilities: 'In other words, one had to "enable" these communities to compete for their place in the sun.'[37]

To Thatcher's ire, Heseltine refuted her assertion that unemployment played no role in the riots, and urged government intervention: 'I argued that this would create jobs, stimulate private investment and reflect the fact that so much cash was flowing as a result of the sale of capital assets.'[38] In his final report, 'It Took a Riot', Heseltine outlined thirteen initiatives he felt would stimulate the local economy. Many of Heseltine's projects relied on substantial state investment, and most were rejected by Thatcher. He recalled:

> They included a town-planning brief to restore the Anglican Cathedral precinct, a scheme for the provision of community workshops for small firms, a government grant of £1 million for sporting facilities (to be matched by private money), a management training scheme for the young unemployed at two separate centres and – the one that caught the headlines – the establishment of the Tate Gallery of the North on the old Albert Dock site.[39]

Heseltine made a personal request of Thatcher to make his position as 'Minister for Merseyside' permanent: 'My suggestion therefore is that you could appoint me and several of my colleagues ... each to exercise special responsibility for one of the conurbations. Our tasks would be to co-ordinate the activities of central government; to act as trouble-shooters and take initiatives; and secure maximum value for money from expenditure programmes.'[40] If his request for permanency went unheeded, at least some of his recommendations came to fruition; most notable was the refurbishment of the Albert Dock on Liverpool's waterfront. Critics claimed that during his brief period as 'Minister for Merseyside' there was more rhetoric than results in combating unemployment in Toxteth. One witness testified before Lord Gifford's committee: 'All we got from Mr. Heseltine was trees in Princess Avenue, and even they were planted by contractors from outside.' The witness also observed that the major showpieces of Merseyside redevelopment, the Garden Festival and the Albert Dock rejuvenation, had little relevance to the economic health of Toxteth's black residents.[41] Thatcher wryly concurred:

> As Secretary of State for the Environment, [Heseltine] did not prove particularly successful in curbing local authority spending ... But Michael was far less interested in local authority finance than in being 'Minister for Merseyside'. In that capacity he made a great impression, which was undoubtedly politically helpful to us. Though for the most part his efforts had only ephemeral results, I would not blame him for that: Liverpool has defeated better men than Michael Heseltine.[42]

Explanations for the Toxteth riots

This chapter began with the suggestion that long-term unemployment and economic deprivation in Toxteth played a leading role in making a minor case of resisting arrest into a major civil disturbance. If the arrest of Leroy Cooper was the unintended spark which set this riot in motion, the question remains then, how could this level of extreme social disorder have been sustained for days, even months, in Merseyside? This section will introduce and analyse each of the reasons most often submitted as the answer to that question.

In Liverpool, as the embers of the Rialto still smouldered, demands had been voiced for an independent inquiry in order to determine the root of this civil unrest. An editorial in the *Liverpool Echo* commented:

> Urban deprivation, police harassment, high unemployment, racial discrimination ... reasons behind Toxteth's nights of rioting and looting are being advanced from many quarters ... It is vital that the cause and pattern of events should be established by an inquiry, and a major effort made to bring changes in the crucial areas, whether they are of human relationships or environmental conditions.[43]

In addition to Lord Scarman's addendum on the situation in Liverpool in his report on Brixton, and Lord Gifford's committee empaneled to investigate urban strife in Toxteth, Liverpool City Council also conducted a thorough survey of the area in the months after the disturbance. It provides a useful tool in deciphering attitudes on race, the economy, and the public's views on the city's governance in this period.

Analysts of the Toxteth riots have suggested numerous causes, ranging from racial tension, over-aggressive policing mixed with selective law enforcement, criminal opportunism – sometimes referred to as the apolitical theory – as well as political exploitation by outside radicals. Still, other observers point directly to unemployment – particularly amongst young, working-class males. It is, of course, possible that all of these situations interacted; contradicting more dogmatic and simplistic approaches that hold only one factor alone sparked the unrest.

The first theory to be explored will be that the violence unleashed on the streets of Toxteth was mainly due to an unforgiving past of simmering racial tensions. The history of Liverpool's black community is unique amongst other British cities. Unlike Greater London, the West Midlands or Manchester, Liverpool attracted the majority of its black population far earlier than the post-war, 'S.S. Windrush generation'.[44] People of colour have inhabited Merseyside in significant numbers since the eighteenth century. Liverpool's black population is largely descended from black male seafarers from West Africa, who married local white women.[45] The majority had not lived the immigrant experience, as had been the case in other cities, but rather, after generations of assimilation, regarding themselves as British citizens rather than British subjects from the Commonwealth.

The size of Merseyside's black population can only be broadly gauged. The 1911 census listed 3,000 black people living in Liverpool; by 1919 that number had increased to 5,000. The 1961, 1971 and 1981 censuses did not include race as a category, so the post-war black population can only be estimated. In 1981 the Merseyside Community Relations Council approximated the black population of Liverpool to be around 40,000, while the Commission for Racial Equality in 1984 suggested the number to be between 12,400 and 18,000, or 4–6 per cent of the city's population.[46]

In 1981, Liverpool's black population was almost exclusively restricted to Toxteth, a small area south of the city centre, sometimes known by its postal code of Liverpool 8. Lord Gifford observed of one of Toxteth's main thoroughfares, Granby Street: 'In terms of amenities, Granby Street used to be a flourishing shopping street, but now presents a dismal appearance. Out of 48 shop fronts, 18 are boarded up or derelict. Sections of Granby Street are nothing but waste ground. Litter and filth accumulate, particularly in areas which are derelict.'[47]

In 1976, the National Housing Survey showed the main area of black settlement was in Granby Ward, where people of colour made up approximately 30 per cent of the population. Other wards comprising Liverpool 8 are Arundel, where black people were estimated to comprise 12.5 per cent of the population, Abercromby, with 10.5 per cent, Smithdown, 10 per cent, and Princes Park, 8 per cent. This data does not suggest ghettoisation, as is often the case of urban areas in Rust Belt America, but it is noteworthy that by 1976 there was virtually no black settlement in Liverpool's Northend – known for its close-knit, working-class, Irish Catholic heritage – or even further afield in Liverpool's more affluent southern suburbs.[48]

Central to the Liverpool black experience have been memories of the city's long, brutal engagement with the slave trade, through which a significant number of the urban elite during the eighteenth and early nineteenth centuries accumulated their prodigious wealth.[49] The monuments and markers throughout the city that commemorate these men were stark symbols of criminality in the eyes of many Liverpool blacks.

Nevertheless, black people had been living in Liverpool for a far longer time than anywhere else in Britain. However, if the bonds of long-term settlement had resulted in better race relations in Liverpool than other British cities, as advanced by some observers, ethnic tensions were far from absent. Ethnic tension and race based riots were recorded in Liverpool in 1919, 1948 and 1972.[50] Such racial strife was often rooted in competition for employment. In 1925 the National Union of Seaman bowed to racist pressure from whites, and denied work to black seafarers. A survey in 1940 disclosed that of 225 black families, 74 per cent of black male heads of households and 44 per cent of black youths under the age of twenty-one were unemployed. Over 50 per cent of black families lived near or below the poverty level.[51]

A culture of racism existed in Liverpool, and black people often felt they could not trust traditional working-class institutions as guarantors of their rights.[52] A black Toxteth resident recalls the difficulties often encountered by people of colour when searching for work:

> When I used to ring-up places about jobs – and I know people have written about this before, and it's been said, but it's actually true. You'd phone up about a job, they'd ask what's your name: blah, blah. 'Where do you live?' ... You'd tell them and they'd say: 'Oh, Liverpool 8.' And if your name sounded one bit foreign, like mine, you never got the job. I never, ever, ever got a job by that way. I had to go down to the place in person and prove myself and my (abilities) if I ever wanted to get hired. There were ways of overcoming it, but there was also the fact that you shouldn't have had to (go above and beyond white job applicants). That went on all the time.[53]

This alienation from the wider working-class community festered over years, and arguably took on even greater salience in the age of Thatcher, as unemployment increased in both black and white communities. There was a reversal in government commitments towards social spending after 1979. In addition to the cuts in welfare and other social programmes during this period of economic uncertainty, there were also increased restrictions placed on immigration. These actions were viewed by many people of colour as a Conservative affront to the black vote.[54] A former Granby Ward councillor testified to the feelings of Toxteth's black community:

> My memories were of a people who were frustrated. They were so disappointed. They felt they were treated different from the rest of the community. Although unemployment was very high in every community, the ethnic minority felt it was exceptionally more applied to them. And it got so they just couldn't live with it.[55]

This estrangement was exacerbated through broadened police powers within a criminal justice system operated and controlled by whites. Thatcher's 'law and order' agenda did not sit well with a population who regarded themselves as the victims of injustice and exploitation.[56] Especially irksome was the introduction of the 'stop and search on suspicion' law, more commonly referred to as the 'SUS laws'. Taken down from an archaic section of the Vagrancy Act of 1824, it was revitalised in 1981 with the passing of the Criminal Attempts Act. This law empowered police to stop and search any individual they deemed suspicious, without meeting any further criteria of just cause. Blacks, and black youths in particular, felt they were targeted for harassment, further increasing their sense of alienation from the wider British society. A black Toxteth resident who was seventeen at the time of the riots recalled:

> Certainly with my generation of first-born, black British, as kids we were used to being on the streets. It got to the point where we felt there was so little for us to aspire to because we were marginalised a great deal ... It's worth mentioning that there was a dichotomy between us and our parents' generation. Our parents came to this country and experienced all sorts of racial problems. But of course, they lived with colonialism. They lived a life from birth told that this was the natural order of things. Basically, they lived in a survival mode. For us, we were born in Britain. And although life was extreme for us in terms of racism and being marginalised, we still lived in a place where you weren't thrown in prison just for complaining about something. Back in the Caribbean or Africa, our parents' parents and grand-parents would tell them if you speak out of

> place, you'd be whipped. But for us here, that seemed to be an experience so far removed from us, simply because we lived in a different country. Of course, we suffered racism, but we could complain about it. You could remonstrate about it. You weren't thrown in prison or publicly flogged. Most importantly, we were watching television, we were going to school with white kids and we saw how they thrived. Now for us, the differences were so vivid and unfair. This was Britain, and supposedly we were all equal, we were all supposed to treated the same. At least in colonial Africa or Jamaica you were told you were a lesser person. But here our expectations were built up from school. And so when you went out into the wider world and you found there was a massive contradiction, the automatic reaction is anger and frustration. Our parents would say, look, just knuckle-down, wear your best suit and just appeal to these people. But our reaction was, why should we have to try harder than anybody else? Why can't we be judged on merit like everyone else?[57]

One local critic claimed such selectivity of enforcement made many of Toxteth's black youths feel as though 'they were classed as foreigners, as far as their rights were concerned, and they were born and bred here'.[58]

This perception of separateness amongst Liverpool's black community was compounded by the systematic de-industrialisation occurring on their doorstep during this period, which some observers suggested was the real catalyst for civil unrest.[59] As alluded to previously, even Conservative Party stalwart Michael Heseltine suggested that racial tension was merely a symptom of the larger economic problems, which had persistently plagued the city.[60] Lord Gifford was more forthright: 'Black people in Liverpool have been denied access to jobs, even low-paid jobs, more systematically and comprehensively than in any other major city of Black settlement ... There has been a unique conjunction in Liverpool of both exceptionally high unemployment and patterns of racial discrimination.'[61]

Another explanation often cited for the high level of public discontent in Britain's inner cities that summer puts the blame on a systematic pattern of heavy-handed policing. This theory frequently discards race as a major factor and usually downplays evidence of existing tensions between ethnic groups as the driver of the conflict. It often ascribes that those who blame racial strife as the main catalyst for the eruption in Toxteth to be heavily influenced by right-wing and reactionary media sources in the Murdoch press.[62] Many middle-class liberals placed blame instead on what they portrayed as an over-aggressive police force, unleashed by a Conservative government obsessed with law and order. According to the Social-Democratic Party MP for Toxteth:

> If there is any small comfort to be gained, it would appear that this was not a case of racial strife ... I do not believe that unemployment was the cause of the trouble, nor is it correct to blame it on the housing in that area. The area of the rioting has many thousands of new houses. I believe that these events came about because, rightly or wrongly, there is a genuine belief, not only in the black community, but in the white community that in that area the enforcement of law and order is not even-handed.[63]

Robert Kilroy-Silk, Labour MP for Ormskirk, defied his party's official position on the cause of the riots when he echoed a similar sentiment:

> Although disturbances of this kind may have some connection with the social and economic conditions referred to by my right hon. Friend [Roy Hattersley, Labour Shadow Home Secretary], may I point out to the right hon. Gentleman that if this were just a matter of the high level of unemployment an outbreak of violence of this kind would have happened first in Kirkby, in my constituency, where there is greater social deprivation and a higher level of unemployment? Will not the right hon. Gentleman accept that there may be something seriously wrong about the relationship of the police with this community, as has been suggested by me and others of my hon. friends on a number of occasions? Will not he now demand an investigation into the policing of that area? Unless he is prepared to discover the causes he will be dealing only with the symptoms.[64]

David Alton, MP, voiced the Liberal Party position: 'The "SUS" laws and stop-and-search methods had been over-used by police and there were too few policemen on the beat. A chemistry of events came together to create the kind of explosion we saw in the city of Liverpool.'[65]

During the riots, journalists reported that the source of the violence was simply that local youths were no longer willing to obey a police force whom they felt were selective in the enforcement of unjust laws. One community activist commented on the first evening of the riot: 'It became clear last night that these terrible events are a question not only if race, but of young people, both black and white, both expressing their resentment against the police. Unless the authorities accept this, they will block any efforts of making an understanding response to the problem.'[66] In contrast, one police constable defended their application of the law:

> Most of the kids down there [Toxteth] didn't like us because, well, they got stopped a lot, they got searched a lot, and they got arrested a lot. But it shouldn't have come as no surprise to them ... because in those days the SUS laws made it very easy to arrest somebody who was merely 'hanging around' with a little bit of intent ... Look, we didn't arrest somebody just

> because they were standing on a corner, we'd arrested them because we saw them going up and down the street trying car door handles.[67]

Specific issues may also have had a bearing on police and community relations in the months prior to the riots. There had been a high number of robberies and muggings in the area. Detectives assigned to a squad established specifically to deal with this problem were expected to make arrests by whatever means necessary. One of the detectives assigned to this unit recalled:

> There were a few places there that brought a lot of influential people from wealthier areas of Liverpool into contact with Toxteth. There was a huge synagogue that brought Jewish people back to Toxteth who moved onto better parts of Liverpool. There was the Racquets Club, which brought in a lot of rich people, and there was the famous Rialto Theatre, all close by to one another ... Well, anyway, it was rife with street robberies because of this. At one time we were getting something like ten handbag robberies a week. The M-O was usually when a lone woman was in her car and stopped at the traffic lights, the robbers would come alongside her car while on a bike or a motorcycle, punch out her car's window, punch her, take her handbag off the front seat and then flee the area. The other trick was to mug older Jewish people coming in and out of the synagogue every Saturday morning, or they'd mug the rich people as they were coming in and out of the Racquets Club. It had gotten so bad they formed a special squad of six detectives to concentrate exclusively on all these strong-armed robberies going on in Toxteth. The squad was disbanded after the riots because our work was seen as being instrumental in causing them. We had a target group of suspects of thirty-three youths and all were black. Out of this we got twenty-seven arrests, most of whom pled guilty, resulting in none of them getting less than three years' imprisonment. There were four or five more outstanding suspects, who were running these gangs of purse snatchers, two of whom, by the way, were the Cooper brothers [Leroy and Paul] ... both were instrumental in kicking off the Toxteth riots in the first place ... Before the arrests were made, however, we were sure to pass on all our information to the local bobbies on the beat to keep an eye out for these people and pull them whenever they could because we know they're all involved in the rash of street robberies.[68]

Police officers were under pressure at the time to generate arrests. A retired Merseyside Police Inspector recalled: 'Certainly police officers in those days were under heavy pressure to achieve targets and meet certain figures for arrests. Recruits in their first two years were especially put under a lot of pressure to make arrests. The unit I belonged to, for instance, the Operational Support Division, there was a lot of pressure to produce arrests.'[69]

Many of those stopped and searched under the SUS laws were not members of street gangs or even engaged in criminal activity. A former assistant chief constable observed the SUS laws did nothing more than take potential criminals off the street for 'only a couple days, and if the law was abused then all it did was embitter' young people.[70] What troubled many local residents was the frequent deployment of this law in working-class neighbourhoods.[71]

Nevertheless, a large number of observers felt the explanation for the Toxteth riots lay not in over-aggressive policing but in criminal opportunism. Proponents of this 'apolitical' theory postulate that the riots were caused by local criminal elements seizing the opportunity to commit crimes while chaos reigned.[72] Chief Constable Oxford articulated this hypothesis:

> This was not a race riot, simply black hooligans trying to provoke the police by indulging in criminal behaviour. This was completely different from Southall or Brixton. There was no racial connotation whatsoever. It is just a group of black hooligans with some criminal elements amongst the whites streaming in to help, who were hell-bent on provoking the police.[73]

This opinion was aired in the local media, which influenced television and radio coverage of the riots. Oxford argued that much of the violence would not have occurred had parents been stricter in their children's upbringing. He scolded Toxteth parents, saying they had 'a duty to stop their people going on a rampage', and that 'parents and the community had a responsibility to discipline or control their young people. Among the rioters were children as young as 12 or 13, who saw it all as a huge joke or game'.[74]

As the rioting shifted from the predominantly black area of Upper Parliament Street, Lodge Lane and Princes Road to the largely white, Park Road neighbourhood of the Dingle, Oxford altered his message slightly but continued to blame criminal opportunism:

> Announcing 75 arrests, Mr. Oxford described the incidents in Park Road as having no connection with weekend disturbances ... 'There was a group of 100 or more ... no less than 21 were juveniles arrested at midnight for thieving, looting and heaving petrol bombs. Their ages ranged from eight to 16, so what in the name of goodness were these people indulging in at that time? Is there no discipline brought to bear on these people – are their parents not interested?'[75]

Chief Constable Oxford was not alone in blaming criminal opportunism. Many of those on the political right also cited an endemic culture of criminal behaviour due entirely to lack of personal accountability. It is interesting to note that this view also served as a useful buffer often deflecting criticism from the police.[76] Prime Minister Thatcher, of course, was a staunch proponent of the 'apolitical' theory. Keeping her economic agenda in sight, Thatcher never once acknowledged that unemployment and economic deprivation might lie at the root of the problem:

> Welfare arrangements encouraged dependency and discouraged a sense of responsibility, and television undermined common moral values that would have once united working-class communities. The results were a steadily increasing rise in crime (among young men) and illegitimacy (among young women) ... Authority of all kinds ... had been in decline for most of the post-war years. Hence the rise in football hooliganism, race riots and delinquency over that period.[77]

There were allegations that local criminal elements had a hand in much of the disorder. Heseltine felt organised crime was interwoven in the fabric of Toxteth:

> There were many ties which held this community – or parts of the community – together: colour and racial bonds, of course, although a substantial proportion of the residents were white; but also a shared feeling of hopelessness born of low attainment ... a sense of grievance against the police and a belief that even a home address in Toxteth was a certain barrier to employment. But there was something else. Toxteth was the centre of numerous criminal activities. Many of the most powerful people in the area at the time were deep into drugs, prostitution and protection rackets.[78]

The line between 'community activists' and known criminals sometimes became blurred. Police sources claimed that two West Indian born brothers, Michael and Delroy Showers, were the main narcotics dealers in the area. The authorities made every attempt to discredit the Showers brothers as legitimate spokesmen for their community, but often to no avail. Ten years after the riots, police were quick to point out to community leaders and the media alike that Michael Showers was eventually convicted for being at the centre of a £2 million drugs plot and sentenced to twenty years' imprisonment. Delroy would later be sentenced to an eight-year prison term in the Netherlands for narcotics distribution.[79]

Yet it was the Showers brothers who many of Toxteth's black community looked to for leadership. Michael Showers became noticeably vocal in the media and at meetings of Liverpool City Council, especially about all matters involving the Toxteth area and the state of race relations. A founding member of the Liverpool 8 Defence Committee, Showers vociferously criticised Oxford: 'The major problem is the intransigence of the present chief constable, who believes everybody is at fault for the riots except him and his men at the top – he must take the blame.'[80] One retired police officer reflected prevailing opinion amongst the Merseyside force at the time:

> Michael and Delroy Showers were certainly known by the police as being criminals. And we were kind of like gobsmacked, we were amazed in fact, that these people were given free rein with the media to spout off. The only credibility they had going for themselves was that they were black or half-caste themselves. It was just so weird to us how people like these could be put up on pedestals when we knew them as just complete gob-shites. They just jumped on the band-wagon because they saw [an opportunity].[81]

The police also suspected that the Showers brothers had a vested interest in promoting looting during the riots. According to one police source: 'It was always rumoured, but we had no concrete evidence one way or another, that people like that [Michael and Delroy Showers] were stoking the fires [of the riot] by running around, handing out money to people so they could go and buy petrol to make petrol bombs or line their pockets for stolen goods and that sort of thing.'[82]

Suggestions that organised crime had coordinated much of the street fighting and looting during the Toxteth disturbance lacks corroborating evidence. A more plausible explanation of why the riots pressed on for weeks may be attributed to this reason offered by one observer: 'For an unemployed black teenager, bored, frustrated, and resentful of the police, the temptation to go out with a few friends to join in the excitement and the looting was intense.'[83] This interpretation, therefore, implies that the 'apolitical theory' is open to criticism.

A counter-argument to the apolitical theory suggests that crime, street violence and rowdy behaviour are normal aspects of urban life, and such disorder is contained in pockets. For minor disturbances to escalate into a major riot the situation would require greater participation from residents, and not just those routinely engaged in criminal or anti-social behaviour. The prevailing conditions would need to be so tempestuous that non-criminals would willingly risk criminalisation along with habitual lawbreakers. A riot calls for a variety of people, most of whom are normally law-abiding, to actively battle against the authorities. Critics of the apolitical theory conclude that mere escalation of anti-social behaviour from known criminals could not sustain the urban strife unleashed in Toxteth over the summer of 1981. They maintain that urban unrest of that magnitude involved people who were normally law-abiding and not usually prone to criminal activity.[84]

While some advocates of the apolitical theory, including many police officers, felt organised crime played a role in escalating the riots, others believed outside fringe political groups were responsible. Factions cited ranged from anarchists to Irish Republicans. No evidence suggests outside radical political elements converged on Liverpool at the start of the riots or immediately afterward, but this notion of conspiracy persists. A retired police sergeant, heavily involved in squashing the riots stated: 'I am convinced that a cell of anarchists formed somewhere, and then travelled to Bristol, to Birmingham, to Brixton, to Manchester, to Liverpool and started these riots throughout the country in an effort to promote anarchy.'[85] Another senior officer had similar suspicions:

> Once [the riots] kicked off people flooded in from all over to join in ... there were also people there, who I would say, that maybe come from Northern Ireland. They knew what they were doing. They knew how to set a building on fire, people who knew how to riot. They knew how to make petrol bombs, all those things, you know, that the local population wouldn't have had the tactical expertise or experience in doing ... There were black activists as well, who were dressed like Black Panthers in black combat gear and balaclavas ... You got to remember the Communist Party was still big then, anarchism was still big, the IRA was strong, so there were still a lot of radical elements in Britain at this time.[86]

Whether outside radical political groups played any role in the orchestration of the unrest in Toxteth is uncertain, but no evidence supporting such suspicions was submitted to later inquiries into the Liverpool 8 disturbances.

The final possible explanation for the high level of urban unrest that summer revolves around the role of youth unemployment and economic deprivation. It must be understood that those born into the final years of the baby-boom generation lived a completely different experience than their elder siblings who came of age in the era of full employment. Unlike those born in the immediate post-war years, people born in the early and middle 1960s had known nothing but economic stagnancy and dwindling prospects. As one Toxteth resident born in 1964 recalls:

> There was always that bit of a generational divide ... For us, we had friends who were older than us. And they enjoyed a period of time when

> work was available. I remember hearing all the stories of how people could walk out of one job and walk straight into another job. So the impression I had – I left school in 1980, a year after Thatcher came into power – meant we had more struggles with being unemployed and problems we were going to later have with the police.[87]

An older Toxteth neighbour of the above informant confirmed this notion, but added a further dimension to the argument:

> As Jimi said, up to about 1973, it was that kind of a thing. You could go into a job, the place would close down or whatever, and you could walk into another. But in those days there was no such thing as redundancy (pay) to speak of because most places didn't keep you long enough (to collect redundancy pay). But us coming from Liverpool we were used to that sort of thing (casual labour) ... It goes back to the days of going down to the docks, standing in queues, hoping to get picked for a day's work ... So my generation, while we had work, we were always brought up knowing that there was no such thing as security in employment.[88]

This generational divide undoubtedly played a key role in fanning the flames of alienation and angst amongst Liverpool's youth in 1981, particularly with those who were most disenfranchised.

The rate of unemployment and poverty in Toxteth was generally greater than other Liverpool neighbourhoods. The 1971 census reported that 19 per cent of the economically active adult males in the Granby Ward were seeking work. The other two wards making up Liverpool 8, Abercromby and Princes Park, had similar figures of 20 per cent, while the city as a whole averaged 9.1 per cent.[89] By 1981, these numbers doubled: Granby then displayed a figure of 39.6 per cent for adult males and 34.6 for all economically active people seeking work.[90] The rate of unemployment for all adult males for Toxteth that year was 31 per cent, compared with 18 per cent for Merseyside.[91] Moreover, between 1971 and 1981 the Abercromby Ward lost 28.6 per cent of its population, while Granby's population dropped by 37.8 per cent – a far steeper fall compared to 16.4 per cent for Liverpool as a whole. Both wards had become needier, as those residents who could afford to relocate left the area, leaving behind a more impoverished neighbourhood dependent on welfare relief.[92]

In September 1981, Liverpool City Council conducted a survey of residents within the Liverpool 8 area, distributing 3,750 questionnaires. *The Toxteth Survey Technical Report*, published in February 1982, was based on a 50 per cent response rate.[93] It found that in an area roughly coterminous with the boundaries of Granby Ward, 46 per cent of all those between the ages of sixteen and nineteen were unemployed; 89.7 per cent of the respondents felt unemployment was the principal problem in the community.[94] Surprisingly, only 3.4 per cent of the unemployed who responded felt racial discrimination was restricting opportunity, whereas 54.8 per cent felt the lack of jobs was the major issue.[95]

The survey also discovered that the predominantly white area of the Dingle reflected a lower level of joblessness compared to the largely black areas of Granby Street and Lodge Lane. This differential in youth unemployment rates was as high as 20 per cent in some areas. 'Attitudes of the police' were not universally regarded as positive. Approximately 17 per cent of the respondents from the predominantly black areas felt poor police attitudes were the greatest problem confronting the area, while the largely white sections hovered near the total average of 11 per cent.[96] The former figure is far lower number than the 54.8 per cent of jobless blacks who said they were mainly troubled by unemployment beyond any other concerns.

The Department of Education (DOE) also conducted a study of the Liverpool 8 neighbourhood. Published in March 1982, its conclusions echoed many of the findings in the City Council's survey. The number of Toxteth children in local authority care was six times higher than the city average. The rate for 'illegitimacy' was four times greater, while other standard measurements ranking deprivation, such as parental job instability, unemployment, infant mortality, delinquency, infestation and rates for various parasitic diseases were twice the city average.[97]

The few jobs being generated at this time were located in outlying areas, relatively inaccessible by public transport. The 1981 census showed that 83.2 per cent of the households in the Granby and Abercromby wards did not have access to a car, compared with 61.8 per cent for the city as a whole.[98] Education, the traditional route out of poverty, was increasingly seen as irrelevant. The DOE report concluded: 'There is not a large number of vacancies waiting to be filled even if the poorly qualified young people in this group (about 90 per cent of that total) were to improve their qualifications.'[99]

The presence of de-industrialisation was evident, as this trend meant that a lack of opportunity and widespread joblessness was becoming a permanent aspect of working-class existence. A foreign correspondent for the *New York Times* commented on the shortcomings of the Thatcherite economic agenda:

> The riots in Liverpool this week, stemming partly from the worst unemployment Britain has experienced since the Depression of the 1930's,

> are grim evidence of the failure of what was once regarded as a brilliant innovation in economic policy.[100]

Labour's Shadow Home Secretary Roy Hattersley offered his party's perspective on the reasons underlying the Toxteth riots:

> I do not believe that the principal cause of last week's riots was the conduct of the police. It was the conditions of deprivation and despair in the decaying areas of our old cities ... unemployment in the inner cities is monstrously high, even by the standards of July 1981 – perhaps 40 per cent or more of the whole working population – and with youth unemployment, of which I believe the riots are a direct product, particularly breeding despair. The Secretary of State for Employment said in Cheshire last Friday: 'Undoubtedly the present high level of unemployment is a fruitful breeding ground for the sort of thing we are seeing. We must recognise that to have such numbers out of work leads to a disaffected people'.[101]

The possible causes for the breakdown in civil order in the summer of 1981 have been examined in detail. As noted above, we should not seek mono-causal explanations. More probably, mass unemployment, aggressive policing and selective law enforcement, brewing racial hostilities, criminal opportunism and political neglect all intersected. However, an overarching factor ultimately appears to have been the very high levels of unemployment in Toxteth. This can be borne out by analysing the rioters' backgrounds, as certain patterns of consistency emerge.

Who were the rioters?

Data on those arrested during the disturbances provide a glimpse into the make-up of the rioters. However, as noted above, during the height of the violence few arrests could be effected.[102] Therefore, we must bear in mind that these statistics have evident limitations and do not necessarily reflect a representative sample of the rioters. Nevertheless, the relatively high numbers do permit informed conclusions to be drawn.

During the period 3 July to 15 August 1981, Merseyside police arrested a total of 530 people for a variety of offences connected with civil disturbances. Nearly half of the arrests, 244, were made in Toxteth. The remainder, 286, occurred in various other parts of the force's jurisdiction. Most of the Toxteth arrests, 157, took place between 3 and 7 July 1981, whereas in the rest of Merseyside only twelve such arrests took place during this period. Most arrests elsewhere in the city, 271, occurred in the week following the major outbreak of violence in Toxteth, between 8 and 17 July 1981.[103]

Table 5.1 Arrests on Merseyside for civil disorder, July–August 1981

	Toxteth		Elsewhere	
Type of offence	%	N	%	N
Violence against the person	15.5	38	9.4	27
Theft act offences	55.7	136	9.7	28
Criminal damage over £200	2.8	7	5.2	15
Riot	0	0	6.6	19
Public order act	23.7	58	48.9	140
Disorderly behaviour	0.4	1	7.3	21
Criminal damage less than £200	1.6	4	10	31
Other summary offences	0	0	1.7	5
Total	100	244	100	286

Source: Merseyside Police Special Return, November 1982 in Paul Cooper, 'Competing Explanations of the Merseyside Riots of 1981', *British Journal of Criminology*, vol. 25, no. 1 (January 1985), p. 67.

Not all of these defendants were necessarily engaged in riotous behaviour during the street disturbances in Toxteth and elsewhere, but it can be assumed that a high percentage was involved. Table 5.1 illustrates the difference in scale between the events as they unfolded in Toxteth, as opposed to elsewhere in Merseyside. There were fewer arrests for violent acts than for property offences. This evidence and the oral testimony of several officers suggests that once the police were no longer involved in quelling street violence directed against them and other emergency service personnel, they concentrated on arresting offenders engaged in looting. There were fewer crimes against the person in other areas of Merseyside.[104]

The role attributed to race in some explanations of these disturbances requires analysis of the ethnic origins of those arrested. Table 5.2 provides data for those detained for serious public disorder in Merseyside between 3 July and 15 August 1981. Table 5.2 clearly demonstrates that the vast majority of those arrested in Toxteth and elsewhere in Merseyside were white. These findings corroborate much of the oral testimony collected from eyewitnesses. One retired police constable recalled: 'Most of my time detailed there I spent in front of the burning Rialto. I was probably never more than 5 to 10 yards from the front line ... but during my entire time there I never saw one black face. Everyone I saw during the riot was white.'[105]

The area of primary residence of those arrested during this period is described in Table 5.3. This shows that 83.1 per cent of those arrested in

Table 5.2 Ethnic origins of those arrested for public disorder on Merseyside, July–August 1981

	Toxteth		Elsewhere	
Ethnic origin	%	N	%	N
White	69.6	170	96.8	277
West Indian/ African	7.3	18	0.3	1
Mixed	13.5	33	1.0	3
Not Known	8.1	20	1.7	5
Other	1.2	3	0	0
Total	100	244	100	286

Source: Merseyside Police Special Return, November 1982 in Paul Cooper, 'Competing Explanations of the Merseyside Riots of 1981', *British Journal of Criminology*, vol. 25, no. 1 (January 1985), p. 66.

Table 5.3 Residential patterns of those arrested for public disorder, Merseyside, July–August 1981

	Toxteth		Elsewhere	
Address of defendant	%	N	%	N
Residing in area of incident	60.6	148	45.4	130
Adjacent area	22.5	55	46.5	133
Elsewhere in Liverpool	14.7	36	4.5	13
Elsewhere	0	0	2.7	8
Not in Merseyside	0.008	2	0	0
Not known	1.2	3	0.6	2
Total	100	244	100	286

Source: Merseyside Police Special Return, November 1982 in Paul Cooper, 'Competing Explanations of the Merseyside Riots of 1981', *British Journal of Criminology*, vol. 25, no. 1 (January 1985), p. 65.

Toxteth and nearly 92 per cent of those detained throughout the remainder of Merseyside were arrested within walking distance of their homes, indicating the riots were very much a home-grown affair and refuting assertions regarding 'outside agitators'.

Age is another characteristic that helps illuminate motivation. Table 5.4 shows that a clear majority of those arrested for serious public order offences in Toxteth and elsewhere in Merseyside between 3 July and 15 August 1981 were under the age of twenty-one. Press

Table 5.4 Age distribution of those arrested for public disorder on Merseyside, July–August 1981

	Toxteth		Elsewhere	
Age group	%	N	%	N
Over 21 years	44.2	108	27.2	78
Between 17 and 21 years	32.7	80	51.4	46
Under 17 years	22.5	56	22.7	62
Total		244		286

Source: Merseyside Police Special Return, November 1982 in Paul Cooper, 'Competing Explanations of the Merseyside Riots of 1981', *British Journal of Criminology*, vol. 25, no. 1 (January 1985), p. 64.

accounts from the time consistently report that most rioters were in their late teens, while others describe children as young as '12 or 13 throwing bottles and stones'. An eyewitness claimed that 'the bulk of the rioting youths were aged from about 16 to early twenties'.[106] A list of names, addresses and ages of defendants brought before magistrates on one random day indicates that the vast majority were young males ranging in age from recent school leavers aged sixteen, to those in their late twenties.[107]

The ages of the defendants listed parallels the normal range for males involved in criminal activity. However, when prior criminal records are examined, it is striking that 41.4 per cent of the 244 defendants arrested in Toxteth had no previous convictions, and 24.5 per cent of the 286 arrested elsewhere in Merseyside similarly had no known previous criminal involvement. This demonstrates that a large percentage of those arrested were not habitual criminals. The data support the view that the Toxteth riots were fuelled by powerful forces of protest, so much so that even normally law-abiding citizens felt compelled to engage in outbursts of criminality.[108]

Of particular relevance to this study is the employment status of those who were arrested. Table 5.5 reveals that only 13.5 per cent of the 244 defendants in the Toxteth group were employed, and only 23 per cent of the 286 people arrested elsewhere on Merseyside had jobs. These figures are significant because they illustrate that the vast majority of those who were active participants in the civil unrest that summer on Merseyside were unemployed. In sum, these figures demonstrate that the majority of the rioters were unemployed, white males, between the ages of sixteen and twenty-one.

Table 5.5 Employment status of those arrested for public disorder on Merseyside, July–August 1981

	Toxteth		Elsewhere	
Employment status	%	N	%	N
Employed	13.5	33	23.0	69
Seeking work	51.6	126	47.2	135
Enrolled in education	16.3	38	5.8	17
Housewife	6.1	15	0	0
Not known	12.2	30	22.7	65
Total	100	244	100	286

Source: Merseyside Police Special Return, November 1982 in Paul Cooper, 'Competing Explanations of the Merseyside Riots of 1981', *British Journal of Criminology*, vol. 25, no. 1 (January 1985), p. 64.

Martin Luther King Jr. famously observed: 'Riots are the voice of the unheard.'[109] Historians George Rudé, Eric Hobsbawm and E. P. Thompson all argued that riots should not be condescended to as irrational outbursts by an unruly mob; nor should they be considered directionless, but instead, they signify purpose and reveal strategies that accurately identify the rioters' major grievances.[110] When a section of society comes to believe their community has been marginalised, as was arguably the case for the young, unemployed residents of Toxteth and the wider working-class community on Merseyside, their frustration will be directed at the perceived source of their anger. We should therefore note one more time that the landmarks and structures selected for destruction by the rioters in Toxteth were the exclusive Racquets Club, the Westminster Bank and the upmarket Rialto Ballroom, symbols of Liverpool establishment and a culture of consumption from which many of the rioters were excluded because of social class and the fact that most were unemployed.[111]

Conclusion

Undoubtedly, a variety of incendiary forces collided in Toxteth during the summer of 1981. Having reviewed the evidence, this study concludes that while racial tensions with police may have initiated this civil unrest, it was other more determining factors such as long-term unemployment and societal alienation amongst Liverpool's mainly jobless youth which fuelled the rampage and looting. Marginalisation and feelings of hopelessness can be the only explanations of why the violence and destruction reached such unprecedented levels in Toxteth.

If the motivation to riot was exclusively down to bad relations with the police, then such protest would have erupted in Toxteth before 1981. The oral sources disclose that a policy of aggressive policing was firmly in place long before this date. As Liverpool's economy plummeted in the late twentieth century, accusations of political neglect could prove persuasive, and it is also true that a large criminal cabal flourished on Merseyside. Nevertheless, these elements were unlikely to engender extreme and sustained disorder had there not been epidemic levels of long-term joblessness and an overwhelming perception by young, working-class males of a complete lack of opportunity and feelings of despair. What emerges from the evidence presented in this chapter is the immense frustration of a generational cohort forced to live most of their lives with structural unemployment.

The majority of these rioters were young, jobless males with limited levels of educational attainment and little chance of ever completing a university degree. Compound this fact with the idea that unemployed youths were not likely to be trade union members; thus, conventional working-class institutions for advocacy were not available to them. If we take this one step further we can surmise that many were not even old enough to vote, and so were also denied access to political expression. Therefore, it becomes apparent that the seemingly irrational act of rioting emerges as the only rational means of effective protest available to Toxteth's army of unemployed, angry and desperate youth. It is even more comprehensible when we see this response in the context of Liverpool, as it was in the summer of 1981.

And once again, we are reminded that the worst riot of the tumultuous summer of 1981 did not occur in London, Manchester, Birmingham, Sheffield or Leeds; it happened in Liverpool. This suggests that no other British city was feeling the effects of Thatcher's revolution more painfully than long-suffering Liverpool. One does not need to look further than the ferocity of this uprising to realise that a large percentage of the local population were despondent to the point of violence and anarchy.

Toxteth was the first spark of rebellion. As Thatcher's revolution was tearing down many of the pillars of the welfare state, large segments of Liverpool's working class no longer sought answers from Westminster. As we shall see in the following chapter, those disgruntled most by the rising tide of neoliberalism now felt the answers lay in wrestling control of local politics.

Notes

1 *Liverpool Echo*, 4/5 July – 31 July 1981. See also: Lord Gifford QC *et al.*, *Loosen the Shackles: First Report of the Liverpool 8 Inquiry into Race Relations in Liverpool* (London, 1989), p. 50.
2 Clive Unsworth, 'The Riots of 1981: Popular Violence and the Politics of Law and Order', *Journal of Law and Society*, vol. 9, no. 1 (Summer 1982), p. 65.
3 Rt. Hon. Lord Scarman, *The Brixton Disorders, 10–12 April 1981* (London, 1981).
4 Lord Scarman, *The Brixton Disorders*, p. 13.
5 Paul Cooper, 'Competing Explanations of the Merseyside Riots of 1981', *British Journal of Criminology*, vol. 25, no. 1 (January 1985), pp. 60–9.
6 Gifford *et al.*, *Loosen the Shackles.*
7 Interview with Michael Evans.
8 Interview with Michael Evans.
9 *Liverpool Echo*, 6 July 1981.
10 Interview with Robert Fisher.
11 *Guardian*, 7 July 1981. See also *Liverpool Echo*, 6 and 7 July 1981.
12 *The Times*, 7 July 1981.
13 Interview with David Potts.
14 *Liverpool Echo*, 6 and 7 July 1981.
15 Interview with Clive 'Dixie' Dean.
16 *Liverpool Echo*, 6 and 7 July 1981.
17 *Liverpool Echo*, 6, 7, 8 and 9 July 1981.
18 Letter from Detective Constable Brian Smith, Merseyside Police (Retired), written to his mother in the summer of 1981. The exact date of the letter is unknown.
19 *Guardian*, 6 July 1981.
20 *Liverpool Daily Post*, 9 July 2007.
21 *Liverpool Echo*, 9 July 1981; *Liverpool Weekend Echo*, 11/12 July 1981.
22 Hansard, House of Commons, 16 July 1981, vol. 8, c. 1397.
23 *Observer*, 2 August 1981; *Guardian*, 28 July 1981; *Liverpool Echo*, 27, 28 July 1981.
24 *Liverpool Echo*, 30, 31 July 1981.
25 *Irish Times*, 30 July 1981.
26 *Irish Times*, 30 July 1981.
27 *Irish Times*, 30 July 1981.
28 Liverpool and Merseyside Record Office (LMRO), 352 MIN, City of Liverpool, *Proceedings of the Council – 1981–1982*, vol. 2, July–November, p. 130.
29 *Liverpool Weekend Echo*, 11/12 July 1981.
30 *Liverpool Echo*, 13, 14 July 1981.

31 Margaret Thatcher, *The Downing Street Years* (London, 1993), p. 144.
32 Thatcher, *Downing Street Years*, p. 145.
33 John Benyon, 'The Riots, Lord Scarman and the Political Agenda', in John Beynon, ed., *Scarman and After: Essays Reflecting on Lord Scarman's Report, the Riots and Their Aftermath* (Oxford, 1984), p. 5.
34 Scarman, *The Brixton Disorders*, p. 13.
35 Gifford *et al.*, *Loosen the Shackles*, pp. 82–3.
36 Thatcher, *Downing Street Years*, p. 423.
37 Michael Heseltine, *Life in the Jungle: My Autobiography* (London, 2000), p. 209.
38 *Liverpool Weekend Echo*, 11/12 July. See also Heseltine, *Jungle*, pp. 219, 228–9.
39 Heseltine, *Jungle*, p. 224.
40 National Archives; Kew, London (NA), HO3106/48ptE, Personal letter from Michael Heseltine to the Prime Minister, 13 August 1981, 2 pages.
41 Gifford *et al.*, *Loosen the Shackles*, p. 50.
42 Thatcher, *Downing Street Years*, p. 424.
43 *Liverpool Echo*, 6 July 1981.
44 For a thorough historical analysis of race relations and the Afro-Caribbean experience on Merseyside see: John Belchem, *Before the Windrush: Race Relations in 20th-Century Liverpool* (Liverpool, 2014).
45 Mark Christian, 'An African-Centered Approach to the Black British Experience: With Special Reference to Liverpool', *Journal of Black Studies*, vol. 28, no. 3 (January 1998), pp. 293, 298. See also: Alfred B. Zack-Williams, 'African Diaspora Conditioning: The Case of Liverpool', *Journal of Black Studies*, vol. 27, no. 4 (March 1997), p. 530; Gifford *et al.*, *Loosen the Shackles*, p. 26; Cooper, 'Competing Explanations', p. 60.
46 Gifford *et al.*, *Loosen the Shackles*, pp. 28, 37. See also Zack-Williams, 'African Diaspora', p. 531.
47 Gifford *et al.*, *Loosen the Shackles*, p. 40.
48 Gifford *et al.*, *Loosen the Shackles*, p. 39.
49 Christian, 'African-Centered Approach', p. 294.
50 Christian, 'African-Centered Approach', p. 295.
51 Gifford *et al.*, *Loosen the Shackles*, p. 31.
52 Zack-Williams, 'African Diaspora', p. 533.
53 Interview with Joe Farrag.
54 Zack-Williams, 'African Diaspora', p. 535.
55 Interview with Mohamed Ali.
56 Zack-Williams, 'African Diaspora', p. 538.
57 Interview with Jimi Jagne.
58 Interview with Mohamed Ali.
59 Zack-Williams, 'African Diaspora', p. 541.
60 Heseltine, *Jungle*, p. 219.
61 Gifford *et al.*, *Loosen the Shackles*, pp. 82–3.
62 Benyon, 'Riots', p. 6.
63 Hansard, House of Commons, 6 July 1981, vol. 8, c. 24.

64 Hansard, House of Commons, 6 July 1981, vol. 8, no. 135, cc. 24, 30. See also Benyon, 'Riots', p. 6.
65 *Guardian*, 17 July 1981.
66 *Liverpool Echo*, 6 July 1981.
67 Interview with Clive 'Dixie' Dean.
68 Interview with James Rafferty.
69 Interview with Michael Evans.
70 Interview with Ian MacDonald.
71 Richard J. Terrill, 'Margaret Thatcher's Law and Order Agenda', *American Journal of Comparative Law*, vol. 37, no. 3 (Summer 1989), pp. 437–8. See also Unsworth, 'The Riots of 1981', p. 69.
72 Cooper, 'Competing Explanations', p. 61.
73 *Liverpool Echo*, 6 July 1981.
74 *Liverpool Echo*, 6 July 1981.
75 *Liverpool Echo*, 7 July 1981.
76 Unsworth, 'The Riots of 1981', pp. 78–9.
77 Thatcher, *Downing Street Years*, pp. 146–7.
78 Heseltine, *Jungle*, p. 220.
79 *Liverpool Echo*, 24 January 2002. See also *Liverpool Echo*, 26 July 2010.
80 *Guardian*, 19 September 1981.
81 Interview with David Potts.
82 Interview with Frank Trevor.
83 Richard Clutterbuck, 'Terrorism and Urban Violence', *Proceedings of the Academy of Political Science*, vol. 34, no. 4 (1982), p. 170.
84 Cooper, 'Competing Explanations', p. 61.
85 Interview with Robert Fisher.
86 Interview with Ian MacDonald.
87 Interview with Jimi Jagne.
88 Interview with Joe Farrag.
89 Gifford *et al.*, *Loosen the Shackles*, p. 40.
90 Gifford *et al.*, *Loosen the Shackles*, pp. 40–1.
91 Cooper, 'Competing Explanations', p. 60.
92 HM Inspectors, Department of Education and Science, *Educational Provision by Liverpool Educational Authority in the Toxteth Area*, March 1982, p. 1.
93 Liverpool City Council, *The Toxteth Survey*, Preface and section 2.1. See also Gifford *et al.*, *Loosen the Shackles*, pp. 40–1.
94 Gifford *et al.*, *Loosen the Shackles*, pp. 40–1.
95 Liverpool City Council, *Toxteth Survey*, section 3.21.
96 Liverpool City Council, *Toxteth Survey*, section 4.33.
97 HM Inspectors, *Educational Provision*, p. 1.
98 Gifford *et al.*, *Loosen the Shackles*, p. 70. See also HM Inspectors, *Educational Provision*, p. 1.
99 HM Inspectors, *Educational Provision*, p. 1.
100 *New York Times*, 8 July 1981.

101 Hansard, House of Commons, 16 July 1981, vol. 8, cc. 1408–9.
102 Cooper, 'Competing Explanations', p. 63.
103 Cooper, 'Competing Explanations', pp. 63–4.
104 Cooper, 'Competing Explanations', p. 66.
105 Interview with David Potts.
106 *Liverpool Echo*, 6 July 1981.
107 *Liverpool Echo*, 30 July 1981.
108 Cooper, 'Competing Explanations', pp. 64–5.
109 Cooper, 'Competing Explanations', pp. 62, 67–8.
110 Stan Taylor, 'The Scarman Report and Explanations of Riots', in Beynon, *Scarman and After*, p. 21. See also David Smith, 'Tonypandy, 1910: Definitions of Community', *Past and Present*, vol. 87 (May 1980), pp. 158–84.
111 Benyon, 'Riots', pp. 67–8. See also Zack-Williams, 'African Diaspora', p. 539; Cooper, 'Competing Explanations', p. 62.

6

The Militant Tendency and Liverpool City Council's fight to save 'jobs and services', 1983–86

At a time when public discontent was rife on the streets of Liverpool and rebellion was in the air, it is not surprising that local politics was also revolving. Suffering the effects of severe long-term unemployment and widespread poverty, Liverpool's local political establishment seemed inept in finding solutions to these problems. A void in local leadership had been created by this fracture, but this gap was soon filled by a new order.

In this chapter an analysis is made of the political landscape of Liverpool in the 1980s. It explores how a Trotskyist, 'entryist' organisation – the Militant Tendency – could commandeer the local Liverpool District Labour Party (DLP) and realign its agenda to meet what the Militant Tendency perceived to be the needs of an increasingly disadvantaged working class. Militant's leaders progressively found themselves in conflict with both the Tory government in Westminster and the national Labour Party based in London. Labour's national leadership, under Neil Kinnock, was committed to steering the party towards the political centre, and therefore opposed the radicalism and revolutionary zeal emerging on Merseyside.

Along with the Miners' Strike of 1984–85, the actions taken by Liverpool City Council (LCC) can be counted as one of the most significant challenges Thatcher faced in fulfilling her economic agenda. Yet despite the Militant-led LCC's ability to attract considerable negative press, there is evidence that the strategies it employed proved effective in fighting job loss – at least initially – in a city heavily dependent on public sector employment.

The economic context

It has been previously emphasised that Liverpool lacked the manufacturing tradition of many other northern cities. During the post-war period private sector employment in Liverpool played a diminishing role in the local economy. The public sector soon emerged to be the largest employer on Merseyside. However, by the 1970s, local councils were pressured by both Labour and Conservative central governments to rationalise jobs and services in order to reduce rates. Therefore, it should be noted that this decline in public sector employment was not restricted to the age of Thatcher, as government jobs in Liverpool fell by 7 per cent between 1976 and 1979 during Callaghan's Labour government.[1]

By the late 1970s, over 70 per cent of all jobs in Liverpool were service sector occupations, with nearly half of those in a public entity. LCC alone accounted for nearly one-third of all public sector jobs. By 1985, after cuts in other government spheres, LCC was responsible for over 40 per cent of all public jobs in the region. Because of the unique character of the local economy, Liverpool was more dependent on public sector employment than most British cities, and therefore more sensitive to shifts in Westminster's policies towards local government.[2] Prior to 1979, central government had maintained high levels of expenditure through grants and subsidies.[3] From 1974 to 1979, the total income paid to LCC that was raised locally fell by 18 per cent. Income from rates dropped by 25 per cent in that period, demonstrating the Council's increasing financial dependence on Westminster.[4]

Fiscal policies from central government after 1979 sought to lessen this dependence. In 1979, Westminster's contribution to LCC amounted to 62 per cent of its total revenue, with the Council's local income – generated almost exclusively from local rates – amounting to 37 per cent. By 1983, the central government in London contributed 44 per cent of the total, while LCC raised 55 per cent.[5] When private industry abandoned much of northern England, the government role as chief employer remained, or as one academic commentator stated: 'The Conservative Government's view was that public employment increased taxes, which drove out the private sector. The Labour Party argued that the private sector had abandoned the city anyway, and that public employment was not part of the problem, but part of the solution to it.'[6]

To offset this decline in income from central government, local authorities had a limited number of options: raise rates, cut public sector jobs or reduce municipal services. Doing nothing would lead to fiscal bankruptcy, but by the mid-1980s, this had become the favoured alternative of the newly elected, Labour-controlled LCC. Many Labour councillors viewed this course as the only available means to challenge the Conservatives' economic policies. The battle lines were drawn in Liverpool between the principles of neoliberalism, espoused by Thatcher, and the role municipal socialism had previously played in Britain's larger cities. Elsewhere, in local authorities such as Manchester, Sheffield, the

Greater London Council and Lambeth, the movements opposed to Thatcher's policies were often associated with democratising tendencies and commitment to identity politics, inclusive of groups such as women and ethnic minorities, rather than purely class-based approaches. Once again, Liverpool was distinctive in the respect that its political left was not entirely reflective of the 'new left' movement emerging elsewhere. The new identity politics saw gender, race and ethnicity as equally reflective of barriers to power within the economic order than the old left's exclusive concern with class struggle. Bucking political trends to some degree, the Liverpool DLP was increasingly influenced and penetrated by a radical-left, Trotskyist-inspired group known as the Militant Tendency. As radical as Liverpool's Militant Tendency was, it was still overwhelmingly representative of the 'old left', and not the 'new left' as it was emerging politically elsewhere at this time.[7]

The political establishment of the local Labour Party faced challenges to its leadership in the mid-1980s. There are two explanations for this shift in power. The Toxteth riots were still fresh in the minds of most Liverpudlians. By 1985, there was seemingly little progress made in rectifying the problems of unemployment and housing, which many felt had sparked the unrest in the first place. This sense of ineffectiveness, of course, further alienated sections of the local working class.[8] This lack of faith in Liverpool's political leadership was also felt by the Conservative government in Westminster. As one former Liverpool politico wrote of the Thatcher government:

> It regarded the city as expensive, inefficient and badly run – incapable of responding adequately, politically or administratively, to the scale of the problem it faced. Even though it can be argued that central government was equally responsible for recent failures of urban policy, the Government thought Liverpool missed the opportunity it was given to help itself, classically blaming the victims for their misfortunes. But most crucially, by the mid-1980s the Conservatives saw Liverpool as the power base of the Militant Tendency. And they wanted to defeat it. The scene was set for a political confrontation.[9]

This leads to the second important factor: the rise of the Militant Tendency. In order to explain this phenomenon, we must first briefly examine Liverpool's political traditions.

Liverpool's political traditions

Liverpool politics cannot be understood without considering the enormous impact of post-famine Irish immigration. The immense influx of destitute Irish Catholics created a strong tradition of sectarianism within the local working class. This sectarianism played a significant role in slowing the evolution of a local Labour Party on Merseyside. Until the 1920s, the leading opposition to Conservatives and Liberals on Merseyside was not the Labour Party, but the Irish Nationalist Party. Indeed, it was Liverpool's Scotland Road constituency which elected the sole Irish Nationalist MP in mainland Britain, T. P. O'Connor, who served from 1885 until 1929. It was not until after Irish independence and partition that Liverpool's many Catholics slowly drifted into the local Labour Party. This transfer was not occasioned by new-found commitment to socialism; rather, the Labour Party was viewed as the only available political expression for the poor and working class.[10]

The vast number of Catholics within Liverpool's working class meant that once the issues surrounding Irish independence were partially resolved, this group would come to dominate the local Labour Party. They would never control it exclusively, as smaller factions consisting of the skilled Protestant working class and left-wing socialists maintained some semblance of visibility. Nevertheless, the left was never able to counter the growing conservative Catholic influence on local Labour Party politics prior to the Second World War.[11] This engendered a personality driven politics and a system of bossism ruled by patronage and corruption, much of which was still in evidence as late as the 1980s.[12]

The most famous of the city's Labour bosses in the post-war years were the husband-and-wife team, Jack and Bessie Braddock. Restricted recruitment into the local party machine excluded anyone perceived as an outsider or troublemaker. One authority cites a contemporary account of the Liverpool machine during that period as one of the few illustrations in Britain of American-style Tammany Hall politics, comparing Liverpool to Mayor Daley's Chicago by calling it 'Cook County, UK'.[13]

While sectarianism largely vanished from Liverpool's political culture with residential desegregation, following the post-war extension of social housing, the remnants of its influence were evident within the work culture of LCC as late as the 1970s and 1980s. One former Council worker recalled:

> If you go through Liverpool's history, the sectarianism was obvious – I mean it's disappeared now – but it was bad. Certain departments of the Council were either all Catholics or all Protestants. And, where you were hired depended on whether you were an Orange Lodge member (Protestant) or a member of the Knights of St. Columba (Roman Catholic).[14]

Catholic dominance of the local Labour Party meant some of the Protestant working class continued to vote Conservative into the 1960s.[15]

Nevertheless, sectarianism became less of an influence on the local political culture of Liverpool, as the issue of housing became a central concern of the city's working class. The availability of reasonably priced, adequately maintained public housing carried far more weight amongst working-class voters than more abstract issues. One study found that in the LCC's debates, housing was the matter most often raised by councillors representing working-class wards. Councillors from predominantly working-class wards raised the issue on 50 per cent of council agendas, while councillors from middle-class wards introduced the matter of housing on only 5 per cent of the occasions.[16]

It was on the housing front that the class war incurred its fiercest battles. Inner-city wards were usually the centres of Labour Party support, while inner-ring and outlying suburbs often voted any party other than Labour in local elections.[17] Until the late 1960s large-scale urban renewal programmes and new housing schemes were a local priority. Central government, in partnership with a Labour-controlled LCC from 1955, were instrumental in transforming entire inner-city areas, often re-housing residents in what were typically large tower blocks in new towns on the periphery of Merseyside. Shifting entire communities of inner-city dwellers to distant and isolated localities became increasingly unpopular, and it created mistrust of the local Labour Party by sections of Liverpool's working class. As the early 1970s dawned, this problem was exacerbated by the city's underfunding. This denied the Council the means to adequately maintain these new housing developments.[18]

By the 1960s, the Liberal Party had a revival on Merseyside, largely because of its policies on housing. Expanding from beyond their middle-class base, the Liberals aspired to become not only the party of choice amongst white-collar, middle-class homeowners, but also a political voice for the upwardly mobile, skilled, working class. Like their middle-class counterparts, they too were increasingly becoming mortgage holders in suburban terraced neighbourhoods, such as Allerton, Wavertree and Aigburth. In the 1970s, the working-class vote was so divided that the LCC did not enjoy majority control by any party for almost ten years. Between 1974 and 1983, there was a series of Liberal–Conservative coalitions, often with the Liberals as senior partner. Their delicate balance bred instability and uncertainty, rendering long-term planning practically impossible, thus stunting construction and commercial development. The main concern of the Liberals was to keep rates as low as possible for homeowners and small businesses – the bedrock of their electoral base. To do so, expenditure on public services was kept to a minimum, to the detriment of the provision and maintenance of public housing. One observer perceptively judged: 'Local ideological conflict over housing and spending in the 1970s sowed the seeds of a national confrontation in the 1980s.'[19]

While the Liberals' frugality kept rates low for property owners, the corresponding cuts in jobs and services had a negative effect on already deteriorating public housing stock. A former Liverpool city councillor recalled the city's finances under the Liberal regime during the 1970s and early 1980s:

> In one year I think they cut the rates by only one penny, but still not a single house was built. Rents [of council housing] were going through the roof. Rates were forever being cut. Because, the more you cut in local authority finance, the more the government cut ... they [the Liberals] tried to appeal to their middle-class base. Inevitably, when you play it this way services will suffer and the fabric of society will suffer. If you pander to people's prejudices and the backwardness – I mean nobody wants to pay rates, nobody wants to pay tax, but who's going to maintain the infrastructure?[20]

While the Liberal–Conservative coalitions were leading the council, the local Labour Party was beginning to transform itself from a largely reactionary bastion of blue-collar, Irish-Catholicism to a party led by younger, better educated activists with a more left-wing outlook. The new generation of local Labour leaders sought to broaden the party's base beyond trade unionists and advocated a far more radical agenda in order to combat the lingering spectre of structural unemployment and sweeping de-industrialisation.[21]

The emergence of the radical left on Merseyside

A small Trotskyist sect, the Revolutionary Socialist League (RSL), created the Militant Tendency out of supporters of its publication, *Militant*. The RSL's central philosophy was revolutionary Marxism, and its principal strategy was a commitment to move the Labour Party further left through 'entryism', infiltrating the Labour Party by recruiting 'supporters'. A cadre of RSL members and their supporters could then dominate the organisation and steer its agenda in their favour.[22] Militant's origins date to 1964 when Ted Grant (born Isaac Blank, 1913–2006), a South African, helped establish the *Militant* newspaper in London.

Militant made noticeable inroads in the Labour Party youth movement and gained increasing support in certain Constituency Labour Parties – Liverpool Walton being the most notable.[23] Its policies included nationalisation of major industries – particularly those threatening redundancies – as well as Britain's private financial institutions, the electronic media and the press. It also advocated a thirty-five-hour work-week with no loss in pay; a guaranteed job for youths after education and training; an increase in the construction of affordable housing and public works projects; and guarantee of absolute equality for all no matter what their race, ethnic group, religion, gender or sexual orientation.[24] These policies, together with such revolutionary proposals as the elimination of the monarchy, an established Church and the House of Lords, incurred extreme hostility from many in the Labour Party leadership.[25]

There were other reasons for this antagonism between Labour's National Executive Committee (NEC) and Militant, notably the clandestine nature of the Militant Tendency. Militant never claimed to be an established organisation, for if it had, it would have breached Labour's constitution. Its supporters maintained they were merely like-minded individuals who subscribed to *Militant* because it reflected their left-wing politics. One former Labour Party councillor for Granby Ward described Militant differently: 'I think the problem with Militant was they were actually a party within a party, and that's not allowed in any political party ... They tried to keep their existence clandestine, but there were too many people involved, and as they were getting more publicity they were becoming more and more scrutinised.'[26]

Militant's members portrayed themselves as a broad-left coalition, whose only aim was to keep the Labour Party true to its socialist roots. Labour's leadership, on the other hand, suspected Militant was, instead, an underground revolutionary movement with a radical agenda and possible connections to subversive Communist groups.[27] Indeed, amongst senior officials in Labour Party headquarters there was widespread belief that Militant was a front for covert revolutionary agitation inside the party.[28] However, two prominent Militant supporters described such allegations as completely false, representing 'media hysteria':

> The charge of 'entryism' against *Militant* supporters, who had been members of the Labour Party for decades, was repeated *ad nauseam* by the press. It is only the press and their right-wing shadows within the Labour Party who can entertain the idea that the ordinary workers who make up the Labour Party membership are like putty to be manipulated by small, secretive, conspiratorial groups of Marxists.[29]

Table 6.1 indicates that Militant displayed some growth by the late 1970s. Nevertheless, these figures are only estimates due to Militant's secretive practices. The Labour Party commenced expelling leading

Table 6.1 Estimated membership of Militant by year

Year	Number
1965	100
1971	217
1972	354
1973	464
1974	517
1975	775
1976	1,030
1977	1,193
1978	1,433
1979	1,620
1980	1,850
1981	2,545
1982	3,438
1983	4,313
1984	c.6,000
1985	c.7000
1986	8,100+

Source: Michael Crick, *The March of Militant* (London, 1986), p. 315.

Militant activists after 1983, so any membership statistics listed after that date may be less accurate. One author suggests that by 1986, Militant was effectively Britain's fifth largest political party, even larger than the British Communist Party.[30]

Militant's strongest support came from within local constituency party organisations. By the late 1970s, the Liverpool DLP was especially ripe for the Militant message. Trotskyist propaganda on Merseyside can be traced back to the 1940s. Its main proponent at that time was a trade unionist and shipyard electrician from Birkenhead, Jimmy Deane. With assistance from Grant in London, Deane, along with others on Merseyside such as *Militant* editor Peter Taaffe and rising young trade unionists, Tony Mulhearn and Terry Harrison, slowly carved out a base for Militant on Merseyside. By the early 1970s, their message was influencing young, working-class, left-wingers, frustrated with the parochialism and right-wing nature of Liverpool's Labour politics, as well as young trade unionists also disillusioned with the bureaucracy and inertia within their own movement.

A dramatic shift emerges in the Liverpool DLP from the Conservative election victory in 1979 onwards. The Braddocks and their generation had passed, and in the absence of a coherent right-wing there emerged a left front, comprising the Militant Tendency and grassroots socialists frustrated after years of neglect. An additional element was the growing influence of the public employee unions.

Militant's Tony Mulhearn assumed leadership of the DLP in 1979, after serving as vice-president for the previous eight years. He was subsequently elected to LCC in 1984. At the same time, an intelligent former seminarian from South Liverpool, Tony Byrne, became active in the broad-left movement sweeping Liverpool Labour. Elected to the Council in 1980, he quickly rose to a position of dominance within the Labour group. While never a member of Militant, Byrne was a committed socialist and a strong advocate for the mass expansion of public housing on Merseyside. Along with Mulhearn, he became a leading voice in the LCC of the 1980s.

Probably the most recognisable personality to emerge was a former city fireman and youth worker turned politician, Derek Hatton. Hatton's verbal flamboyance and ready wit guaranteed media exposure. He became synonymous with Militant and LCC, of which he eventually was elected deputy leader and its most powerful force. It has been suggested that Hatton was never especially committed to Militant, nor were Militant's leaders terribly impressed with Hatton's grasp of political philosophy. Nevertheless, there was a marriage of convenience formed, as Hatton needed a political base, and Militant found him useful in popularising their message.[31]

As alluded to previously, it should be emphasised that the Militant Tendency on Merseyside had a distinctive character, not entirely comparable to the radical new left movements developing in London or in the provincial centres. These differences were most evident in matters not specific to class, such as gender and race. In many ways the Liverpool version retained the orthodox view prevalent in trade unions and Labour clubs, which was in assuming that by taking control of the local Labour Party, they automatically articulated the interests of the working class. Elsewhere in Britain, the left had learned the importance of alliances with the feminist movement and black community organisations. Consequently, because of their philosophical leanings, it can be surmised that the majority of Liverpool's faction of the Militant Tendency were white, male and working class.

Opposing this assumption, Mulhearn insists the Liverpool Militant Tendency was much more broadly based: 'In the early years, I mean to get 100,000 votes for Labour wasn't just working-class votes. We won in the middle-class areas of the city too.'[32] Nonetheless, even if Liverpool's Militant Tendency never extended its base beyond the white working class, it may very well be that this homogeneity actually gave the movement a degree of legitimacy within Liverpool's working-class community. This, in itself, is not necessarily detrimental to the cause of fighting unemployment and economic deprivation.

The racial discord which exploded on the streets of Toxteth in 1981 proved that some segments of Liverpool's working class felt alienated from the larger society as a whole. Militant's 'colour blind' Marxist orthodoxy discounted such sensitivities and prevented a significant section of the city's working class from supporting its political message. This alienation felt by people of colour and some women towards the Militant Tendency in Liverpool was in so many ways contrary to the ethos of the new municipal left-wing who were assuming control of councils in other major cities.

The incident that best illustrated this dissonance between Militant in Liverpool and left-wing elements elsewhere occurred once the Militant-influenced Labour group assumed power in 1983. The 'Sam Bond affair' involved the appointment of a twenty-six-year-old Londoner and Militant supporter to lead LCC's Race Equality Unit. The selection of Bond to lead this sensitive committee infuriated Liverpool's black community for a number of reasons, including his lack of experience in campaigning for racial equality, as well as his non-involvement in any of the mainstream black organisations in either Liverpool or his native London.[33] His appointment reeked of the old-fashioned political cronyism of Liverpool Labour's old right-wing. The fact that an inexperienced young man, whose primary credential only appeared to be his active support for the Militant Tendency, was to oversee race relations in a city that recently experienced the worst riot in memory – a riot that involved many members of Liverpool's black community, seemed unthinkable to Liverpool's Black Caucus. This decision also did not go down well with many local trade union and Labour activists.[34]

Nevertheless, with regard to Liverpool Militant's white working-class majority, it is not difficult to comprehend how Militant's clear message of hard-line socialism exerted a simple appeal. Poverty was not unique to Liverpool, and the economic deprivation of the area was not the only reason that so many of its working-class inhabitants were drawn to vote for Militant. Liverpool's history of trade union radicalism also played a major role in broadening Militant's support.[35]

Local authority trade unionism

By the 1970s and 1980s, in the context of a declining manufacturing sector, trade unions representing public sector employees became more prominent within the labour movement. In 1950 public sector employees represented nearly a quarter of the total British workforce, but this figure rose to over one-third by the mid-1970s. The public sector employees coming under the umbrella of trade union membership were not only blue-collar workers but also those in white-collar occupations.[36]

Because their membership lists were often highly diverse in terms of both occupation and class, some observers felt this, and their lack of experience within trade union networks, meant the public sector unions were slow in advancing their collective power, particularly with regards to the role of shop stewards. They had a reputation for passivity, undoubtedly much of this was due to the fact that their collective bargaining was often done on a nationwide basis rather than at local levels. In addition, shop stewards were not officially recognised in public sector industrial relations until 1969.[37]

Due to government wage controls and price inflation, the mid-1970s witnessed public sector unions emerging as a leading voice in the labour movement. Indeed, it was the escalating militancy in public sector unions that brought forth the 'Winter of Discontent' of 1978–79. However, due to their highly sectionalised and hierarchical structures, some labour leaders doubted such unions could maintain solidarity over an extended period of industrial action. Nevertheless, in the 1980s, LCC's unions would disprove this notion.

In an effort to cut costs, the Liberal-controlled council in the 1970s reduced personnel from 34,000 to 30,000. While these 4,000 jobs were eliminated through attrition and not compulsory redundancies, this loss in manpower put increased strain on the remaining workforce. It was precisely this increased tension in the workplace that spurred local authority employees to greater union and political activism. A more left-leaning Liverpool DLP was eager to attract their votes.[38]

In 1979, Liverpool's local authority workers formed a combine of the various trade unions representing city council employees. As a reaction to both the job cuts from the Liberal-controlled council and the threat of less government funding after the election of the Conservatives, the Liverpool City Council Shop Stewards' and Staff Representative Committee was established. This body realised from its inception that it must represent all unionised council employees, and that the combine should be active politically if it were to exert any influence. The committee made history as the first large joint shop stewards' combine to be formed outside private industry. Especially significant was its diverse membership, which included trade unions representing blue-collar workers, white-collar workers, professionals and even supervisors. The combine included eleven unions representing over

25,000 workers. Ian Lowes, a city forestry department tree feller and convenor for the General, Municipal, Boilermakers and Allied Trade Union (GMB), was chosen to lead the committee. It was founded as a means of politically advocacy; therefore, its main goal was to contest further redundancies and lobby against the expected reduction in grants and revenues from Westminster. Lowes recalled its inception:

> What prompted us to form it was that we had a Tory government nationally. We just went through the Winter of Discontent where we were taking it from a Labour government. And we realised ... that we had to get better organised. Different unions were doing different things, so we realised we needed to pull people together. And obviously when the Tory government was elected in '79, Thatcher's government and her programme of cuts, we needed to organise ... And we knew there were going to be attacks on us from the national government, and we knew we'd get attacked by the local Liberal/Tory council, so we formed the Joint Shop Stewards Committee. The history behind the formation of our Joint Shop Stewards Committee is quite amazing ... I mean these kind of things [joint shop stewards' committees] were traditional in private industry – particularly the car factories, where they have combine committees, but not in local authority employment ... What we were able to do, which was quite unique was that, traditionally, any organisation that was at shop stewards' level was either the manual unions – to themselves, or the manual and craft unions organising. It was quite unprecedented to actually have white-collar staff, and teachers, and professionals actually all lumped together in one joint stewards' committee.[39]

Bidding for their support was a local Labour Party already heavily influenced by the Militant Tendency. There were pledges of increased pay and a rise in budget allotments made by the DLP if a Labour-controlled council were elected. There were also guarantees of hiring more personnel and, in addition, unions were unprecedentedly promised a 50 per cent say in who would be hired. This would later lead to allegations of cronyism and 'jobs for the boys', but it was an enticing proposition in an era of mass unemployment, when scores of union activists had been made jobless and blacklisted from worksites.[40] Despite such criticism, Lowes defended the hiring policy that came into place after Labour's takeover of the Council:

> We [the Committee] were allowed to put forward names of candidates for employment with the Council. Now bear in mind, we had a lot of people who were made redundant from industry, who had been blacklisted. There were also people who never had a job, never been in a union – young

> people ... Providing you were willing to join the union if you got the job, we'd be more than happy to nominate them for a job ... Now this system took a lot of criticism – stories of 'jobs for the boys' and all that. But what they fail to understand is that before Labour took back the Council in 1983 it was always the other way, it was jobs for their boys ... If you listened to these critics you'd have thought everyone who got a job on the Council at this time was a raving Trotskyist. While it's true some activists found employment, the vast majority of the people who found employment with the Council were just ordinary men and women who had never been involved in anything [political], but were just desperate for employment.[41]

In return for saving and even adding jobs to the Council payroll, Labour asked that unions politicise their members and encourage them to vote Labour. In the years from 1980 to 1983 there was debate within the committee as to whether they should support Labour in such an active way. The trade union representing many of the white-collar workers and supervisors, the National and Local Government Officers' Association (NALGO) and the National Union of Teachers (NUT) were not affiliated with the Labour Party and were not in favour, while the manual unions, particularly those representing the building trades, were staunchly in Labour's camp. The former president of the Liverpool DLP recalled:

> The NUT rank-and-file were supportive of us, but their leadership adopted a more neutral position. They weren't as enthusiastic, shall we say. They [NUT] were under the leadership of the Communist Party. And again, while the national leaders of the Communist Party may have been hostile toward us, the rank-and-file were the salt of the earth. They supported us through thick and thin.[42]

A further complication was the fact that many of the teachers and other white-collar employees were homeowners, residing in the suburban wards, and therefore unenthusiastic about Militant's promise of expanding its public housing policy. Ultimately, the combine gave its support to Labour. Lowes recalled how the combine slowly became more politicised:

> If you look at the early '80s, those of us in the manual unions – the Labour Party affiliated unions – took a conscious decision to actually become active in the Labour Party, recognising you could have industrial disputes, but there's really only ever going to be a political solution to the problem. So we took a conscious decision to actually encourage people to join the Labour Party and send delegates, because the GMW [GMB] – as it was called then, and the council's T&G branch were, of course, affiliated with the Labour Party. But we [LCC union activists] never really played

> an active role within the Liverpool District Labour Party ... So after we became active we actually had a heavy influence in the Labour Party in Liverpool. We helped shape policies that [Labour] would fight the election on in 1983 ... In the end we felt it was better to support a Labour council on a radical programme that would defend council workers' interests, than to have to keep fighting a Liberal/Tory council. They [Militant and NALGO] became reluctant allies ... As long as the local Labour Party was acting in the interest of its workforce, we'd support them. But, we drew a line. If they ever did anything that was not in the interest of the workforce, we'd be in conflict with them. And I think we all agreed that we had to maintain some independence.[43]

A Labour-controlled city council

This partnership between the local authority trade unions and the Labour Party would be tested in time, but it was clear that the initial element uniting both groups was preservation of jobs. Their joint mission was encapsulated in the slogan of the day: 'No cuts in jobs and services, and no increases in rents or rates!' By 1979, Labour had emerged as the largest party on the council, but it still did not have an overall majority. Nevertheless, Labour's voice was growing stronger on the council, and after 1980 its message was increasingly directed by Militant. The first noticeable sign of this came in March 1981 when the council's Labour leader, John Hamilton, proposed a budget containing a 50 per cent rate rise. Hamilton and many of the older non-Militant Labour members of the council saw such a rate rise as a last resort, but they felt there was no other way around making up revenue lost after Thatcher's drastic cuts in aid to local authorities.

Opposition to Labour's proposal came not from the Tories or the Liberals, but from one of Hamilton's own backbenchers, the newly elected councillor Derek Hatton. Hatton insisted that due to the region's economic deprivation and dependence on public employment, 'the plight of the city lies squarely in the lap of the Government'. Consequently, in Hatton's opinion, the Labour Party ought to be proposing a budget with a rate rise limited only to the current level of inflation, which at that time was 13 per cent. He also demanded Labour councillors should insist on a policy of no redundancies or cuts, and that the council should unite with the trade union movement, 'to fight for the money needed from the Government'. Hatton's motion lost overwhelmingly that year, but in testimony to Militant's growing influence, in the following year, Hatton's proposal would become DLP official policy; and within a further year, Hatton would become deputy leader of the council.[44] Hatton's daring proposal in 1981 changed the face of Liverpool politics forever, leading to an inevitable collision with Thatcher.

In 1981 the government introduced a new baseline system of allocating grants to local authorities. Largely because the Liberal–Tory coalitions on LCC had kept rates low in previous years, Liverpool suffered a heavy loss in revenue from Westminster. The new system also did not take into consideration the long-standing economic decline and loss of population suffered by the city. Refusing to consider such factors, Westminster reconfigured Liverpool's allocation. The new policy was meant to curb what Conservatives considered overspending by Labour-controlled councils, but Liverpool did not fit this description in 1981, nor had the city resembled this picture in the preceding decade, due to the peculiarities of its political structures and demographic trends. Any loss of jobs at LCC – the region's largest employer – would be catastrophic. Indeed, it was Thatcher's neoliberal policies that helped mobilise Liverpool's working class, as Tony Mulhearn recalled:

> Between the mid-1970s and Labour taking control of the council, [May 1983] the Liverpool economy had collapsed – 65 per cent of the Liverpool economy had collapsed ... Thatcher actually cut something like £300 million – from when she got in [1979] to when we took over [1983] – from the Liverpool budget ... There's no question that her policies graphically aggravated the problems faced by working-class people. Now we articulated that concern. We said 'Vote for us, but we're not going to implement any of these cuts. That's not our job. If you want people who are going to implement her cuts then vote for the Liberals or vote for the Tories' ... And when we did take control we said, 'We are not prepared to carry through these Tory cuts, or increase rates and rents to compensate for these Tory cuts', and that was the basis of our programme. When we did take control there was something like 30,000 people on the council housing waiting list. The public corporation rents in Liverpool were the highest in the UK outside of London. The previous administration had not built a single unit of council accommodation in the previous two years. We said, 'We're going to reverse that. We're going to tackle that problem' ... That was Thatcher's contribution to raising people's class consciousness and allowing us to explain and educate the people the process of what was going on. We said, 'There's no need for all of this. There's tremendous wealth in this country, which has been proved time and time again. In a crisis, capitalism always finds enough funds to fight a war, or two wars, or bail out the banks; the money always seems to be there'. So our campaign was to get the money back into Liverpool which Thatcher had stolen from the city.[45]

Privatisation of public services was especially feared, as it would mean greater loss of jobs, yet this was the route encouraged by the Conservative government. It became a rallying cry for the local authority trade unions, in hope their members would mobilise politically. The threat from the Liberal–Tory council to privatise refuse collection was what finally provoked many public employee trade unionists to take an active political stance, as Ian Lowes remembered:

> What brought everything to a head was in 1983 when the Liberals wanted to privatise the refuse collection and street cleansing. Well, we mounted an effective campaign against that ... And we encouraged council workers to turn out, and their families to vote Labour in the May elections. Now the consequence was Labour actually swept in to power. You can't underestimate the influence the council's own workforce had.[46]

If jobs were a primary concern, so too was housing, as Liverpool after so many years of neglect was in dire need of urban renewal. Liverpool had some of the worst housing conditions in all of Europe. After years of refusing to raise rates, the Liberal–Tory controlled council found it increasingly difficult to maintain the limited public housing stock available, much less build additional estates. While this had the effect of keeping private property values high, it aggravated the demand for affordable public housing. The dilapidated housing stock also increased pressure on the decreasing number of council workers charged with its maintenance.

Along with jobs and housing, education was also a growing concern, as cost-cutting schemes included closing and consolidation of some neighbourhood schools. The Liberal–Tory controlled council's decision to close a comprehensive school in the impoverished Croxteth neighbourhood infuriated many local residents, who soon gained the attention of the Militant Labour group. In protest, parents, alumni and neighbourhood activists occupied the school in August 1983, demanding it be re-opened, but in the meantime they ran the school themselves. Croxteth, one of the poorest neighbourhoods in the city, where there was an unemployment rate of 40 per cent and where approximately 98 per cent of the sixteen- to nineteen-year-olds were without work, was especially vulnerable to government cuts.[47]

Recognising this problem, Militant threw their support behind the cause, winning further loyal converts to Militant Labour. Militant also promised that if a Labour-controlled council were elected they would give their strongest backing to not only keeping Croxteth Comprehensive School open, but Labour also gave assurances that the building of new schools would encompass 'a system of "community" comprehensives with existing and new schools, open to anyone who wants to attend, young or old'.[48]

Defending jobs and services

Jobs, housing and education became the three primary concerns of the working-class electorate of Liverpool in an age of increasing cuts from Westminster. Militant Labour shrewdly tapped into these anxieties, and by the time of the council elections in May 1983, it was Labour – now under Militant influence locally – that was seen by many voters as the only alternative. Once elected, Labour pledged there would be no privatisation of council services, a £2 per week cut in council house rents and no further cuts in municipal spending. There was also a greater commitment to necessary repairs on public housing, and the promise of 6,000 new council houses and the institution of an additional 4,000 council jobs.[49]

Working people in Liverpool voted enthusiastically in the local elections in 1983: turnout was 'more than 40 per cent and, and in some wards, as high as 53 per cent'.[50] These figures can, in part, be attributed to Militant's efforts to radicalise the council workforce, as well as local reaction to unpopular government policies. According to the *Liverpool Echo*:

> Liverpool woke up to a new Socialist administration to-day, following Labour's spectacular capture of the city council ... Labour won an overall majority on the council, wrestling power from the minority-ruling Liberals. The result gives the city its first council for 10 years on which any party has an overall majority. The new administration of 51 Labour councillors against 30 Liberals and 18 Conservatives will be hard-Left. It contains about 10 Militant Tendency supporters and a majority in sympathy with their Trotskyite aims. The party is pledged to slashing council rents by £2 a week, a massive council-house build for rent scheme, vast job creation and official re-opening of the rebel Croxteth School.[51]

Although the estimated number of Militant-affiliated councillors on LCC only ranged from ten to sixteen out of Labour's fifty-one members, they exerted control on the leadership of the Labour group through tight organisation and complete unity within their caucus.[52]

This now largely radicalised local Labour Party realised they had to live with – at least for the following year – a budget inherited from the previous regime. The pending budget would become a battle of wills between LCC and Westminster from May 1983 until the summer of 1984, and the council also were well aware that they needed both the electorate and the council workforce firmly behind their cause. Militant chose to use this interregnum to further politicise the council workforce and win the trust of their trade unions. According to Tony Mulhearn:

> The level of political [consciousness] of the working class can be judged in a number of ways. Physically, and that's judged by demonstrations and the number of people coming out into the street – by their willingness to take action. Now we demonstrated this graphically before the '83 election. We had a demonstration in which 25,000 people turned up in the streets of Liverpool demonstrating against Thatcher's cuts. Now, when we actually took control we had demonstrations, where 10, 20, 30,000 people – we had one occasion when we had 50,000 people in Castle Street, outside the Town Hall, demonstrating in support of the policies put in place by the Labour controlled Liverpool City Council ... And then, of course, the other way to judge [the level of political consciousness] is the ballot box. We got the highest Labour votes in '83, '84, '85 that had ever been recorded in the city of Liverpool. We got more votes in a local election since 1945. And that's in spite of the population of the city declining from 700,000 to 460,000 ... On one occasion we got a 62 per cent turnout in a local election. That's unheard of; it's unprecedented! In these days if you get 11 to 20 per cent in a local election you're lucky. That, then, is a clear indication of how the consciousness of workers can be raised if the leadership is given and the issues are clearly explained.[53]

One of Labour's first priorities was to assure the workforce their positions were secure, and that more council jobs would be created. Labour councillors realised that they needed to keep their campaign promises, even if that meant the creation of a financial deficit and the submission of an illegal budget based on insufficient rates. They had to prepare not only for the resulting battle against the government but also an internal struggle with Neil Kinnock and the Labour Party leadership. This required the Liverpool DLP to further politicise and mobilise large segments of Liverpool's working class.

Upon taking control, the Labour group under Hamilton and Hatton announced their new 'Urban Regeneration Strategy', a massive scheme of public housing construction. Labour Councillor Tony Byrne took special interest in this project, ensuring that quality of life issues were considered and construction targets met. Over 5,000 new homes were built during Labour's term of office between 1983 and 1987. In the first eighteen months, the council built 1,000 homes, the largest public works project in Britain at that time.[54] This zeal to build more council houses, parks, hospitals and schools created additional jobs on LCC's payroll and boosted private construction employment. Mulhearn insisted that the Urban Regeneration Strategy had a 'dramatic impact' on the local economy:

> We created something like 16,000 [private sector] jobs in the construction industry ... 2,000 local authority jobs were created ... We took on more apprentices during our period than any previous comparable period. So it had an enormous impact on the local economy, on kids getting work ... What this demonstrates is what can be done if the will is there. The resources are there, the money is there, what is required is the political will to drive it through ... You've got to translate socialism into the language of housing, the language of jobs, the language of social service, the language of nursery schools, and education. So you got to translate the ideas into action which people can understand and identify with.[55]

Public support from the local authority unions was seen as essential if the Liverpool DLP was to resist government policies.

'Budget day' had arrived in March 1984, and despite apprehension from some white-collar union leaders, the council pushed ahead with a budget that they knew would guarantee conflict with Thatcher. The consensus amongst the Labour group was that if they chose to implement the cuts in jobs and services demanded by government, the city would become unmanageable. With recent memories of the Toxteth riots, many Labour councillors felt sharp cuts and the corresponding jump in rates and rents was too much to ask of a city whose population was already suffering some of the worst social and economic conditions in Western Europe. The Labour group proclaimed they were not elected to carry out the Conservatives' draconian cuts on an impoverished city, heavily dependent on public sector employment and services: they would not present a balanced budget. They planned to spend more than the revenue received to deliberately bankrupt the city, forcing government to restore previous levels of funding.

The planned budget was declared illegal because its expenditures were higher than its income. Labour's budget was £296.7 million, £80 million above the target set by Whitehall. A rate rise of over 126 per cent would be required to support it, but the council proposed a rise of 9 per cent, leaving a deficit of £190 million, probably more when government penalties were taken into account.

On 19 March 1984, District Auditor Lesley Stanford warned the council that a 9 per cent rise in rates would lead to fiscal collapse, as the city would run out of funds for services. He also cautioned that councillors voting in favour of such a budget could be held personally accountable, subject to fines, imprisonment and/or a ban from public office for five years. Labour maintained that the government should raise the city's spending target by £55 million. A further complication was that any rate the council submitted in their budget was binding and could not be altered or rescinded later in the fiscal year. Consequently, once the 9 per cent rate was approved, LCC would have to live with limited revenue for an entire year, inevitably causing massive cuts in jobs and services – which the council pledged never to do – or municipal bankruptcy, which, it was hoped, the government would not allow.[56]

The illegality of Labour's plan was excused by its proponents who argued the £279 million lost over the previous four years from government cuts had been 'stolen' from Liverpool in the first place, so accusations of criminality should rather be levelled at Thatcher's ministers.[57] While the Labour group and the DLP considered their response to the situation legitimate, the national Labour leadership regarded it with dismay, fearful that the tactic could backfire and create larger problems for both LCC and the electability of the Labour Party at large. At this time, a growing tendency within the Labour Party was attempting to cultivate a more centrist image. The future architects of New Labour were courting the middle-class electorate and discouraged any regression to Labour's radical past.

Despite pressure from Transport House and national union leaders, overwhelmingly negative coverage from the press and threats of fines and even imprisonment from a district auditor, the council's Labour group presented their 'illegal' budget on 29 March 1984. Outside the council building, 50,000 supporters rallied in full support of Labour's stance. However, a problem erupted when six Labour councillors sided with the Tories and Liberals and voted down the 'illegal' budget.

The Labour group had ruled with a majority of six votes in 1984, and the defection of what the media labelled the 'Sensible Six' and the left termed the 'Scabby Six' eliminated this control. The defectors were largely remnants of the Labour's old right-wing, and their desertion did not come as a complete surprise to the Militant Tendency group. Hatton publicly threatened their future political careers, eliciting the response from one defecting councillor: 'Labour have taken on the Government and they have lost. I am not going to be intimidated by threats from people I see as extremists.'[58]

The Labour group's strategy shifted to delaying tactics, in the hope of securing a greater majority for Militant Labour by the next round of local elections in May. This was a dangerous ploy, since running the city without a working budget and setting a legal rate had never been attempted before. However, most of the left-wing of the DLP and the Labour group felt the city could function adequately during the month and a half until the elections. The gamble was whether Labour's left-wing could mobilise the voters once again in order to restore their majority. Moreover, the left needed a second mandate to silence their critics in Transport House and the TUC. One-third of the ninety-nine council seats were up for election that year, meaning one seat in each of Liverpool's thirty-three wards.[59]

During the election campaign, Liverpool's 30,000 local authority workers were mobilised. More than 80 per cent voted in that election and many took active roles in Militant Labour's campaign.[60] A massive 51 per cent turnout put an additional seven Labour councillors into office, giving Labour fifty-eight out of ninety-nine council seats. The Liberals and Tories attained only forty-one seats. Significantly, this victory for Labour's left-wing came about when the national party was losing votes in parliamentary elections, thus, temporarily silencing Kinnock and other party leaders.[61] Tony Mulhearn, President of the Liverpool DLP, accused Kinnock of a serious misjudgement by insisting Labour councils should adhere to the law: 'We have been the trailblazers and Mr. Kinnock should surely now recognise that fact. Our success will be a tremendous boost for a united front for Labour local authorities and trade unions in defence of jobs and services.'[62]

Liverpool versus the government: part I

Westminster also took notice. Thatcher assigned Environment Minister, Patrick Jenkin, the task of monitoring and controlling the situation in Liverpool. It was not an easy undertaking. Mulhearn recalled the state of affairs at the time of Jenkin's arrival:

> Well, he came to Liverpool, and he's one of these patrician Tories, you know, one of the old, blue-blooded style Tories. He never had seen a council estate in his life. So we took him on a tour around the city centre and in the old Scotland Road docks area where I was brought up. Some of the most miserable housing you ever seen, and he was visibly shaken. He just couldn't believe that people were forced to live under these conditions. So there's about 2,000 people following him on this tour of an estate, and when the tour was over we organised a press conference. And his famous quote was, 'I've seen housing today the likes of which I have never seen in my lifetime. And I will do my very best to ensure that funding is made available to overcome this problem'.[63]

By the spring and summer of 1984 Thatcher was engaged in a civil war against the National Union of Mineworkers. Mulhearn recalled it in this context:

> We always said we owed a debt of gratitude to the miners. [The government] were focused on defeating the miners. And by no means at that

> same time did they want to open up another front. But once they defeated the miners, they were, of course, gung-ho, and we knew she was coming after us.[64]

It has been argued by some observers that the government would not have contemplated bargaining with LCC had Thatcher not recognised the growing influence of the Joint Shop Stewards' Committee, particularly amongst other trade unionists. Conducting a highly controversial offensive against the miners rendered doing battle against a rebel provincial city council, backed by a highly politicised workforce, unthinkable, at least for the time being.[65]

Meanwhile, Hatton and his colleagues, fresh from their landslide victory in May and aware of the government's predicament, saw that the budget crisis, if handled deftly, was an opportunity to further politicise Liverpool's working class. The government understood that if it allowed Militant to win this confrontation, other councils would also follow Liverpool's lead. Conversely, if the government disbanded Liverpool's council and administered the city by a board of commissioners – which was its legal right – it would have the burden of overseeing a city on the brink of revolt. Since this might create a political disaster for the government, the Liverpool DLP realised it had the upper hand. A series of negotiations between Jenkin and the council were approved by Thatcher in order to find a way to save face and reach a workable solution.[66]

Labour argued that the neoliberal economic principles espoused by the government were inapplicable to much of the impoverished, de-industrialised north of England, and especially to Liverpool. Dependence on government funds and public sector employment was its only lifeline. Nevertheless, Jenkin insisted that 'the local authority was not a system of outdoor relief' and 'if unemployment was the price of economic growth, it would have to be paid'.[67] Such entrenched attitudes precluded any negotiated settlement. Both parties agreed to allow a panel of independent civil servants the opportunity to examine the city's finances. The subsequent report sided heavily with the council's position, giving its cause greater moral and technical authority. Some rationalisation was recommended, but the Labour group maintained its opposition to central government cuts.[68]

The government, weary of the situation and still engaged in its brutal battle with the miners, eventually capitulated to some of the council's demands. Under the headline '"Generous" Jenkin offers way out to Liverpool', the *Guardian* reported: 'Mr. Patrick Jenkin has presented a package of concessions to Liverpool City Council which is far more generous than any of the participants believed possible a few weeks ago.'[69] Mulhearn recalled the circumstances:

> [Jenkin] arranged to meet us in London, and he made concessions. Now, the way the rates of support grants worked was if we overspent by £1, then we lost two quid from the government. But what he said was he would make money available which would allow us not to overspend. So, he conceded by way of various measures something like £30 million pounds. Now, in addition to the money we didn't lose that was worth something like sixty million quid to the city. This was a significant achievement. Now that allowed us with our policy of continuing to build houses, creating jobs and keeping the rents and rates low.[70]

If the contest with the miners weighed heavily on the government's decision to compromise, mobilisation of local authority trade unions may have also made an impact. Lowes retrospectively assessed events:

> Thatcher was obsessed with smashing the miners ... She wasn't going to be deflected from that. And the situation in Liverpool was a diversion. There's no doubt in my mind that if the Miners' Strike hadn't been on, then I think the Tories would've had a go at Liverpool, and Liverpool wouldn't have got anything. So, I think one of the reasons why we were able to get some concessions out of them was the Miners' Strike, but also because they were terrified that the movement in Liverpool ever spread out to local councils elsewhere they'd have problems. What we were trying to do was build links with other workers elsewhere. We had a flourishing joint shop stewards' committee, and we were reaching out to workers in other councils, and we were saying, 'Look what we achieved in Liverpool; you could do the same'. So I think they were terrified there was going to be a major movement. Because, as you can imagine, what the consequences of a well-organised government workforce could do – and if that was extended nationally, well, you can imagine.[71]

The compromise put together by Jenkin was the product of complicated, and some would say, creative accounting. Nevertheless, it met nearly all the demands of the Labour group, while at the same time the government could save face in that it forced LCC to raise its original rate of 9 per cent to 17 per cent. This was still much less than the 170 per cent rise initially demanded by Whitehall and caused consternation within establishment circles.

No matter how much the Tories insisted otherwise, the agreement was widely regarded as a triumph by the Liverpool DLP over the formidable Margaret Thatcher. It secured the Labour group's position on the council, giving it an even stronger mandate to implement its spending agenda. Derek Hatton appeared to take special delight in publicly humiliating Jenkin and Thatcher over their apparent surrender. Hatton later recalled Jenkin's reaction after he prematurely released details of the agreement to the media:

> Jenkin was furious. He believed, in his own words, that we had 'danced on his political grave' and Liverpool had become his personal *bête noir* ... It is true though that the episode soured our relations with Whitehall from that day on. Jenkin vowed to deal with every single matter relating to Liverpool personally – even the smallest of details.[72]

Vitriolic exchanges in the press did little to build lines of communication for future budget talks, considering that the council and government were likely to encounter the same situation the following year. The national Labour Party leadership also received vicious attacks in the press from Hatton and Mulhearn, which created an even wider gulf between the party elite and certain DLPs – many of which were now turning to people like Liverpool's Hatton and Mulhearn for leadership and advice.[73]

Critics of Militant and LCC contend that their victory over the government was not as overwhelming as Hatton and others proclaimed. They assert that the government budget deal with LCC was merely a compromise, and nowhere near the 'revolution' that the colourful Hatton was claiming in the press.[74] The complexities of local government finance render definitive assessment of these claims difficult. Nevertheless, it is apparent that the Labour group won the propaganda war. In doing so, it convinced Thatcher and her government that they could never give in to the demands of Liverpool or any other local authority in future. Thatcher's eventual victory over the miners in 1985 buoyed her government's confidence and virtually sealed this decision.

Liverpool versus the government: part 2

Confident it could beat Thatcher once again in 1985 LCC funded a massive housing scheme, and by December 1984 had signed contracts totalling £88 million, £11 million short of its budget. The council gambled that the government would increase housing grants that year; instead, it lowered them. Liverpool was especially hard hit, with a 20 per cent cut, by far the largest decrease of any local authority on Merseyside.

Many observers felt this was Jenkin's revenge, while others saw this as a clear sign that Downing Street had finally had enough of Liverpool and Militant Labour. Whatever the motives, the cuts were devastating for Byrne's Urban Regeneration Strategy. Defiantly, Byrne told the press: 'We will not reduce our building programme by one single unit.' Byrne then successfully negotiated a loan from a Parisian bank.[75] With the budget for 1985/1986 looming, the Labour group maintained plans for no cuts in jobs and services, and to carry on with its commitment of more and better public housing.

Nevertheless, the once unlimited support the Labour group enjoyed was beginning to fray. A number of factors eroded Militant's standing. Hatton's flamboyance and arrogance alienated some within Militant's inner-circle, yet he proved almost indispensable because of his media savvy and close connection with the voters.[76] Another fissure stemmed from the rift between the Labour group and Liverpool's black activists over the Sam Bond affair. This situation also created tension on the Joint Shop Stewards' Committee, where NALGO representatives were sympathetic to the arguments against the appointment.[77] Taaffe and Mulhearn countered that the Black Caucus was swayed by Liberal Party activists and a local black criminal element seeking political patronage.[78] Other problems included complaints from local authority trade unions regarding changes in work policies that increased employees' workload. Tenants in council housing complained of a decline in maintenance services.

These were the conditions under which the Labour group was operating in June 1985, when it submitted a budget proposing only a 9 per cent rate increase. Hatton recalled:

> Budget Day was almost a formality. Tony Byrne announced that we required £265 million for the coming year. But the Government said we must not spend more than £222 million. So, he announced, we would not set a rate – and we didn't. We knew there was no legal requirement to do so until June, so we postponed the decision until then. But a move in the game which was totally outside our control was about to change events. The Audit Commission, whose job was to monitor local government finances, appointed a new district auditor, Tim McMahon ... Now McMahon came down on us like a ton of bricks, and it was his report which would eventually land us in court, fighting the legal battle against surcharge and disqualification.[79]

It was an illegal budget since its rate increase did not come close to covering the enormous expenditures expected in the following fiscal year. On 14 June 1985, after only two hours of debate, it was approved by the council, whose fate would now rest in the hands of the government-appointed district auditor, Timothy McMahon.[80]

Patrick Jenkin made it known that 'If a loss occurs as a result of a deliberate deficit, councillors may be liable to be surcharged or disqualified'. Byrne countered that a balanced budget was impossible 'without carrying out Thatcher policies' and that 'to comply with government targets would mean dismissing staff, which could not be considered in an area with 60,000 unemployed'. The council leader, John Hamilton, contended:

> Our budget says to the Government: This is what Liverpool needs, this is what is reasonable to regenerate the area and to provide for the needs of the people through council jobs and services and in the private sector. If we do go down and are defeated in legal terms, in terms of decent humanity we will win. We have right and justice on our side.[81]

Mulhearn struck a similarly defiant note: 'for the first time, elected members are prepared to put on the line their resources and houses and risk imprisonment and bankruptcy because they believe that the attacks on the city and its people had to be halted'. While council unions sought mandates to strike in the event of legal moves against councillors, Hatton railed against 'those elements in the party and trades unions who betrayed us last year [whose] days are numbered'.[82]

On 26 June 1985, McMahon initiated legal proceedings against the forty-nine defiant Labour councillors, accusing them of wilful misconduct. Exercising his judicial powers, he later found all forty-nine guilty of setting an illegal budget and negligent in incurring debts of £1.2 million in interest, for which he held them personally liable.[83] Mulhearn recalled:

> We weren't defeated by the ballot box. We weren't defeated on the streets. We were defeated by a manoeuvre put on by the Thatcher government ... [McMahon] came into Liverpool like Thatcher's hired gun. He was in this city for three months and couldn't find any improprieties. He couldn't find anything inappropriate at all. So what he seized on, what he got us on – and it was a frame-up, and I've said this publicly – was the fact that we delayed setting the rate. We didn't set it until June. Now he used that against us, although that in itself wasn't illegal ... [but] no money went into the bank. Now, McMahon argued had we have set a rate, we would have got that money, we would've put it in the bank, and that would have generated interest of £106,000 ... He doesn't have to convince a jury. He makes his judgement as an individual. And he made a guilty judgement,

> and it was on that basis we were removed from office. It was all so totally anti-democratic.[84]

McMahon gave the council three options in order to rectify the situation. The first was massive cuts in jobs and services in order to live within the 9 per cent rate already set. The second option was to appeal to the High Court for the 9 per cent rise to be overturned, and then prepare an amended budget that worked within the new government guidelines. The third choice offered was, 'You can start preparing 30,000 redundancy notices'.[85] LCC was not prepared to accept any of the three alternatives and instead requested that it be allowed to borrow £25 million from the government. The government refused the council's request.

Without funding, the council felt it had no alternative but to issue ninety-day redundancy notices to its 31,000 employees. The council leadership had hoped that this action would rally its workforce to mount a general strike against the Westminster cuts. In order to gain as much media coverage as possible, Hatton and his colleagues hired a fleet of black cabs to hand-deliver the notices to workers' homes.[86] But the tactic backfired, as many workers who supported the Labour-led council reacted strongly against them. Hatton recalled how the situation evolved:

> The redundancy notices were, of course, only ever intended as a technical device to give us breathing space ... The ninety-day notices would take us on to the end of December, and would keep us within the law. Our own officials pointed out that if we continued to employ people when the balance sheet said we would not have the cash to pay them, we would be breaking the law. But under the Employment Protection Act if we gave three months' notice we stayed within the law. Not that we ever intended sacking anyone, and let's remember that we didn't. On September 6th, 1985 we announced the decision. How it backfired on us. The trade unions revolted, their national officials went for us, and at Labour Party headquarters the decision was seized upon as a stick with which to beat Militant. We argued that by issuing redundancy notices we could also hammer home the sharp reality of our arguments: that unless more money was available to Liverpool from the central funds, then jobs really were on the line.[87]

The council's decision created divisions within the Joint Shop Stewards' Committee. NALGO, NUPE and the NUT argued there should be no redundancies, and money earmarked for housing should be redistributed to pay council employees. Housing was a priority for the Labour leadership, and especially important to blue-collar unions who saw it as important to job security. What the Labour group failed to appreciate was that making people redundant, even temporarily, would have profound effects on their lives, and the issue damaged the group's reputation among even its most loyal supporters. The entire Liverpool DLP was soon suspended. Hatton and forty-seven of his colleagues on the council were removed from office and eventually expelled from the party.

At the Labour Party's annual conference in 1985, Neil Kinnock denounced the Liverpool councillors in his now famous 'Grotesque Chaos' speech, in which he attacked the radical left within his own party. Mulhearn expressed his disgust at the turn of events:

> The only reason why we were all defeated was because we were isolated. Because we were involved in a major campaign nationally with many other major local authorities, they all eventually, one by one, split away from us, gave in to the government and made cuts. We were left on our own ... We developed a tremendous level of unity, of which we are rightly proud. Many critics accused Militant of being sectarian, or this and that, but the contrary was true; otherwise, we couldn't have developed such a massive campaign and received such marvellous results on the streets and in the ballot box. So I think we did all we could, under the circumstances, to develop the massive unity of the Liverpool working class.[88]

Conclusion: Liverpool Labour's achievements and support

While many of the failures attributed to Liverpool's Labour council of the 1980s are today lampooned by political observers from the right and centre, their achievements are often forgotten. LCC made noticeable improvements in the quality of life for a good majority of Liverpool's working class, including:

- 6,300 families rehoused from dilapidated tenements, flats and maisonettes
- 2,873 tenement flats demolished
- 1,315 walk-up flats demolished
- 2,086 flats/maisonettes demolished
- 4,800 houses and bungalows built
- 7,400 houses and flats improved
- 25 new Housing Action Areas developed
- six new nurseries built
- 17 community comprehensive schools established following a massive re-organisation
- £10 million spent on school improvements

- five new sports centres, one with a leisure pool attached, built
- 2,000 additional jobs provided for in LCC Budget
- 10,000 people per year employed on Council's Capital Programme
- three new parks built
- rents frozen for five years.[89]

In addition there was the political legacy bequeathed by a socialist council. It demonstrated that, in spite of the government's restrictions, deep-seated problems affecting working people could be easily rectified if there is the funding and the political will.

Considering the scale of these accomplishments, it is surprising that the widespread support once enjoyed by the Labour council could evaporate so quickly. Perhaps the answer lies in the leadership of the council itself. Certainly, Hatton's perceived narcissistic persona and egomaniacal tendencies would eventually test the loyalty of even his most fervent supporters; however, the city was no stranger to larger-than-life leaders. Vivid personalities had been running Liverpool even before the days of Jack and Bessie Braddock or T. P. O'Connor. The same can be said for Liverpool's association with American-style machine politics, a characteristic often attributed to the Militant-dominated Liverpool DLP.

The answer may lie beyond individual leaders and more in Militant's taking for granted such assumptions as the working class's unquestioning support of Labour and the privileging of class issues. Not all the workers who initially supported the Labour council shared common attributes and concerns. It was the Militant Tendency's failure to recognise such differences that blinded them from certain realities.

Broad segments of society in Liverpool, ranging from blue-collar unions, white-collar unions, middle-class professional bodies, organisations from the black community, feminist groups, tenants' associations, voluntary societies and charities all had views on what the city needed and each wanted to contribute. The Liverpool DLP, while encouraging support from everybody, insisted on the exclusive right of forming party policies. While it would have been difficult to maintain unity amongst such a broad coalition; nevertheless, rejecting the input of all outside the Labour Party banner was a recipe for alienation and the eventual factionalism that followed.

Despite the tragic fall of the Labour-led council and the Militant Tendency, perhaps we should not discount the fact that they had, albeit for only a brief period of two or three years, fundamentally altered the political landscape in Liverpool. While it is still fashionable amongst most observers to discard – even lampoon – the efforts of this group, we should judge their accomplishments outside the narrow constraints of the irksome media personalities of one or two of its leading lights. It should be remembered that it was their mobilisation and politicisation of large sections of Merseyside's working class which helped effect many positive changes in Liverpool's deprived communities, not least of which was the preservation of jobs and prevention of further economic decline.

There is little evidence of any other British city in this period produced a council with the same level of emphasis on class-based radicalism in its agenda as the Militant Labour controlled council in the 1980s Liverpool. Indeed, while other Trotskyist-inspired and Militant-led local authorities existed at this time, few could claim the unprecedented measures Liverpool's council dared. The revolutionary programme and far-reaching perspective of this body has yet to be seen from any local council since its departure. Once again it proves abject poverty and relentless high-unemployment make an excellent breeding ground for revolutionaries.

Notes

1 Michael Parkinson, *Liverpool on the Brink* (Hermitage, 1985), p. 13.
2 Parkinson, *Liverpool on the Brink*, p. 13.
3 Parkinson, *Liverpool on the Brink*, p. 10.
4 Parkinson, *Liverpool on the Brink*, p. 14.
5 Parkinson, *Liverpool on the Brink*, p. 10.
6 Parkinson, *Liverpool on the Brink*, p. 14.
7 Hilary Wainwright, *Labour: A Tale of Two Parties* (London, 1987), Chs 1 and 2.
8 Peter Taaffe and Tony Mulhearn, *Liverpool – A City that Dared to Fight* (London, 1988), pp. 50–2.
9 Parkinson, *Liverpool on the Brink*, pp. 17–18.
10 Michael Crick, *The March of Militant* (London, 1986), p. 38; John Bohstedt, 'More than One Working Class: Protestants and Catholic Riots in Edwardian Liverpool', in John Belchem, ed., *Popular Politics, Riot and Labour: Essays in Liverpool History 1790–1940* (Liverpool, 1992), pp. 173–216; John Belchem, 'Liverpool in the Year of Revolution: The Political and Associational Culture of the Irish Immigrant Community in 1848', in Belchem, *Popular Politics, Riot and Labour*, pp. 68–97; Sam Davies, *Liverpool Labour* (Keele, 1996); P. J. Waller, *Democracy and Sectarianism: A Political and Social History of Liverpool 1868–1939* (Liverpool, 1981); John Belchem, *Irish, Catholic and Scouse: The History of the Liverpool-Irish, 1800–1939* (Liverpool, 2007), pp. 299–300.
11 Reginald Bevins, *The Greasy Pole: A Personal Account of the Realities of British Politics* (London, 1965), pp. 11–13, 18; Davies, *Liverpool Labour*, Chs 1 and 2.
12 Parkinson, *Liverpool on the Brink*, p. 18.

13 Crick, *Militant*, p. 39.
14 Interview with Ian Lowes.
15 Crick, *Militant*, p. 38.
16 Barry Hindess, *The Decline of Working Class Politics* (London, 1971), p. 70.
17 Hindess, *Decline*, pp. 49–53, 70. See also Parkinson, *Liverpool on the Brink*, pp. 20–1.
18 Parkinson, *Liverpool on the Brink*, pp. 19–20.
19 Parkinson, *Liverpool on the Brink*, p. 21.
20 Interview with Tony Mulhearn.
21 Parkinson, *Liverpool on the Brink*, p. 25. See also Hindess, *Decline*, pp. 57–67.
22 Crick, *Militant*, pp. 2–3, 23–4.
23 Crick, *Militant*, pp. 8–11, 13–15.
24 Crick, *Militant*, pp. 70–3.
25 Eric Shaw, *Discipline and Discord in the Labour Party* (Manchester, 1988), pp. 218–20. See also Crick, *Militant*, pp. 73–4.
26 Interview with David Leach.
27 Crick, *Militant*, pp. 75–7.
28 Eric Heffer, *Never a Yes Man: The Life and Politics of an Adopted Liverpudlian* (London, 1991), Chs 18, 19. See also: Shaw, *Discipline*, pp. 224–8.
29 Taaffe and Mulhearn, *Liverpool*, p. 64.
30 Crick, *Militant*, p. 2.
31 Crick, *Militant*, pp. 224–9. See also: Bruce Spencer, *Remaking the Working Class? An Examination of Shop Stewards' Experiences* (Nottingham, 1989), p. 81; Parkinson, *Liverpool on the Brink*, p. 33; Derek Hatton, *Inside Left* (London, 1988).
32 Interview with Tony Mulhearn.
33 Liverpool Black Caucus, *The Racial Politics of Militant: The Black Community's Struggle for Participation in Local Politics, 1980–1986* (London and Liverpool, 1986).
34 Wainwright, *Labour*, pp. 132–3
35 Taaffe and Mulhearn, *Liverpool*, pp. 70–1.
36 Spencer, *Remaking*, pp. 16, 77.
37 Bruce Spencer, 'Post-War Trade Unionism: Its Role and Significance', *Studies for Trade Unionists*, vol. 13, no. 52 (December 1987), pp. 7–10. See also Spencer, *Remaking*, pp. 77–9.
38 Parkinson, *Liverpool on the Brink*, pp. 40–2. See also Taaffe and Mulhearn, *Liverpool*, pp. 162–70.
39 Interview with Ian Lowes.
40 Crick, *Militant*, pp. 240–1. See also Taaffe and Mulhearn, *Liverpool*, pp. 162–70.
41 Interview with Ian Lowes.
42 Interview with Tony Mulhearn.
43 Interview with Ian Lowes.
44 Crick, *Militant*, pp. 224, 228. See also Parkinson, *Liverpool on the Brink*, pp. 29–30.

45 Interview with Tony Mulhearn.
46 Interview with Ian Lowes.
47 Taaffe and Mulhearn, *Liverpool*, pp. 71–2.
48 *Observer*, 19 June 1983.
49 'Liverpool: What Went Wrong', http://archive.workersliberty.org/publications/readings/trots/liverp.htm.
50 *Liverpool Echo*, 6 May 1983. See also Taaffe and Mulhearn, *Liverpool*, pp. 78–83; Parkinson, *Liverpool on the Brink*, p. 42.
51 *Liverpool Echo*, 6 May 1983.
52 Crick, *Militant*, pp. 229–34.
53 Interview with Tony Mulhearn.
54 Taaffe and Mulhearn, *Liverpool*, p. 159. See also *Guardian*, 7 August 1984.
55 Interview with Tony Mulhearn.
56 Parkinson, *Liverpool on the Brink*, pp. 54–5; *Liverpool Echo*, 29 March 1984.
57 Parkinson, *Liverpool on the Brink*, p. 38; for discussion of the complexities of local authority finance see pp. 79–83.
58 Parkinson, *Liverpool on the Brink*, pp. 49, 54–6; Crick, *Militant*, pp. 243–4.
59 Parkinson, *Liverpool on the Brink*, pp. 59–60.
60 Parkinson, *Liverpool on the Brink*, pp. 69–71.
61 Parkinson, *Liverpool on the Brink*, pp. 59–60. See also Taaffe and Mulhearn, *Liverpool*, pp. 107–27, 135–9.
62 *Guardian*, 12 July 1984.
63 Interview with Tony Mulhearn.
64 Interview with Tony Mulhearn.
65 Spencer, *Remaking*, pp. 85–6; Crick, *Militant*, pp. 239–40.
66 Parkinson, *Liverpool on the Brink*, pp. 72–80; Margaret Thatcher, *The Downing Street Years* (London, 1993), pp. 306, 309, 642–7. See also *Guardian*, 9 May 1984, 18 May 1984 and 20 June 1984.
67 Parkinson, *Liverpool on the Brink*, p. 9. See also *Guardian*, 9 March 1985.
68 Parkinson, *Liverpool on the Brink*, pp. 103–5.
69 *Guardian*, 9 July 1984.
70 Interview with Tony Mulhearn; Taaffe and Mulhearn, *Liverpool*, pp. 146–58.
71 Interview with Ian Lowes.
72 Hatton, *Inside Left*, p. 85.
73 Parkinson, *Liverpool on the Brink*, pp. 107–10; Spencer, *Remaking*, pp. 89–93. See also *Guardian*, 12 July 1984 and 14 July 1984.
74 Wainwright, *Labour*, pp. 129, 132.
75 Parkinson, *Liverpool on the Brink*, pp. 132–7. See also *Guardian*, 21 December 1984 and 7 August 1984.
76 Crick, *Militant*, pp. 248–51; Taaffe and Mulhearn, *Liverpool*, pp. 170–2.
77 Crick, *Militant*, pp. 250–1; Spencer, *Remaking*, pp. 88–9.
78 Taaffe and Mulhearn, *Liverpool*, p. 55.
79 Hatton, *Inside Left*, pp. 94–5.
80 Parkinson, *Liverpool on the Brink*, pp. 156–60; Crick, *Militant*, pp. 257–60. See also *Guardian*, 15 June 1985.

81 *Guardian*, 15 June 1985.
82 *Guardian*, 15 June 1985.
83 Parkinson, *Liverpool on the Brink*, p. 163. See also *Guardian*, 28 June 1985.
84 Interview with Tony Mulhearn.
85 Parkinson, *Liverpool on the Brink*, p. 166.
86 Spencer, *Remaking*, pp. 89–92.
87 Hatton, *Inside Left*, pp. 98–110.
88 Interview with Tony Mulhearn.
89 Socialism on Trial: www.liverpool47.org/menu/Menu.htm (website produced by Tony Mulhearn and John Kennedy).

7

Sit-ins and factory occupations: a case study of Cammell Laird's shipyard

The mid-1980s proved to be a pivotal period in British labour history and the trade union movement in particular. The crux of Thatcher's Employment Acts had become clear to most trade union leaders by this time, and many saw no way around their far-reaching tentacles. The Miners' Strike was lumbering along in 1984, and while the miners were still holding on, many trades unionists foresaw a bleak future for organised labour. Pessimism was on the rise, and much of the old fire which was captured in the early 1980s was beginning to wane after the Conservative victory in the election of 1983 and the overall public support Thatcher received for her new set of labour laws. Nevertheless, not everyone had bought into the 'new realism', and shop-floor activism still remained strong in some quarters. The workplace occupation by striking shipyard workers at Cammell Laird Shipyard in Birkenhead, Merseyside is a perfect illustration of these changing times.

Workplace occupations as a form of industrial protest have been a method of remonstration increasingly used by British workers during the latter half of the twentieth century. Commonly referred to as a 'sit-in' or 'sit-down strike', it became an accepted alternative to picketing within the British labour movement after some notable uses in Europe and the United States. This course of action was often seen as the last resort by trade unionists resisting permanent redundancies and factory closures, as was the case at Cammell Laird.

Factory occupations: theoretical background and legal implications

Whilst factory occupations can take a variety of forms, for the purposes of this study this term is defined as being a type of industrial action in which workers refuse to leave their workplace at the end of their agreed hours of employment. In doing so, the workers exercise control over both plant and machinery, preventing management or their agents from gaining access to the means of production. It fundamentally challenges managerial control, and it also raises legal issues regarding private property rights and the commodification of labour under capitalism.

The commodification of labour means that workers' toil is regarded as having a value that can be bartered in exchange for wages, in the same way that capital is financed in exchange for interest, or the way materials are acquired from wholesalers at an agreed price. Proponents of the legality of worker occupations believe workers are entitled to halt production and assume control of workplaces when contractual agreements are disregarded, or when rationalisation procedures and redundancies are unilaterally introduced without first being mutually agreed upon by both labour and capital. Such ideas came into vogue during the heyday of shop steward-led activism from the 1960s onwards.

Along with this notion of workers possessing a right to stewardship over the sale of their labour, and included with that awareness a say in the control of production, also came the idea of all people having a fundamental right to work. In the post-war context of political commitments to full employment, it was believed by both organised labour and government that if capital could not provide the needed jobs, then it was the responsibility of government to ensure that paid employment was available to all who were willing to work. This meant more than cross-party support for the welfare state. To many of those on the left of the trade union movement, work was a fundamental human right. However, by the end of the 1960s, this principle was challenged by right-wing tendencies in both the Conservative and Labour parties.

Along with the shift in bargaining power to the shop floor in the 1960s, a movement also developed at this time advocating greater industrial democracy. Many on the left began questioning traditional methods of industrial action, as government gradually became focused more on lowering inflation and seemingly less interested in maintaining full employment.[1] Shop stewards were an important component in inspiring their members to opt for a sit-in over traditional forms of strikes and picketing, as it is certain that a large percentage of factory floor shop stewards were more to the left politically than their union officials.

The Communist Party of Great Britain provided necessary support and counsel in some cases involving workplace occupations.[2] The Institute for Workers' Control (IWC), a group promoting greater industrial democracy, formed in 1968 by a group of British academics and union activists, led by Ken Coates, was also influential in its advocacy of factory sit-ins.[3]

The choice of occupation over that of picketing was usually the result of intimation of workplace closure rather than disputes over wages or conditions. In contrast to conventional disputes, an 'end-of-the-line' mentality and a 'nowhere else to go' group psychology were common attitudes preceding decisions to occupy. The most effective occupations involved a considerable amount of planning. Solidarity and resources from other trade unions and the wider community at large was paramount. Strong leadership was vital to any successful occupation, as was the ability of that leadership to articulate convincingly the group's demands through an effective use of the media. As with traditional strikes, maintaining solidarity was the highest priority, but in addition, an occupation carried the added burden of detailed planning for bedding, provision of meals, washing facilities and entertainment.[4]

There are numerous tactical advantages of a sit-in compared with traditional picketing outside the workplace. Several writers have suggested the enhanced sense of agency experienced by workers exercising control over material, plant and production. One observer noted that having the power to lock-out management did wonders for workers' morale.[5] Strikers remaining inside a factory meant production could not be carried on with blackleg labour. Another important advantage of occupations was that workers controlled the employer's assets, which prevented any movement of production to alternate facilities. Additionally, sit-ins alleviated the tedium of manning a picket at the mercy of the elements, twenty-four hours a day, seven days a week.

Historical examples of factory occupations

Early recorded instances of factory occupations occurred during the 1905 Russian Revolution, and again during the Russian Revolution of 1917. The tactic spread throughout Europe, being used by strikers in Italy in 1920. It was also a favoured method of protest amongst supporters of the left-wing Popular Front in France during the mid-1930s. These examples all had political overtones, but as the tactic developed, the labour movement soon recognised its usefulness for resolving economic disputes. Factory occupations were used successfully against the General Motors Corporation (GM) by American workers seeking recognition of their newly formed trade union, the United Auto Workers. The famous Flint, Michigan, Sit-Down Strike of 1936–37 demonstrated the effectiveness of the sit-in to the wider world.[6]

However, sit-in strikes did not resurface with any frequency until the nationwide French protests of May 1968. Sparked initially by student unrest over conditions in French universities, the civil disorder quickly spread to factories and workshops, as the French workers protested with their own set of grievances. The French working class, long resentful of de Gaulle's authoritarian, right-wing regime, barricaded themselves in their places of employment, protesting that they were the second lowest paid in the European Common Market and worked the longest hours, while paying the highest taxes. This civil and industrial unrest did not topple de Gaulle, nor did it overthrow capitalism; however, the protests made workers in Britain aware of the usefulness of well-organised, highly publicised workplace occupations.[7]

By the early 1970s, de-industrialisation and rising unemployment stimulated new campaigns of resistance. Taking their cue from tactics used by the new left and student activism, British labour rediscovered the sit-in strike. In 1971, over 16,000 British workers were involved in workplace occupations. By 1972, that number rose to over 53,000. From 1973 to 1975, over 22,000 British workers on average, per year, took part in approximately 100 different sit-in strikes. From July 1971 to December 1975, nearly 150,000 British workers participated in over 200 workplace occupations.[8]

The largest and most publicised of these sit-ins was something novel: its organisers at the Upper Clyde Shipbuilders (UCS) called it a 'work-in'. From 30 July 1971 to 9 October 1972, the workers of the UCS, fighting mass redundancies and closure of shipyards on Clydeside, barricaded themselves inside and continued to work their usual shifts. Redundant employees were instructed by the strike committee to disregard their redundancy notices and report to work as usual. Instead of drawing pay packets from UCS, the redundant workers received strike pay from funds raised by the unions.[9]

The leaders of the UCS strike committee devised the 'work-in' because they realised a strike would not halt or delay closure. They also knew such an innovative tactic would generate widespread publicity and draw attention to the argument, long advanced by syndicalists, that workers were capable of managing the means of production.

Additionally, it should be noted that shipyards are unique in that much of the production process is completed by a variety of skilled tradesmen often working independently of one another. Consequently, shipyards are renowned for sectionalism between the different unions representing the sometimes opposing interests of these trades. Despite UCS management's attempts at exploiting these internal divisions, observers noted the high degree of solidarity forged by the UCS workers amongst the array of British trade unions represented in that shipyard. These workers were faced with the prospects of losing their livelihoods in an area of the world that offered little alternative to the only work they knew. Some analysts felt that fact alone provided the motivation needed to keep the disparate workforce unified.[10]

By October 1972, the persistence of the UCS workers was rewarded with an accord from management that agreed to keep all four yards open with no loss in jobs. Ultimately, the demonstration at UCS proved that the effective use of a 'work-in' could save jobs. After the UCS occupation, worker takeovers became a new weapon in labour's armoury. Following the victory of UCS workers, AUEW president Hugh Scanlon declared, 'A beacon has been lit ... The takeovers will continue'.[11]

The sit-in strike at Cammell Laird shipyard, Birkenhead

Cammell Laird's Birkenhead facility had been in existence as a shipyard since 1824. The company had a long history as a major employer in the region, and it was one of the few durable goods manufacturing companies indigenous to Merseyside. The Aircraft and Shipbuilding Industries Act, 1977, effectively nationalised all but one of Britain's shipbuilding companies, placing Cammell Laird under the umbrella of the British Shipbuilders' Corporation.

Prior to nationalisation, Cammell Laird, like most shipbuilders, was heavily dependent on government subsidies. The government often supplied funding, but in return it demanded rationalisation programmes as a measure of security for public investment. Whitehall administered this control through the Industrial Reorganisation Commission (IRC). By 1983, after only six years, Britain's nationalised shipbuilding industry was coming to an end. The move to privatise shipbuilding had gained ground, and by 1983, a bill was introduced which allowed the government to disinvest its assets in that industry on a piecemeal basis. MPs representing shipbuilding constituencies throughout Britain lobbied the government to spare their local yards from disinvestment.

In February 1984, Labour MP for Birkenhead, Frank Field, reminded the government during a Commons debate about the precarious employment situation in Merseyside, and that closure of Cammell Laird's would have grave effects on an already dying local economy:

> I wish to remind the House of the sufferings endured by Birkenhead. In the first two years of the Government's life we lost 1,800 jobs. That was bad enough for a town which already had high unemployment, but since then job losses have speeded up until they are now out of control. The latest figures which the Government can give are for the mid-point of 1983.

> If we take the period from 1979 to 1983, we find that there have been more than 20,000 job losses in the Birkenhead area ... In many streets in Birkenhead, unemployment is now well over 40 per cent.[12]

Workers at Cammell Laird's detected rumours that their shipyard was one of several earmarked by the government for closure. Nevertheless, others were more optimistic because of the company's numerous national defence contracts. There were divisions within the workforce, and this difference in outlook manifested itself in a number of ways as this situation developed.

Lol Duffy, who worked as a plater at the shipyard, served as a GMB shop steward and was an active participant in the eventual occupation at Cammell Laird's, recalled what some people were thinking in the spring of 1984:

> There was a fairly strong, sort of right-wing element within the workforce there that thought a closure would never happen. They thought that the government wouldn't let the yards close down. They thought that the Tories would keep us – you know, because we built Navy ships and all the rest of it, and they just wouldn't let the place shut.[13]

Meanwhile, the press reported the loss of two important contracts for the Birkenhead shipbuilder:

> British shipbuilding and offshore construction yards face a new threat to lost business with the decision by Sun Oil, the American oil company, to place a £125 million order for a revolutionary North Sea oil production vessel overseas. The company and its partners in the Balmoral field development met on Monday and reaffirmed their decision to place the order overseas ... The Cammell Laird yard at Birkenhead, which is also part of British Shipbuilders, was among those that hoped to win the order.[14]

A month later there was further disappointing news: 'The future of British Shipbuilders' Cammell Laird yard at Birkenhead looked bleaker last night after a £30 million Royal Navy order to convert a ferry into a helicopter training ship went to Harland & Wolff of Belfast. It leaves the Merseyside yard desperately short of orders.'[15]

On 15 May 1984, citing a lack of orders, company officials announced that half the yard's workforce of 3,300 would face compulsory redundancies. Approximately 100 Cammell Laird workers had been placed on indefinite furlough earlier that year. In response to compulsory redundancies, a number of the shipyard workers launched a strike in late June of 1984. Pickets were set up, barricading the two vessels currently being built in the yard. One of the activists, Billy Albertina, a GMB shop steward and chair of the occupation committee, recalled:

> The redundancies had been going on for a couple of months. We refused to accept the redundancies. The stagers decided to fight against any further redundancies ... We found out that management had plans to move the two vessels, that were being built in the yard at the time, to France during that summer holiday period. And those of us that were against the redundancies, we got together and decided we could not let the vessels leave the yard. Hence, the occupation, or at least the start of it ... Now every other union there and every other department within the shipyard accepted the redundancies.[16]

The physical occupation of the two vessels being constructed occurred almost immediately after the strike was launched. Eddie Marnell, a former shipwright at Cammell Laird, remembered that the decision to occupy came about because:

> We originally just had a picket line, but management abused that situation. We found out they were getting people on board the destroyer and the gas rig and were doing work. So we then said look, we got to use occupation – which had been used numerous times in the past in all kinds of industrial disputes. So we retreated onto the rig ... and barricaded ourselves in so that it was impregnable. We just maintained a picket line on the Type 42 destroyer, for obvious reasons involving national security and avoiding any potential conflicts with the Navy.[17]

Additional indefinite lay-offs were announced on 28 June 1984, the day after these workers initiated industrial action. The *Liverpool Echo* reported:

> Seven-hundred Cammell Laird workers were being laid off today following a shipyard blockade by boilermakers ... Last week a further 800 workers were given 90 days' notice, bringing the total of redundancies announced this year to 1600 – nearly half the Birkenhead workforce ... The 50 boilermakers are refusing to allow a gas rig to move from the yard for completion in France. They also threaten to block *H.M.S. Edinburgh* leaving for sea trials on July 7.[18]

The *Guardian* summed up the situation:

> The 130 mostly young men preventing two vessels from leaving the ailing Cammell Laird shipyards, Birkenhead, see themselves as part of a national upsurge by working men and women in defence of their jobs. 'It's this or

the dole – and once you're on the dole on Merseyside the odds are you are there for life', says Mr. Billy Albertina, chairman of the occupation committee and one of the 1,600 workers being shed by the firm this year. They have been occupying an accommodation rig and a destroyer, the last two orders in the yard, for the past three weeks and say that they will remain until the company ends its policy of compulsory redundancies. Another 400 notices were issued last week, trimming the workforce to 1700.[19]

It is important to note that there was only a small element within the entire Cammell Laird workforce at the Birkenhead facility prepared to protest against the forced redundancies. Lol Duffy, who was not employed as a stager, but someone who took an active role in the occupation, recalled that national union officials had on a previous occasion fully endorsed any decision by their members to take industrial action in the event of compulsory redundancies:

> There was a national policy that had been set a couple years before, which basically said if there were any enforced redundancies, then the shipbuilding negotiating committee of the Confederation of Shipbuilding and Engineering Unions (CSEU) – which is an umbrella organisation representing all the trade unions involved in shipbuilding, that a strike would automatically get their support. This came about around the time Thatcher came into power, because we knew she was going to get the shipyards privatised, so there would be a lot of forced redundancies. So that was the basis set to let us know we could actually do something about it ... But what we did know was we had a frigate sitting in there and a gas accommodation rig. And we knew once they had gone out, we'd have nothing to bargain with.[20]

British Shipbuilders offered the Cammell Laird workers a monetary settlement if they would accept permanent redundancy. The figures varied according to seniority and pay grade, but Duffy recalled:

> They offered the usual rate for redundancy payments going around at that time, nothing more. They offered a week's pay for every year of service, or a week and a half if you were over the age of forty-nine. And they offered a financial inducement of something like twelve weeks' pay on top of that as well ... It wasn't enough to tempt many people out, but some still took it.[21]

According to Albertina: 'The average redundancy payment offered to my department was around £2,000.'[22] A former employee who was not in the Staging Department, but was relatively junior in seniority recalled: 'I remember finishing out with about £4,000 in redundancy money, but that wasn't that much even then. It got you through a couple months, but that was it.'[23] Nevertheless, pay-outs increased dramatically with age and years of service: 'So the stagers [scaffolders] decided to stand and fight … even though craftsmen in other unions were taking the redundancy money, said to be about £3000 to £4000 for a young man, rising to about £10,000 for long-service men.'[24]

The divisions amongst the workforce over acceptance of the redundancies displayed clear generational and occupational boundaries. Younger workers, dismissive of the relatively meagre amount of money offered in return for their jobs, were mindful of the dismal local economic conditions. They were fearful of never finding work again, at least at the rate of pay they were earning in the shipyard. Older employees saw the package offered to them as generous. They perceived the redundancies more as an opportunity for early retirement, rather than a long desperate life of dole dependency. Albertina, the sit-in leader, commented on this age gap within the workforce:

> The reason being why so many of the stagers didn't accept redundancies and the others did was because it was a very old workforce there. Most of the workers at Cammell Laird's were skilled and between the fifty-five and sixty-five age mark. So because they were near retirement they accepted the redundancies – as a matter of fact they wanted the redundancies. Now the Staging Department, because of the nature of the work – it was the most dangerous job in the yard … the average age of the stagers, I'd say was twenty-two. Not many were over forty. So we knew if we were thrown out of work, we'd have a long time ahead of us being unemployed because of the [local economic] situation … Because of this, it was mainly stagers who decided to fight against the redundancies … And we were told by the management that if we took action we would lose all redundancy payments … [But] we weren't having redundancies forced on us. Their departments might have voted in favour, but we didn't.[25]

Marnell similarly remembered many of the stagers were younger than the rest of the workforce:

> The problem was that most of the people who went out on strike, and subsequently went to jail, were from that one department [Staging] and it was a young department … There were very few skilled tradesmen involved in that sit-in. There were only a handful of us. I was, in fact, the only shipwright. There were one or two platers, but the vast majority were stagers.[26]

There were occupational antagonisms present, as is often the case in shipbuilding. Duffy, a skilled tradesman, summarised the situation:

> There's always been this thing in the shipyards where the skilled trades had to play off the unskilled trades. Like mine or Eddie's [Marnell] trades [plater and shipwright, respectively] were considered elite trades. And then you had the lads in like Billy's [Albertina] section, the stagers, which were considered unskilled. And so there were all these really old antagonisms ... But in shipbuilding especially, it's difficult to bridge solidarity, so when redundancies come down, basically, most people don't care, so long as it affects somebody else ... Most of us in my department thought the stagers and the other unskilled guys would never work again. So the few of us who were sympathetic to their view could see why they felt it was important that we all put up a fight and refuse the redundancies ... I mean we felt we were fighting for future generations as well, but other people were just trying to sell their jobs. And others voted for the redundancies, thinking the redundancies wouldn't affect them personally. So they were agreeing to lay-off a thousand people, thinking it would only be the stagers and the production people, but their jobs would remain safe.[27]

Albertina reflected further on the idea of craft consciousness, and how it affected the situation at Cammell Laird's:

> We [the stagers] were one department, and we were all members of the boilermakers' union [the GMB] even though we weren't skilled. In our department we had anywhere from 80 to 120 men. But what you got to understand in a shipyard there are thousands of craftsmen – by far the majority of the workforce is skilled, which isn't like most factories. Now, because of the craft consciousness, they looked down on the labourers. So besides the stagers, you had mates to tradesmen which were also unskilled ... I mean for years they [the skilled tradesmen] thought they could treat you like a lackey.[28]

This occupational elitism also brought about a high incidence of job demarcation within most shipyards, as each trade competed with one another for job security. An anonymous Cammell Laird employee stated:

> I mean shipyards are loaded with it anyway [job demarcation], and Cammell Laird's was rife with it. It was laughable. There'd be a strike over if somebody did somebody else's job. You know, like only somebody from this union can hold the chalk line, and only somebody from that union can pull the chalk line, and all this carry-on ... I mean in that place I can count out right now at least six trade unions just involved in production alone ... And you had all the little fiefdoms and union officials, and all their carry-on.[29]

This feeling of occupational superiority fuelled an enormous degree of workplace sectionalism. Duffy commented:

> You got to understand, shipyards are different. There's never been a history of solidarity in those places. Now, on the other hand, if you take the dockers, they have a long tradition of sticking together. They fought things in the past and they *won* things in the past as well by sticking together. That's not the case in the shipyards. In the shipyards you got long histories of unions fighting other unions. If ever there was an event where one union thought they were losing out to another one, there'd be a dispute ... Plus, most people are skilled, so you have this old-fashioned thing where everybody thought they were special. You know, 'My craft is special. How could you ever do without my trade'?[30]

It was against this divisive tradition that members of the Staging Department decided to fight against the redundancies and occupy the shipyards. The majority of the workforce voted in favour of accepting the redundancy payments, while approximately one hundred workers, most of who were employed in the Staging Department, refused and called a strike. The sit-in committee cited that this was a lawful strike since Confederation of Shipbuilding and Engineering Unions (CSEU) officials, several months earlier, had claimed they would support any industrial action by a shipyard or individual department in response to forced redundancies. Duffy recalled:

> We had a mass meeting inside the yard, in which it was decided not to fight the redundancies. So a lot of the stagers, and some of the younger lads in other departments like me, who sympathised with them, said, 'Hang on, you can't vote for other people's redundancies'. So we said, 'Let the sections who are facing the redundancies have a vote and let them decide what they want to do'. So the likes of the stagers voted to strike, and once they occupied the gas rig, they appealed to other departments within the yard to support them.[31]

From the outset of this industrial action, management appeared to have had a plan that would counter any resistance, as one of the strike leaders, Eddie Marnell, recounted:

> I'd say close to 800 or 1,000 took the money. Originally there were over a hundred out on strike with us, but the threats [from management] were coming down hard. Where people were supporting the strike, management posted out letters saying that if they didn't come off the strike they'd be sacked immediately. That would mean they'd [the strikers] be guilty of

> gross misconduct, which meant they wouldn't be entitled to any redundancy money. This, obviously, scared off a lot of people. So our numbers went down to about forty-five then.[32]

It became apparent after only a few weeks of occupation that the scant solidarity there was for the sit-in strike began to wane. Albertina described the change in attitudes:

> At first, when we started we had support all throughout the yard. What happened was, when we first went out on strike, the rest of the yard said, 'Well that's up to you. If you lads [stagers] want to fight it [redundancy] that's fine, but we're not going to fight it.' Well, the problems eventually came because, since we were occupying the vessels that meant the men couldn't work on them, so the firm eventually laid them off. It wasn't till they laid them off, is when we got that reaction. Now, at that time the Miners' Strike was going on. And during the mining strike a number of these Back to Work Committees were formed; well, the same thing happened in our shipyard. A number of men got together at Laird's and formed a Back to Work Committee. We do know now that these committees were all Tory funded. Now, this committee at Laird's was secretly connected to a Tory Party group on the Wirral who supplied them with finances.[33]

Marnell claimed any attempt at persuading the break-away group of the importance of maintaining solidarity with the striking stagers was futile:

> The Back to Work Committee was led by a group of right-wing stewards whose jobs were safe, so they weren't worried about anybody else ... We tried explaining the situation to them. The handwriting was on the wall. They said the place would never shut down. We said, 'look, when you have a shipyard with a total of 1200 employees and out of that only 200 are manual workers, the rest are white collar staff, it no longer is a viable situation' ... So there wasn't going to be a yard there anymore.[34]

As is so frequently the case with factory closures, redundant workers often feel powerless against the enormous forces of capital or government, and these same feelings of desperation and hopelessness applied to many of the employees of Cammell Laird during this period. A number of the sit-in's leaders recalled a pervasive, fatalistic attitude amongst many of the workers who took the redundancy money. A clear example of this pessimism can be seen in the sentiments of one worker who voluntarily took the redundancy money. Complaining about the sit-in strikers, he recounted:

> Most of the support they got was from people outside [Cammell Laird] who didn't know what was going on inside that place ... Margaret

> Thatcher just had that yard earmarked for closure. There was nothing they could have done to prevent that. Her and Norman Lamont had it in for that place ... And I'll tell you what, a lot of people are glad that place shut. I mean it really was a twat of a place to work. It was. It was filthy. It was freezing in the fuckin' winter. And it was unsafe as well.[35]

Other observers felt that many of the workers at Laird's didn't necessarily accept that the yard would close outright, but that only certain sections would be eliminated. Some workers believed that the demise of other sections in the shipyard meant that their own jobs would be saved. It was by this logic that some even supported the company's rationalisation plans. This sectional attitude prompted Duffy to comment:

> The Back to Work Committee was led by a guy called Harry Ewers. It was more or less based on self-interest. Harry claimed he was assured by people in the Thatcher government the yard would remain open. And there was also a lot of fatalism. A lot of people just felt any action on their part couldn't win anything.[36]

In an attempt to end the occupation, the leaders of Laird's Back to Work Committee summoned all those who were laid off to a meeting. They confronted the striking workers and demanded a shipyard-wide vote to determine if *all* the workers at Laird's officially supported the sit-in strike. A local newspaper reported:

> A back to work move took a step forward at Cammell Laird today. More than 500 workers at the Birkenhead shipyard turned up at an unofficial meeting organised by the rebels. A large majority voted in favour of petitioning union officials to call a meeting to find out whether most of the 1,700 workforce supported the sit-in on the *H.M.S. Edinburgh* and a gas rig ... Harry Ewers, a boilermaker and a leader of the back to work committee, was cheered when he told Mr. Albertina and the sit-in protesters: 'If you want to fight for jobs, get off the gangways and you will help 1,700 to have jobs'. He said pickets on the gangways of the two vessels were prejudicing chances for future work for the yard. Mr. Ewers said: 'We have got to get work in this yard and the only way is by returning to a working situation'. The sit-ins have resulted in more than 1,000 being laid off.[37]

Ewers further explained the position of the Back to Work Committee: 'We felt that we had to seek the views of all hourly-paid workers and staff ... We believe that the union officials have heard only one side of the story so far, that of the stagers.'[38]

Ewers and his fellow committee members were denied a shipyard-wide vote. The *Guardian* reported:

> Leaders of a back-to-work committee at Cammell Laird, Birkenhead, failed yesterday to win the support of the unions' joint body, Confed [CSEU], in their attempt to end the sit-in by 120 stagers which has halted work at the shipyard for the past seven weeks. District officials of Confed told the committee that while they understood the genuine concern over the yard's future, they were constitutionally barred from interfering in the affairs of an affiliated union. And they pointed out that the stagers' sit-in on the only remaining orders at the yard, an accommodation rig and a destroyer, was in line with Confed national policy opposing enforced redundancies. In the past year the yard has cut its workforce from 3,300 to 1,700, of whom 1,200 have been laid off by the sit-in.[39]

Despite official backing from their national union offices and the favourable decision from the CSEU, some of the strikers and their supporters felt union leaders in London should have taken a harder line against the Back to Work Committee:

> Nobody from our union or any of the others there got involved with trying to discipline these Back to Work Committees in any way. These were the ones who were going against a legitimate job action. But as you can imagine, the mandate from the union was, 'We fight redundancies'. Yet no one took them on; they let them get on with it.[40]

This lack of action on the part of the national union illustrated the schism that still existed between union leaders and local shop-floor militants. Marnell remembered the difference in working relationships the strikers enjoyed between the GMB's London leadership and the union's local Merseyside official:

> Our relationship with the local union leader [Barry Williams] was brilliant. Nationally: not very good ... Barry Williams was the local GMB official right throughout the strike. He supported us 100 per cent ... I mean the [national] union did support us in such a way that we were given strike pay, but in my belief that's all they did for us ... All of us on that strike were members of the same union, the GMB.[41]

Duffy echoed these sentiments:

> The national union didn't want to support us at all. Anything they did do, they were forced into it. Barry Williams, on the other hand, was behind us ... a Communist Party guy, he did a good job of getting it [the strikers' request for official union sanction] in and passed through as official – very quickly, very efficiently, and very much in line with policy. But the national officials were trying to hide behind the fact that the majority of

> the shipyard didn't want to do it. I mean, in a sense, you can understand it, but they never gave any solidarity to us. I mean we were forever dealing with negotiating committees who were, shall I say, very understanding of management's point of view.[42]

Albertina remembered that if it had not been for the active role played by local union officials in fostering public support and trade union solidarity, their sit-in would not have happened:

> Now thankfully, at least locally we had someone like Barry Williams from the union. He was not only the boilermakers' union [GMB] full time official here locally, but he was also President of the Liverpool Trades Council. He was a very influential man. He was also very active in our strike all the way through, as getting as many unions outside the shipyard involved – which was very successful. I mean we may not have had much support from the people working with us at Laird's, but we had tremendous support from the unions outside the yard in the form of sympathy strikes, the manning of picket lines, monetary support ... Nearly every union and branch in Liverpool supported us and donated money in order to keep the strike going. The support from the outside was just fantastic. I'd say all of this overwhelming support came largely through the efforts of Barry Williams.[43]

The miners were involved in their national strike at the same time as the Cammell Laird sit-in was taking place, and both disputes reflected the industrial turbulence of the day. These protests allowed both groups to demonstrate mutual solidarity with their respective campaigns: 'About 200 striking miners picketed the Cammell Laird shipbuilders at Birkenhead yesterday to support workers occupying the yard in protest of job losses.'[44] Albertina remembered that such gestures of solidarity were important in sustaining each other's cause:

> There was a lot of solidarity between us and the miners, especially. I spoke at some of their meetings in mining villages, and some of their lads came here and spoke to our lads. They helped man picket lines at Laird's and gave us tremendous support, so there was a lot of intermingling.[45]

The political consciousness of the sit-in's leaders was developed in the atmosphere of the day. According to Duffy, 'We all had been campaigners in our individual pasts. We were already politicised. Billy [Albertina] was a member of the Communist Party; I was active in Labour Party politics'.[46] Billy Albertina affirmed that he had also been highly politicised prior to his involvement in the sit-in:

> I was a member of the Communist Party ... I was very involved with the Communist Party, so I had been very political prior to this ... I was on the Commune, which is the Communist Party main committee ... I was always very active in the trade union movement. I was a shop steward for the GMB. I was on a couple committees – one national committee. I was also a member of the Liverpool Trades (Union) Council, which was the voice of all the unions on Merseyside.

Their previous political experiences made the sit-in strikers acutely aware of the elements necessary to sustain a successful industrial action:

> The only way you win these things is through solidarity action. You don't win them with food parcels. You don't win them with the public's sympathy. You certainly appreciate the good intentions from others; however, the only way you can beat these things is by way of strike action from other unions ... If there's one thing the trade union movement could learn from our experience is that if all unions work together and show solidarity to one another, you can win anything.[47]

Albertina reiterated these sentiments:

> I gave a press interview once during our strike, and I predicted what would happen. And as it all eventually played out, I was spot on. I said if they allow us, a young department, to lose our jobs none of us would ever work again. I also said if they allow us to go then this place will close. And I knew the government was keeping a special eye on our situation. They wanted to wash their hands of shipbuilding, so I said, 'If Cammell Laird is allowed to close then so to eventually will every British shipyard right, front and centre'. And in the end, that's exactly what happened ... So we did have a sense of class consciousness. We knew this was a working-class fight against a Tory government. We knew the political implications behind it, because it was well known that Thatcher wanted to take the unions on, which she already had done. But we did strike back.[48]

Despite assurances from both company officials and politicians that Cammell Laird's was safe from closure, the sit-in's leaders believed that their shipyard was in line to be privatised. They did not trust government promises that shipyards engaged in defence contracting would not be sold off. The sit-in leaders argued that it was only a matter of time before *all* British Shipbuilders' yards were privatised – defence contractors or not. In a newspaper interview from 1984, Albertina predicted the government aimed to break up British Shipbuilders, selling it to private enterprise, and reducing the whole industry to three yards:

> We are one of the most modern yards in British Shipbuilders – a nice plum for some group to get cheaply. We see the yards like ours, being picked off for the private market, workforces slashed, then the yards reopened with much of the work sub-contracted ... When the whole industry was in private hands, the best three could be selected and the rest sent to the wall.[49]

At least part of Albertina's prediction came to fruition while he and his fellow strikers were occupying Cammell Laird's. *The Times* reported during that summer:

> The Government has decided that shipbuilders should sell its warship building interests, Mr. Norman Tebbit, Secretary of State for Trade and Industry, said in a statement in the Commons. There was a strong Opposition protest at his announcement. Mr. Tebbit said the Government wanted BS to make substantial progress toward privatization of warship building by March 31, 1985 and to complete the process by March 31, 1986. He said that the Corporation accounts for 1983–84 showed a trading loss of £161 million ... 'Accordingly, I [Tebbit] have asked the Corporation to set in hand action to dispose of those parts of the Corporation engaged mainly or wholly in warship building' ... The two yards engaged mainly in warship building are Cammell Laird at Birkenhead and Swan Hunter on Tyneside.[50]

Tebbit's announcement came as a surprise to many of those who were not supportive of the occupation, but it appeared to have only strengthened the resolve of the sit-in strikers. Many of the latter recognised the need for greater political support for their cause. It was also at this time that LCC had shifted sharply to the left, and despite the Birkenhead strikers being outside LCC's jurisdiction, Liverpool's Militant Labour controlled city council gave the sit-in strike at Laird's its full support:

> Locally, Liverpool City Council helped people who had council housing and were late with rents ... The council was under the Militant Tendency at the time and they supported us wholeheartedly ... In fact, Liverpool City Council installed a plaque in the Town Hall dedicated to us and our efforts. It's still there today ... Unlike Derek Hatton and Eric Heffer, the right-wing branch of the local Labour Party weren't as supportive. Frank Field and Peter Kilfoyle just didn't want to know us. Now, Peter Kilfoyle was the MP for Walton, which was where the majority of the people jailed [after the occupation] were his constituents. I'd say most of the stagers were all Scotland Road lads.[51]

LCC leaders appealed to their employees for support of the striking workers at Cammell Laird's:

> Liverpool City Council's 30,000 workers have been urged to join the mass picket outside Cammell Laird's Birkenhead shipyard on Monday morning ... And the plea for action comes from their own Labour bosses, who have pledged no-one will be punished if they arrive at work late [that day] ... City councillor and Liverpool district Labour party president Tony Mulhearn said: 'Young men fighting to save their jobs are being threatened with imprisonment by one of Mrs. Thatcher's judges' ... Personnel Committee chairman Councillor Derek Hatton assured Councillor Pam Bradley (Liberal) that workers who chose not to take part in the picket would not face retribution from Labour.[52]

Albertina reflected:

> You see, politics at that time was really split down the middle. You were either right-wing or left-wing. There was no room for any middle ground in those days. It was the same thing in our union. There was a right-wing, who was in charge of the national offices at the time, and there was a left-wing like Barry Williams and us. Now this was also the same thing in local Labour Party politics. You had right-wingers in the Labour Party like Frank Field, who was the MP for the area where Cammell Laird's was located ... His feeling about Laird's was it's going to happen no matter what kind of fight we put up, so just let it close. On the other end of the Labour Party, you had Liverpool left-wing MPs like [Eric] Heffer and [Eddie] Loyden [Labour – Liverpool Garston], and they gave us fantastic support. They'd show up on our picket lines, visit us when they put us in jail. Now, nationally, probably because of the image of Liverpool, Kinnock and that crowd, they just refused to get involved in our situation.[53]

In spite of the growing support the strikers were gaining from trade unions, the public, LCC and Merseyside County Council, company officials at Cammell Laird decided it was time to put an end to the summer-long occupation. On 23 August 1984, the approximately 100 workers who did not accept redundancy cheques were dismissed for industrial misconduct, ultimately meaning they were no longer eligible for redundancy payments.[54] It also exposed them to the criminal charge of trespassing on company property. Managers were preparing a legal case for the forced removal of the occupiers: 'Management told workers occupying a destroyer and a gas rig that they would be trespassing unless they left by 4.30 p.m. today. But the workers voted unanimously to stay until redundancy notices were lifted.'[55] Cammell Laird management had secured from Manchester Crown Court an injunction ordering them to leave the rig and company property, or they would be charged with Criminal Trespass and Contempt of Court.

Realising that the pressure had been raised to a higher level, and that the strikers would now have to barricade themselves in order to avoid arrest, Albertina warned managers: 'We have plenty of food supplies on board and we have barricaded ourselves in for a long struggle.'[56] He later reflected on this period:

> Eventually they went to court and got a court order, which said if we didn't vacate the rig and leave the yard by midnight of such and such a date we were going to prison for Contempt of Court. If we didn't, anyone caught by police would be arrested and taken directly to prison. It was after that we knew we had to keep inside the rig and not leave it for anything. That's when all the barbed wire and police dogs showed up. There were also loads more police at the gates watching us then too. There was no more coming and going and working it in shifts after this.[57]

The thirty-seven men who chose to continue on with the occupation at Laird's were now subject to arrest. They had been tried in absentia in Manchester Crown Court. A local newspaper reported:

> One of the leaders of the occupation, Mr. Lol Duffy, said the men would continue to defy the court order and not recognise its decision. After hearing that police and court officials had feared for their lives if they attempted to use force to end the sit-in, Mr. Justice Glidewell said the men must end their action by midnight on Sunday or go to prison. Mr. Justice Glidewell was presiding at Manchester Crown Court when he was asked by Laird's management to jail former workers for contempt. The judge agreed with Mr. Charles James, barrister representing Cammell Laird's, that the 40 (*sic*) men had deliberately disobeyed the previous orders ... Mr. Justice Glidewell said if the defendants had felt they had been unfairly dismissed, they could have complained to an industrial tribunal. But they had taken no such action.[58]

Soon after the court order to vacate the premises was issued, a different tone emerged from national GMB officers and CSEU:

> Shipyard union leaders could shortly urge workers to end their 13-week occupation of two vessels at the Cammell Laird shipyards at Birkenhead, following a legal ruling two days ago. The executive of the Confederation of Shipbuilding and Engineering Unions decided yesterday to arrange a special meeting of a national shipyard committee next week to discuss the crisis. Mr. Alex Ferry, the CSEU general secretary, stressed that there had been no disapproval of the men's action in support of jobs. But he made clear that the confederation was unlikely to support action 'clearly in defiance of the law'.[59]

Despite the reticence from the strikers' union, a growing number of miners and other supporters had been forming a picket line for several weeks outside Cammell Laird's gates. On 1 October 1984, sit-in spokesman Lol Duffy and eleven fellow strikers took a chance and left the relative safety of the rig in order to address the throng of supporters gathering at the front gates. Unfortunately for Duffy and the eleven others, this gamble did not pay off, as the police were also there and this move led to their arrest:

> At the main gate supporters set up camp for a round-the-clock picket … About 250 people, including groups from other shipyards, London and local pits responded to a call for a mass picket at the yard … twelve of the striking workers were arrested after they left the gas rig to mount the picket line.[60]

The local press reported: 'The men were trapped in a well-planned police manoeuvre as they tried to dash from the picket line to the accommodation rig.'[61]

Finally, on 3 October 1984, Merseyside Police scaled the accommodation rig with specialised climbing equipment. They confronted Albertina and the remaining sit-in strikers and placed them under arrest without incident. Marnell subsequently remembered the siege of the gas rig:

> Suddenly, one day these people appeared all dressed in black and they started erecting their own staging that we couldn't get to. I don't think they were police, but they were sure connected to the government some way. So we knew something was going on. And out of nowhere this guy appears in front of us looking like he just stepped out of a James Bond film. I mean, he looked like Bobby Charlton dressed in a fancy suit. He said he had orders to take these vessels today. And then he said in taking these vessels that there was a chance some of his men may die. And if that's the case, so might some of yours. So I turned to Billy and said, 'This is getting a bit heavy. I mean, we'll fight for our jobs, but we won't die for them'. So we had a quick meeting amongst ourselves … It was decided then that we had to walk off. There wasn't much choice by that time. We all were told to walk off, one by one, where we were handcuffed … and then driven to Walton Jail, where we were put in a high security wing … They put us on the same wing as mass murderers, drug dealers – the worst … While there we were locked up for twenty-three out of twenty-four hours a day for a total sentence of twenty-eight days.[62]

Marnell reflected much of the bitterness still felt to this day by many of the participants in the sit-in strike at Cammell Laird's:

> We were tried in our absence in Manchester Crown Court ... The only time we were ever allowed legal representation was when we went before a tribunal over our redundancy pay. And the GMB supplied us with a legal officer who was just a young lad ... And to be honest with you, I could have done a better job than what this kid did.[63]

Echoing his former colleague, Albertina observed of the strike and its aftermath:

> The biggest injustice over that whole thing was, number one, jailing us just for fighting for our jobs. The second injustice was them taking our redundancy payments away. I mean, they took our jobs, they took our money, and then they jailed us. And all we did was just follow union mandates ... And I can't tell you how many times over the years I've run into these same people who thought their jobs were safe and opposed us, who now tell me after Laird's shut, 'Oh you were right Billy, you were right'.[64]

Cammell Laird was eventually privatised in 1986 after its sale by British Shipbuilders to Vickers Shipbuilding and Engineering Limited (VSEL). By 1993, the facility was no longer used for shipbuilding, having focused its business instead on maritime maintenance and conversions. The yard was eventually closed for business in 2001.

Reflections of occupations on Merseyside

Factory occupations and sit-in strikes, while arriving comparatively late in Britain, eventually flourished as a form of industrial action in the turbulent 1970s and 1980s. The use of this tactic went on to become especially prevalent on Merseyside. This particular case at Laird's was in many ways emblematic of the local population's acute awareness of the negative impact associated with industrial closure and the devastating effects factory shutdowns were having on their communities.

The sit-in at Cammell Laird shipyards in 1984 has been analysed in depth because it was one of the longest recorded workplace occupations on Merseyside. This case study showed that some workers there were so desperate to keep jobs in a region where unemployment was rife that they were willing to risk arrest and imprisonment. Unfortunately, this protest demonstrated that the thirty-seven men who held out to the bitter end of this dispute did not share the same solidarity and comradeship with their co-workers as the UCS in 1971–72. Arguably this was so because in the case at UCS, the workers were told that the closure of their workplaces was certain, and that *everyone* employed at this facility would be made permanently redundant. All of their jobs were under threat. Desperation, therefore, constructed solidarity, and it healed the past wounds of inter-union conflict and sectionalism at places like Upper Clydeside.

Yet there is arguably a degree of justification regarding the stance taken by those who opposed the sit-in at Cammell Laird's. Considering that the shipyard remained a viable business – despite privatisation – for nine years after the strike, this action by the stagers may be judged premature. At least some of the men from the Staging Department would have been kept on the payroll during this transition. However, despite lingering on for a number of years, Laird's did eventually close its gates forever. Billy Albertina's prediction came true, albeit not as swiftly as he and his fellow strikers initially believed.

This particular factory occupation at Cammell Laird's also demonstrated that the tactic of the sit-in strike was now facing increasing challenges from both capital and government. British courts and management adopted new approaches to counteract the tactic's effectiveness. Nevertheless, this particular sit-in strike will be recorded in labour history as one of the last incidents of an organised, large-scale workplace occupation. Like the national miners' strike that was occurring simultaneously, the defeat of the Cammell Laird occupation signalled the close of an era. The days of powerful shop stewards and wildcat strikes had come to an end, even in Liverpool. However, trade union militancy had not been killed off completely on Merseyside, and new tactics were devised to adapt to the changing times, as will be explored in the following chapter.

Notes

1 Gregor Gall, 'Resisting Recession and Redundancy: Contemporary Worker Occupations in Britain', *Working USA – The Journal of Labor and Society*, vol. 13, no. 1 (March 2010), pp. 110, 120–1.

2 J. A. Mills, 'Worker Occupations, 1971–1975: A Socio-Historical Analysis of the Development and Spread of Sit-Ins Work-Ins and Worker Cooperatives in Britain', PhD thesis, Department of Sociology, University of Durham, England, 1982, pp. 17–18.

3 Ken Coates, *Work-Ins, Sit-Ins and Industrial Democracy: The Implications of Factory Occupations in Great Britain in the Early 'Seventies* (Nottingham, 1981), pp. 27–9. See also: Richard Hyman, 'Workers' Control and Revolutionary Theory', in Ralph Miliband and John Saville, eds, *The Socialist Register, 1974* (London, 1974).

4 John E. Kelly, *Rethinking Industrial Relations: Mobilisation, Collectivism, and Long Waves* (London, 1998), pp. 24–6, 34. See also: Gall, 'Resisting Recession', pp. 108, 111, 116–18; Mills, 'Worker Occupations', p. 17.
5 Andrée Hoyles, 'The Occupation of Factories in France: May 1968', in Ken Coates, Tony Topham and Michael Barrat Brown, eds, *Trade Union Register, 1969* (London, 1969), p. 288. See also: J. Greenwood, *Worker Sit-in and Job Protection* (Farnborough, 1977), pp. 29–33.
6 Sidney Fine, *Sit-Down: The General Motors Strike of 1936–1937* (Ann Arbor, 1970); see also: Dave Sherry, *Occupy! A Short History of Workers' Occupations* (London, 2010), pp. 75–81.
7 Sherry, *Occupy!*, pp. 95–112. See also: John Gretton, *Students and Workers: An Analytical Account of Dissent in France, May–June 1968* (London, 1969); Alain Touraine, *The May Movement: Revolt and Reform: May 1968, the Student Rebellion and Workers' Strikes, the Birth of a Social Movement* (New York and Toronto, 1971).
8 Alan Tuckman, 'Occupation, Worker Co-Operatives and the Struggle for Power: Britain in the 1970s', unpublished paper at the 28th International Labor Process Conference at Rutgers University, New Jersey, March 2010.
9 John Foster and Charles Woolfson, *The Politics of the UCS Work-In* (London, 1986), p. 172.
10 Bruce Spencer, 'The Case for Workers' Take-Over: GEC and UCS', *Political Quarterly*, vol. 43, no. 4 (24 August 2005), p. 433. See also: Willie Thompson and Finlay Hart, *The UCS Work-In* (London, 1972), p. 80.
11 Spencer, 'Case', p. 436.
12 Hansard, House of Commons, 23 February, 1983, vol. 37, cc. 994–6.
13 Interview with Lol Duffy.
14 *The Times*, 22 February 1984.
15 *The Times*, 3 March 1984.
16 Interview with Billy Albertina. A 'stager' is a shipyard term meaning a scaffolder – a builder of scaffolds used during the construction of a ship. They were sometimes incorrectly referred to within contemporary news reports as 'boilermakers'. This occurred because they were members of the boilermakers' union although not engaged in that trade.
17 Interview with Eddie Marnell.
18 *Liverpool Echo*, 28 June 1984.
19 *Guardian*, 23 July 1984.
20 Interview with Lol Duffy.
21 Interview with Lol Duffy.
22 Interview with Billy Albertina.
23 Interview with an anonymous Cammell Laird employee.
24 *Guardian*, 23 July 1984.
25 Interview with Billy Albertina.
26 Interview with Eddie Marnell.
27 Interview with Lol Duffy.
28 Interview with Billy Albertina.

29 Interview with an anonymous former Cammell Laird employee.
30 Interview with Lol Duffy.
31 Interview with Lol Duffy.
32 Interview with Eddie Marnell.
33 Interview with Billy Albertina.
34 Interview with Eddie Marnell.
35 Interview with an anonymous Cammell Laird worker.
36 Interview with Lol Duffy.
37 *Liverpool Echo*, 13 August 1984.
38 *Guardian*, 14 August 1984.
39 *Guardian*, 16 August 1984
40 Interview with Billy Albertina.
41 Interview with Eddie Marnell.
42 Interview with Lol Duffy.
43 Interview with Billy Albertina.
44 *Guardian*, 7 September 1984.
45 Interview with Billy Albertina.
46 Interview with Lol Duffy.
47 Interview with Lol Duffy.
48 Interview with Billy Albertina.
49 *Guardian*, 23 July 1984.
50 *The Times*, 26 July 1984.
51 Interview with Eddie Marnell. Some members of LCC attempted to bestow on the thirty-seven sit-in strikers the distinction of Freemen of Liverpool. The motion was narrowly lost in a council vote: *The Times*, 10 and 11 October 1984.
52 *Liverpool Echo*, 28 September 1984.
53 Interview with Billy Albertina.
54 *The Times*, 24 August 1984.
55 *Guardian*, 23 August, 1984.
56 *Guardian*, 23 August, 1984.
57 Interview with Billy Albertina.
58 *Liverpool Echo*, 26 September 1984.
59 *Guardian*, 28 September 1984.
60 *Guardian*, 2 October 1984.
61 *Liverpool Echo*, 1 October 1984.
62 Interview with Eddie Marnell.
63 Interview with Eddie Marnell.
64 Interview with Billy Albertina.

8

The Liverpool dock strike of 1995–98: the end of the line?

In many ways, what became of the docks and dockland community of Liverpool is emblematic of the region's decline. Stevedores and dockers were the backbone of the city's maritime-based economy. In order to grasp the fate of Merseyside in the second half of the twentieth century, it is necessary to examine Liverpool's waterfront. The main focus of this chapter is on unemployment and underemployment in dock work, and specifically how workers reacted to these changing circumstances in the Liverpool dockers' strike of 1995–98.

Commencing this chapter will be an outline detailing the pattern of industrial relations on the docks, the dockers' work culture and the challenges to it produced by technological change. The remainder of the chapter explores the consequences of the abolition of the National Dock Labour Scheme (NDLS) and, ultimately, the Liverpool dockers' strike of 1995–98. A question is probed whether this long dispute represented the last great manifestation of working-class militancy in Liverpool. The conflict certainly marked the end of an era, symbolising, perhaps, the last challenge by a radicalised working class in Liverpool, and their fight against the miseries and degradations associated with a lifetime of unemployment and casual labour.

Dock work in the immediate post-war era

The overriding theme on Liverpool's docks during this period was industrial conflict. The most pressing concern of Merseyside's dockers was freedom from casualism. Due to the erratic, unpredictable nature of marine transport, casualism was seen as the most profitable operating system by shipping companies. The work practices derived from it bred a 'feast or famine' mentality among dockworkers, and the uncertainties of underemployment were an omnipresent aspect of dockers' daily lives. This hand-to-mouth existence, along with a collective memory of famished times, fostered a trade-union militancy, which gave particular emphasis to the local autonomy of the work group.

The Second World War prompted the government to encourage decasualisation in order to instil a system of stability on the docks. In 1947, the Labour government introduced measures extending wartime decasualisation by way of a new system of worker protection called the NDLS. Despite these measures, dockwork still had not provided the steady employment desired by the majority of its employees. The NDLS instituted a system of 'fall-back' money in order to ensure steadiness in dock employment; nonetheless, it was far from the end of casualism.[1]

The NDLS also retained the wartime protocol of mandatory registration for dockers. This meant only dockworkers registered with the National Dock Labour Board (NDLB) could be employed in most British ports, therefore eliminating any threat of surplus labour or encroachments from strike-breakers. In order to obtain work, one had to be registered, and in order to get on the register a potential docker had to first be a member of either the TGWU or the National Amalgamated Stevedores and Dockers Union (NASD). This led to accusations of nepotism, especially as dockwork was becoming better paid and more sought after during the growing affluence of the 1960s. One newspaper column observed:

> Getting a job as a docker is a process as cumbersome and complicated, though not of course as expensive, as getting one's son into Eton: and it depends, much more than the chances of the three-day-old prospective Etonians depend, on the old boy network, and the fact that father was also there ... Both sides of the docks defend the rigid nepotism of their recruitment. They say that being a docker is a family business, and they want people in the docks who have a stake, and an interest and a tradition there. Being a docker, far more than being an Etonian goes back in a family for generations.[2]

Preference was given to dockers' sons for jobs, but as one docker argued: 'There weren't a lot of people looking for those jobs until the late 1960s and 1970s when the wages became very, very, very good.'[3] Dockworkers' wages increased in this period, and by the 1960s, they ranked amongst the highest paid wage earners: 'as entry to this occupation became more difficult for outsiders; its privileged aspect was more accentuated'.[4]

The NDLB was a bilateral consortium comprising representatives from Britain's largest shipping companies and delegates from the major dockers' union, the TGWU. The union was put in a powerful but contradictory position, since it had a major say in the hiring, firing and disciplining of dock employees. In the immediate post-war period, discontent often emerged from this arrangement, as rival waterfront unions such as the NASD, known as the 'Blue' union, because of the colour of its membership cards, demanded representation on the Board. This inter-union rivalry was a major catalyst of the labour strife on Merseyside's waterfront throughout the 1950s. The TGWU, sometimes referred to as the 'White' union, battled with the 'Blue' union for a closed shop and complete control of the docks. It was the TGWU's dominance and new role with management that prompted rank-and-file defections to the smaller Blue union.[5]

Industrial conflict and the reform of employment relations

Labour disputes were rife throughout many of Britain's docks, but Merseyside's were often the most volatile. Change came with Harold Wilson's first Labour government in 1964, and its commitment to advancing into the 'white heat of the technological revolution'. Waterfront managers were aware that enormous technological transformations were on the horizon for the UK. They also knew that to capitalise on these developments traditional labour practices required alterations. Consequently, the government commissioned Lord Devlin to investigate these issues in 1964.

Lord Devlin's committee cited casualism as the primary cause of labour disputes, and it was the high degree of industrial action in Liverpool, which took particular prominence in the committee's findings.[6] Table 8.1 indicates Liverpool's docks were second only to London's in the number of days lost due to industrial action. Liverpool also placed second in the number of workers involved in strikes at British ports between the years of 1947 and 1955. In order to alleviate these disruptions in trade, Lord Devlin's committee recommended decasualisation and implementing a weekly wage, sick pay and a modest pension scheme.[7] However, with these benefits for dockworkers, Lord Devlin also called for stronger disciplinary powers for management, which included the lessening of certain labour restrictive practices. Nonetheless, union officials demanded and received protection for all dockworkers from involuntary redundancies due to the introduction of any new mechanised processes.[8]

When Lord Devlin's recommendations were implemented in 1967, the majority of dockers celebrated decasualisation. However, not all shared this view. Whilst casualism was far from a steady means of employment, its lack of structure did provide many of the dockers with a sense of agency, freedom and independence not afforded to workers in factories.[9]

Table 8.1 Dock strikes by principal ports, July 1947 to July 1955

Port	Total registered dockers in 1955	Number of disputes	Number of workers involved	Strike days lost
London	31,045	213	203,149	1,497,527
Liverpool	18,173	46	82,855	735,626
Hull & Goole	4,739	25	11,982	101,552
Glasgow	3,288	66	20,722	18,728
Manchester	3,102	13	16,223	157,977
South Wales	3,067	39	4,043	4,520
Bristol & Severn	2,526	38	9,803	44,401
South Coast	2,350	17	7,525	20,542
East Scotland	2,200	13	1,131	1,314
Grimsby & Immingham	2,146	1	40	40
Tyne & Wear	1,922	9	889	4,846
Middlesbrough & Hartlepool	1,625	15	3,715	18,079

Source: Peter Turnbull et al., *Dock Strike: Conflict and Restructuring in Britain's Ports* (Aldershot, 1992), p. 16.

Some changes in work practices were too drastic for a vocal minority of Liverpool's dockers. Consequently, a series of unofficial strikes broke out until a new set of work rules could be negotiated.[10]

According to some dockers, one of the more irksome of concessions agreed to in the post-Devlin arrangement was the attempted elimination of the time-honoured work practice known as the 'welt'. This was a system where half a gang would take turns at work, while the other half rested. It had been a long-accepted custom by dockers, and bosses had normally turned a blind eye to it for generations. The practice served several purposes, but most importantly it allowed relief breaks in what was obviously a physically demanding occupation. It also maintained manning levels, and therefore protected jobs. The welt could also be deployed as a system of reverse discipline too. If the shipper was unreasonable or difficult, then that obstinate company paid for their inflexibility through the penalty of an increase in docker overtime.[11] One docker and shop steward remembered the welt as an essential component of the job culture:

> You see in them days they might send you over to Vestey to unload a coal ship. And they'd never give you enough protective gear to go around for the entire gang. These ship owners would try to make everyone go down

> there with no safety equipment. They'd try to make lads go down there with just fuckin' bags around their shoes. Well, we would have none of that, and so we'd share the safety gear in shifts ... You see, you never got anywhere with these ship owners without a fuckin' struggle. They never gave you anything, and you had to fight them tooth and nail all the way.[12]

Nevertheless, the times were changing, and in 1970 the Mersey Docks and Harbour Board (MDHB) became insolvent. The Board found itself in need of a means to lower expenditures and secure an immediate infusion of revenue. The 1971 Mersey Docks and Harbour Act was the Heath government's answer. This Act privatised 79 per cent of the Board, which in turn, transformed the Board into a private company. Thus, the MDHB became the Merseyside Docks and Harbour Company (MDHC) and was thereafter listed on the London Stock Exchange.

Containerisation and job loss

Containerisation is a system of transporting cargoes in massive metal boxes on the decks of ships. It was a radically different system of shipping compared to the old method of transporting goods. Prior to containerisation, bulk cargo was usually packed into small crates, placed on wooden pallets, and buried deep in the holds of ships. Containers, on the other hand, are offloaded by large overhead cranes and then placed directly onto the beds of trailers attached to lorries or offloaded directly onto flatbed rail cars, which are later transported and unpacked at their final destinations.

The number of man hours needed to unload a containerised ship is considerably lower than that for a conventional vessel. For instance, it took 10,584 work hours to remove 11,000 tonnes of cargo from a conventional freighter, yet a containerised ship needs only 546 man hours to offload 11,000 tonnes of containers.[13] With containerisation, a ship can be turned around and back at sea within twenty-four hours. Previously, a ship might sit for weeks before it was completely unloaded.[14]

The size of work gangs needed to service a containerised vessel was very different, as one docker explained: 'Now, with a freighter carrying standard cargo you need eight holdsmen, two deckhands, five porters, a hatch boss, two crane drivers and a checker, for a total of nineteen. A container ship only requires one crane driver, two spotters, and a checker for a total of four.'[15] Because fewer dockers were needed with containerisation, a system of voluntary redundancies was negotiated

Table 8.2 Numbers of registered dockers, 1947–89

Year ended	National register	Liverpool
1947	79,769	
1957	75,700	16,085
1967	56,808	11,530
1969	49,225	11,100
1971	43,645	10,427
1973	34,590	7,550
1975	31,884	7,326
1977	29,168	6,402
1979	25,770	5,202
1981	18,219	3,402
1983	13,813	2,151
1985	11,922	1,862
1989	9,400	1,100
De-registration		

Source: Bill Hunter, *They Knew Why They Fought* (London, 1994), p. 135.

between unions and the MDHB – as Devlin recommended. In spite of redundant dockers collecting generous pay-outs at this time, there were now far fewer jobs available on Merseyside.

The container revolution also held serious implications for Liverpool's wider community. Containerisation meant not only far fewer dockers, but this revolution in commercial transport also brought redundancies in the seafaring trade, as containerised ships required fewer mariners to man them. This, in turn, meant less work for those employed in marine maintenance and supply as well, since both of these trades formed important branches of the local economy. Indeed, the entire dockland community changed drastically during this period. The container revolution had a lasting effect on a community whose way of life was anchored in eighteenth-century traditions and rhythms.[16]

After 1971 and the opening of the new container port in Seaforth, most Merseyside ship traffic was diverted away from the older docks to this newer facility north of the city's traditional maritime centre. Containerisation brought thousands of redundancies: the number of dockworkers in Merseyside during the 1970s and 1980s plummeted. Table 8.2 shows that in 1967 there were 11,530 people employed as dockers in Merseyside; by 1979 that number had dropped to 5,202.[17] By 1993, only 800 dockers remained.[18] Sons of dockers were unable to get on the Register, and a way of life disappeared forever for many

Liverpool families. When older workers took voluntary redundancy, their posts vanished.

The loss of so many jobs had a devastating effect on Liverpool's dockland community. All along the Dock Road and the neighbouring area around Scotland Road, the economic blight trickled down from large concerns, such as wholesale ship supply companies to small family businesses, like neighbourhood pubs.[19] One docker remembered that period:

> Yeah, it was around this time when you noticed that everything just closed down. You see, Liverpool is a really social city, so there's a love for pubs. I suppose that's the Irish in us. There's an old saying that on the end of every street in Scottie Road [Scotland Road] there's a pub. Well, the first thing you saw when unemployment was going up in the 1970s, and things were getting bad, was when the pubs started closing down. In Scotland Road there was, in my day, over thirty pubs. Well, I think there's only three now.[20]

Abolition of the NDLS

The Thatcher government's prescription to remedy Liverpool's unemployment epidemic was more free-market neoliberalism and less government regulation. Some within the government cited the militancy of the Liverpool workforce as the root of the problem. Thatcher's latest round of constraining employment legislation curbed any enthusiasm amongst union leaders for industrial action. Therefore, it is quite clear that it was this succession of restrictive laws that placed the dockers in a much weaker bargaining position, thus allowing the government a legal foothold to rid the docks of costly labour practices. Indeed, this is precisely what the Tory government did in 1989 when it used the legislative process to abolish the highly prized NDLS.

Dock employers claimed that by 1988 the average docker earned over 50 per cent more than the earnings of a typical manual worker in manufacturing. Others complained the high wages came with low productivity, since cumbersome work practices from the era before containerisation remained. Old customs such as the welt were still employed despite it being officially prohibited after 1967. Many shipping companies complained management systems in the Port of Liverpool were weak and ineffective. There was a growing feeling amongst stevedoring companies that the NDLB was a toothless tiger, since the union exercised significant control over it. They argued the TGWU and the dockers themselves held more sway in the day-to-day running of Liverpool's docks than the employers, and this system was cutting into profits. One observer summarised the MDHC's view of that arrangement:

> The imposition of a flat-rate levy on employers to finance the scheme meant that efficient employers subsidised the inefficient, and that ports with large variations in labour needs were subsidised by ports with more regular schedules. Substitution of labour with more efficient capital investment was the exception rather than the rule. The normal commercial criteria for profit-seeking businesses were more or less impossible to implement, and the wider Merseyside economy suffered as a result of the missed opportunities for productive wealth-creation and real employment growth.[21]

Pressure was applied to Downing Street by many of the business concerns involved; hence, the Tory government abolished the NDLS in July 1989.[22] This legislation brought back casualism and nullified agreements which had been in effect since Lord Devlin's original recommendations had become law.

The ensuing strike in 1989 proved fruitless. The TGWU, accused by some to be more concerned over threats to the union's finances, gave only limited assistance to Liverpool's dockers, many of whom were angered by the indifferent attitude of their national union:

> The national dock strike was unexpectedly called off last night as Transport and General Workers' Union leaders instructed members to return to work and press for local negotiations with employers. Angry dockers' leaders in Liverpool described the decision as unacceptable and suggested their shop stewards may refuse to recommend that the men go back at a meeting today. The move, a climb-down by the union in the face of the accelerating return to work, was agreed by 18 votes to 12 at a fraught meeting of the union's executive council. Dockers from Liverpool and Tilbury lobbying the meeting were furious. One described it as 'an utter disgrace' ... In Liverpool, Mr Jimmy Nolan, chairman of the unofficial national dock shop stewards' committee, said: 'The general council obviously do not understand dock workers. What they are doing to us is a tragedy, treacherous'.[23]

The context of the decision was the unwillingness of dockers in non-scheme ports to support the strike. Ron Todd, TGWU general secretary, pledged that:

> Reinstatement of sacked dockers and the protection of union organisation would take priority ... the union had to 'face the reality' of widespread returns to work ... The combined force of the Government and

> the 'gangster tactics' used by some employers had attempted to scupper a legitimate dispute ... Sometimes you have to say things that are not very popular.[24]

The reliance on this notion of the 'new realism' as a ready excuse was popular amongst trade union bosses and Labour Party elites at this time. It proved useful in impressing upon union militants that there would be no chance of official organised support for industrial action.[25]

Debates in the Commons illustrate the arguments on both sides of the dispute. Secretary of State for Employment, Norman Fowler, insisted casualisation would not return following the Scheme's demise:

> Dockers are well paid and the enormous changes in the way ships are unloaded – with new technology and with containerisation – has transformed the nature of dock work and virtually eliminated the scope of casual work. Dock work is now highly skilled, specialist work that often requires the use of sophisticated machinery. It requires a permanent and well trained work force. The days when large numbers of unskilled labourers assembled, waiting to see if there was work for them have gone for good – the employers in the present scheme ports have given an assurance that after abolition there will be no return to casual employment. That assurance is, both in my view, important and unprecedented. The reason we have a dock labour scheme is to prevent casualism. Port companies employing 93 per cent of registered dock workers have now given an undertaking that there will be no return to the casual system of working and the practice in non-scheme ports already demonstrates that this is a bogus fear. Those who seek to argue that the scheme should be preserved to prevent casualism should have no public credibility. They are using the argument to cloak other reasons for resisting change.[26]

After repeated interruptions from Labour backbenchers demanding government assurances of an end to casualisation, Fowler continued:

> The reason why ports covered by the scheme want to see those restrictions go is because they want to be able to compete better with ports outside the scheme and to compete with continental ports that have taken too much of our trade, and to compete in the new position created by 1992 and the single market, and with the railway competition of the Channel tunnel ... Let us be clear. Unless those ports succeed in competing, no conceivable dock labour scheme will prevent the relative decline of scheme ports and of employment prospects ... very few people outside the Transport and General Workers Union's docks section have been prepared to defend the detail of the scheme. All kinds of arguments have been used, but I have heard very few people on radio or television defending the scheme itself. The Leader of the Opposition most certainly has not done so.[27]

The only response to Fowler's arguments came from backbench Labour MPs. Bob Parry, MP for Liverpool-Riverside. Parry pledged his support for the dockworkers in his constituency and throughout Britain, and his remarks were to prove prescient:

> [On Liverpool docks] They were treated like cattle, and were employed only if they bought the foreman or the ganger a pint of beer, or even because they were of the same religion. We never want to see such things happen again in the docks ... I believe that employers will jump at the opportunity to make bigger profits at the expense of dock workers ... The port of Liverpool employed 25,000 workers 30 or 40 years ago. Now it employs fewer than 2,000. That does not say much for the argument that jobs are for life, which the House should recognise as a myth ... We will not agree to any system that would bring back casualisation and use dock workers as chattels in the hands of unscrupulous employers.[28]

Some of those employed on Liverpool's docks felt that national union leaders and Labour Party officials were no longer interested in their concerns. Nevertheless, despite this apparent rebuff it has been argued that this perceived feeling of neglect coming after the decision in 1989 reinvigorated a sense of collective struggle and a strong notion of class consciousness, which until this time had been lacking.[29] Nevertheless, dock work, particularly as practised in Liverpool, fostered a greater sense of solidarity than in other manual occupations. When this is coupled with a distinct community that has common family, religious and ethnic backgrounds, it is easy to comprehend how many of the old working-class values such as collectivism and mutualism still flourished, even if any sense of class-consciousness was waning or called into question.[30]

The return of casualism

Dockland recollections of underemployment, abject poverty and managerial intimidation were rekindled with the removal of the NDLS.[31] In the minds of most dockers on Merseyside, the year 1989 marked a turning point:

> Before they got rid of the Scheme it was a real pleasure coming to work. You actually looked forward to it. The tremendous characters, the fun you had off all the lads you worked with. Don't get me wrong, the employers never gave you anything. You still had to work hard and fight for everything you earned, but it was a completely different and more relaxed atmosphere. But after the '89 strike, when we came back to work things

were completely different ... The employers, of course, were all very much aware just how strong the Liverpool branches of the unions were, in comparison to the other ports around the country, especially the smaller ones and the ones down South. I'm sure they took special notice of this.[32]

Despite government assurances, casualism returned to the waterfront, and along with this re-emergence of casualisation came conflict. By 1989, there were additional snares added to the mix. The one saving grace under casualism in the past was that at least the individual docker exerted some control over his life, and he could chose, to some degree, when and where he wanted to work. Now 'management rights' became the mantra of the day, and port managers saw the return to casualism as an opportunity to extend their managerial control.

The MDHC adopted a more aggressive stance concerning employee relations. Workers were placed under stricter regulations. For example, dockers were now required to be available for work at all times, including scheduled days off. These intrusions into their private lives, and the fact that they now had to do more work with fewer people reinforced amongst the Liverpool dockers a heightened sense of grievance.[33] One docker recalled:

> Everything changed completely. In 1989 we in Liverpool were the last port to go back to work after the strike. Well we had a bagpipe band lead us, and we marched to the docks from in town. Well, as soon as we got there I went to my desk, and I was told I didn't work at that desk anymore. I said: 'Yes I do', and they said, 'No you don't. You work out doors now. If you don't like it, you're going to get the sack'. Just like that! Another example is the company bought 1,000 brushes, so when the men would finish a job early; they no longer could sign off and go home. They gave them a brush and told them to brush up and down the quay. Grown men and they're making them do 'busy work'. You had no more protection. They made it a point to harass shop stewards. They'd say over and over and over again, 'Times have changed boys, this isn't the 1960s anymore'.[34]

This same former docker provided a further graphic example of the new managerial style:

> There was one evening I won't forget. I was working as a checker on Hold No. 2 of a ship, and a friend of mine was the checker on No. 3 Hold. Well anyway, he fell and was killed in the hold of the ship. Well, the standard practice when such unfortunate tragedies happen – a custom that goes back hundreds of years – is for us to stop work for twenty-four hours as a symbol of respect and a time to help the docker's family in

any way. Well, on that night he was killed, the company said, 'What are you doing? Everyone back to work. This is a business'. Well that was it for most of us. We now realised we were dealing with the lowest of the low – real cut-throats. We all walked off anyway. Well, they disciplined all of us with something called a written warning for life, which to this day I have no idea what that is. Well, it was after this incident, we think at least, is when the company decided to look for a situation to get rid of all of us anyway they could. They knew if they could force a strike, they would have the means to sack all of us, and put in a much younger and non-unionised workforce. Plus, because of Maggie Thatcher they now had the laws behind them to do whatever they wanted. And this is exactly what they did a couple years later in 1995.[35]

Many of the Liverpool dockers were dismayed at the lack of respect the employers suddenly started extending to their workers:

There was this nice old fellow ... He was a stevedore ... a stevedore is a very skilled job that takes years of experience to learn. A stevedore is not an average docker. He is the fitter, more or less, of how a cargo is loaded, packed and unloaded. He's the one who figures out where and how things are more or less done. Liverpool stevedores are known the world over for their skills ... It takes years of experience, and most stevedores are highly respected by dockers ... Our first day back to work after the strike in 1989 was a tough one. First off, they told us there would no longer be any demarcation between jobs. We would be expected to do any job necessary, regardless of title. In fact, they stripped us all of whatever job title we may have held previously, and called us all POW's, short for Port Operations Workers, or as we called it, 'Prisoners of Work'. I'm sure this title was purposely abbreviated this way just to send us a message as to who was now going to be in charge. Anyway, our first day back, most of us were handed brooms and told to sweep the quay. Dockers never did that before, that was a cleaner's job. 'Not any more', we were told. Well this boss turned to the stevedore I was telling you about, and he said, 'I have a special job for you. I want you to go over there and clean out the toilets'. Well, as you can imagine, the old stevedore said to the foreman, 'I'm a stevedore, I don't clean toilets. That's not my job'. The foreman then shouted so everyone could hear him, 'From now on since the Scheme is gone, you will do what you're told, or go fuck off back to where you came from!' So the old fellow took the cleaning materials and walked toward the toilets. I followed him and tried to give him and everyone else there a little leadership and assurance that things would get better after the first few days. We just had to ride it out. He turned to me and said, 'I can't do this' ... With that he walked back to the office and told the foreman, 'I can't do this. I want to leave. How do I go about applying for retirement'? The foreman looked up from his newspaper and snapped, 'Go fuck off then, we'll send you

> a form'. With that, I could see this poor old fellow was a broken man. I could see it in his body language as he walked back to his car. That was my most lasting memory of how things changed after 1989.[36]

With the resurrection of casualism it became apparent to the dockers and their families that home lives were coming under strain. Since dockers were now permanently on call, many felt imprisoned by their jobs, and it was dockers' families who were often the first to see how these changes at work affected the entire family structure. One docker's wife commented:

> He'd go to work in the morning, come home in the evening. Work would then call at say 9 o'clock at night. They'd say report back to work at 4 o'clock in the morning. OK, then the phone would ring again, and they'd say disregard the last message. A half-hour later the phone would ring yet one more time, and they'd tell him they scrapped the last message, they now need him back on the docks at 2 o'clock in the morning. This would go on day and night. I can't begin to tell you what a terrible intrusion this was into our lives. I mean you couldn't realistically go out for a drink or plan anything ... It was beginning to affect our home life. I mean my husband used to be the life of the party – he was a very funny man. But around this time he just became withdrawn and depressed.[37]

Indeed, surveys at the time demonstrate that the new way of doing business on the docks was taking its toll on the workforce. Morale sank, as a stricter code of discipline was introduced.[38] By the 1990s, over 85 per cent of dockers still in employment on Liverpool's docks complained of longer work hours. Over 70 per cent felt job security had been eliminated, and 82 per cent felt trade union influence had been eradicated, while 54 per cent felt health and safety standards were lowered to a dangerous level.[39]

Accident rates rose considerably too, as longer hours and compulsory overtime increased worker fatigue. Correspondingly, as more of the dockers retired, their jobs were shifted to replacement employees, hired by a sub-contracted work-personnel firm named Torside Ltd. Most of these individuals, while unionised, were working under different contractual arrangements than the original registered dockers. They were usually much younger, relatively inexperienced and untrained at dock work, which in turn, added to the rise in the number of work accidents.[40]

After 1989, Britain's dockers left the trade in droves. From 1989 to 1992, approximately 80 per cent of dock workers left the industry. Between 1989 and 1995, the number of MDHC employees dropped

Table 8.3 Merseyside Dock and Harbour Company's annual profits

Year	Profit in millions (GBP)
1986	3.1
1987	5.0
1988	7.2
1989	8.3
1990	10.8
1991	13.2
1992	15.2
1993	20.9
1994	33.6
1995	31.7
1996	29.6

Source: Merseyside Port Shop Stewards Committee, 'The Case for the Reinstatement of the Sacked Liverpool Dockers': www.labournet.net/docks2/9707/booklet.htm.

from 1,100 to 500.[41] The TGWU was marginalised in most ports and its leading activists were blacklisted and labelled union militants. From the MDHC's perspective these changes were necessary if the Port of Liverpool was to remain profitable in an increasingly competitive and globalised economy. One observer commented:

> One of the most marked changes at Liverpool was a huge reduction in the dock labour force. The registered dock labour force had been on a downward trend for many years, from around 12,000 in 1969 to 6,000 in 1979, to 1,000 in 1989. In the year immediately after abolition, there was a further drop of over 30% to 700, and yet more reductions to reach the current complement of around 450 dock workers. At the same time, trade volumes handled by the port have increased from under 20 million tonnes in 1988 to over 30 million tonnes in 1997, an increase of over 50%.[42]

As Table 8.3 demonstrates, the number of dockers may have been vanishing from the waterfront, but MDHC's profits soared during this period. Between 1988 and 1994, company profits rose by nearly five-fold.[43]

By 1995, it seemed unlikely that dockworkers would ever set up another picket line again. After 1991, much of Liverpool's dock work was sub-contracted to private firms such as Torside, which were able to circumvent union agreements through moving much of their unloading operation off the docks and into private warehouses miles from the port. The union could do little to control this practice.[44] Finally, it must be noted that because of the decreasing number of registered dockers' jobs available, firms such as Torside became the only avenue many of the sons of dockers could use to enter their father's trade. These were the conditions which led up to the strike of 1995 to 1998.

The Liverpool dockers' strike

The dispute began in September 1995 when 500 dockers were locked out after they refused to cross a picket line put together by striking employees of Torside Ltd. The conflict lasted nearly two and a half years and was one of the longest, most bitter industrial disputes in British labour history. Liverpool's reputation for union militancy continued to weigh heavy on the minds of ship-owners after the 1989 strike, perhaps lending some credence to the claims by a number of observers that the 1995 strike was engineered by the employers in order to clear the way for even stricter managerial controls.[45] Nevertheless, MDHC officials apparently felt the time was right to reassert their managerial prerogatives.

The incident that sparked the conflict did not arise from any action taken against dockers employed directly by the MDHC. It involved a picket line set-up by workers employed by the sub-contractor, Torside Ltd. On 25 September 1995, a dispute erupted at Torside regarding overtime rates. The company responded by abruptly dismissing its entire workforce. Consequently, a picket line was organised by the former Torside employees, many of whom were the sons and younger relatives of the dockers working for the MDHC. The MDHC dockers refused to cross this picket line. This act of solidarity cost the registered dockers their jobs, and within twenty-four short hours the company ran advertisements for replacements, albeit at lower rates of pay and under different contracts.[46] According to one local press account:

> Nearly 400 Merseyside dockers were sacked today – for refusing to cross a picket line. A fleet of taxis and despatch riders was hired by dock bosses to issue dismissal notices ... An MDHC spokesman said today: 'The striking men are in breach of their contracts, and we have therefore terminated them. We are in the process of offering new contracts to the majority of the men, but MDHC will be recruiting in the market place' ... Angry striking dockers described today's sackings as 'an abuse of power'.[47]

Whatever the company's ulterior motives, their response came as a shock to the dockers who honoured that picket line:

> We thought they [the MDHC] were up to something just by the way they provoked that strike with those kids at Torside ... They must have known we, the old timers who worked for MDHC, would have honoured that picket line ... Within only forty-eight hours of that incident they had virtually hundreds of dismissal notices prepared and then driven by taxis flying all over Liverpool. And then within that short forty-eight-hour period they could have a new contract drawn up and available to be signed by only a select few of the sacked dockers, who they could personally choose to rehire ... It was a good way they could use to get rid of once and for all the union militants and thorns in their side. And at the same time force the men into working at a far lower rate of pay and even worse working conditions. So yes, it was a shock, but what was really startling was how suddenly they did it.[48]

Another docker added this observation:

> Yes, I was shocked. But I also knew post-1989 we began to regain our strength as an organised unit. Leading up to 1995 we were involved in a number of disputes here locally, and we were winning most of them. We were starting to gain a little self-confidence back. I was beginning to hear some noises from the company that they were getting fed up with us. They hadn't been able to stop or hamper our reorganisation, and I was picking up vibes they were prepared to do something drastic, if necessary. Having said that, when they sacked us all so soon after the Torside incident, it was a shock. We all were in shock at the time.[49]

Despite the unexpected reaction by the MDHC, the vast majority of Liverpool's dockers refused to concede defeat: the Liverpool dockers' strike of 1995–98 had commenced. It would last twenty-eight months and ultimately end in defeat, but it became recognised within trade union circles, not as another defeat for labour, but more importantly for the new and innovative tactics used in fighting for the rights of organised labour in the developing age of globalisation and international capital.

In the remainder of this chapter we will focus on four significant themes: first, problems of support and solidarity from TGWU bosses and other trade unions in Britain; second, the novel tactics adopted to publicise the dispute at home and abroad; third, the high level of support the strikers received from their families and the local community; and finally, the determination and solidarity of the strikers themselves.

The TGWU and the British labour movement

Initially TGWU national officers gave moral support to the Liverpool dockers, although they could not endorse this strike officially, as this trade publication reported:

> Bill Morris, leader of the Transport and General Workers' Union yesterday threw his weight behind the 10-week-old unofficial Liverpool docks dispute and demanded talks to end the lock-out of 500 workers. The alternative, he warned, was 'irreparable harm' to the port of Liverpool. Skating round the legal problems of an unofficial strike, the TGWU executive yesterday voted to set up a hardship fund for the dockers ... Mr. Morris also gave a strong welcome to promises by dockers' unions abroad to boycott ships and shipping lines which used the dispute-bound terminals on Merseyside.[50]

Eighteen months later, the relationship between the striking dockers and Morris had soured. There were numerous pleas for the union to make the dispute official, or at least take a larger role in calling for universal solidarity. Some critics of Morris noted certain snubs on his part which they perceived as intentional. One instance in particular was that the Liverpool dockers' struggle was never once highlighted in the union newspaper, *T & G Record*. Reports also emerged that Morris was under internal scrutiny for allegedly misleading statements regarding his efforts on the strikers' behalf.[51] Suspicions mounted, as a former docker and current TGWU official declared:

> I noticed the big changes in Morris, the political establishment, and with the media in their attitudes toward us right after we set up a picket line outside the London Stock Exchange. We did that a few months into the strike. Up to that point, Morris was making all the right noises, 'I'd like to help you lads, we believe in what you're fighting for up there in Liverpool, but as you know there are legal restrictions on what the union can do, et cetera'. But after our day picketing down at the London Stock Exchange, according to him, we were suddenly the biggest group of scallie Scouse bastards in the world. The establishment had got to him. They scared him, and he turned on us, just like that. In the minds of the rich and the powerful who run things, what we did was a no-no. I learned a valuable lesson that day. I was awoken to the fact of who really runs things in this world, and just how much power they have. So if you ever want to stir things up, just try causing a little trouble and inconvenience for the billionaire bankers down at the London Stock Exchange.[52]

The same union official related another experience that suggested less than enthusiastic support for the Liverpool dockers cause from their union's general secretary:

> One day I was talking to the General Secretary of the Fire Brigades' union, and I was telling him about our money woes, and how we were struggling just to make our needed £50,000 payments a week just to keep the strike afloat. He then turned to me, and said his union had recently decided to

> grant us an indefinite, interest free loan of £250,000 cash, in a box, with no paperwork or attachments. He told me they did the same thing for the miners in '84, and it was a fairly common thing amongst trade unionists. Now remember, the Fire Brigades' union isn't a particularly large union, and for them to even consider loaning us that kind of money, interest free, was very generous. But then he added, 'However, your General Secretary won't let us'. Now we dockers definitely could have used that money, especially at that point in the strike. So that's an example of the kind of support we were offered from other British unions, but were denied by our very own national union leadership.[53]

Morris is often accused by the Liverpool dockers of refusing much needed outside aid on their behalf:

> If we only had more money, I'm certain we could have held on, gathered even more worldwide support and eventually won our jobs back. It came down to money and putting too much faith in Morris and the national union. They kept saying the strike was unofficial, but they always wanted to run it. There were three or four different occasions when offers of international support – and we only found out about this later – and it was always Morris who knocked it back. For instance, we found out later that Morris had told the Americans, 'This union is not asking you to blockade ships going to Liverpool, because if we can't do it ourselves why should we ask somebody else to do it for us'. Well, needless to say, we were furious when we found that out ... This was the same Bill Morris who I remember standing up at a TUC conference when the first of Thatcher's Employment Acts came out and said, 'I will never let trade union buildings and property ever come before the human rights of the individual. The rights of the individual worker are far more important'. But once he was in power the human element became secondary. He thought if union funds or property faced sequestration, then the funds come first, people or workers came last. In other words, if he had to protect the union coffers with the loss of a few hundred jobs here or there, then so be it. That's the attitude we were up against.[54]

Over the long months of the strike, the national media began to take notice of this ever apparent strained relationship between Morris and the Liverpool contingent:

> The Liverpool dockers march through London today. After 14 months, the dockers' dispute is now longer than the miners' strike of 1984–85 and one of the most tenacious in British labour history. Until recently, it was also one of the least known. But now the docker's unfashionable struggle to reclaim almost 500 jobs may become a touchpaper for something their union and New Labour have done their best to contain ... Their union, the

> Transport and General Workers, has provided hardship money and office facilities, but has refused to make the dispute official. Bill Morris, the general secretary, told the TUC conference in September that he would 'die for the dockers'. Dockers' wives, who were prevented from speaking, replied, 'Don't die, just support us'.[55]

Disappointment with Morris and union officials in London was, in some ways, a reflection of the times. Many of Liverpool's striking dockers initially had high hopes after the election of a Labour government in 1997, eager that Tony Blair would use the government's financial share in the MDHC as a way to force the company to back down and reinstate the striking Liverpool dockers. Unfortunately, most dockers initially did not realise the level of commitment New Labour had to maintaining many of Thatcher's neoliberal economic policies. Consequently, many in their ranks soon became disillusioned, as one docker put it bluntly: 'Once that crowd [New Labour] got in office they didn't want to know us. They did absolutely nothing to help us. Our local MP's were helpful, but they couldn't do much for us as individuals.'[56] Another commented:

> We got nothing from those people [New Labour]. From the time our strike was started, right up to when they got in power in 1997, the Labour Party was going through big changes. They wanted the party to associate itself more with trade union reform, so they didn't want to be identified with anything from their past association with unions. In fact, at the time the government owned a 14 per cent share in the Merseyside Docks and Harbour Company – the golden share, as it's called. Well now, all they had to do was use this golden share as influence over the company to get us our jobs back, but they wouldn't do it. Once in power, they didn't even want to know us.[57]

The media campaign and international support

Given the fact that Thatcher's Employment Acts remained operative, the Liverpool dockers appreciated that their room to manoeuvre was limited. Support from other British unions could not be expected, and official backing from their own union would not be sanctioned. Their traditional allies during times of industrial conflict no longer could or would come to their aid. The British media tended to portray the dockers and their cause as dinosaurs from another age.

However, by 1995, fax machines, cyber technology and the Internet were emerging and coming more into common use. Trade unionism needed to catch up in a world that had become smaller and far more technologically advanced. Consequently, the Liverpool dockers were some of the first to embrace this new technology. The message of the striking Liverpool dockers found new channels of communication that circumvented the establishment press.

The British media and public eventually took notice once international labour organisations received word of the dockers' plight through the modern modes of communication via the worldwide web. Once international labour was aware of what was happening in Liverpool, trade unions and labour organisations around the globe began lending their support. According to observers at the time, it was not until the world's press started converging on Liverpool, that the British newspapers finally gave the strike any coverage. Within only a few short months of their first use of the Internet, the Liverpool dockers and their plight became a cause célèbre.[58]

Communications and public relations took centre stage in this dispute. The use of the Internet and cyber-technology played a vital role in this struggle, and this aspect helped project the strike as a model for future grassroots industrial action. The worldwide web allowed the Liverpool dockers a way to appeal to rank-and-file trade unionists across the globe without having to channel their message through union bosses and government officials. It was through this experimentation with the use of emails, personalised websites, faxes and the Internet which helped generate the international solidarity they needed.[59]

It was not long after the strike began that Liverpool's dockers realised the answer to their problems did not lie in Britain, but in the outside world. A campaign was initiated calling on dockers throughout the globe to boycott the loading and unloading of ships travelling to or from the Port of Liverpool. It was also decided that Liverpool dockers would picket in foreign ports at the presence of Liverpool ships, since they could not legally set up secondary picket lines in Britain. According to one docker who helped organise this strategy:

> We were still living under the shadow of Thatcherism. She no longer was in power, but her policies and laws were. So we knew there was no chance we were ever going to be able to get other unions here to come out and support us. It dawned on us one night that maybe it would be best if we tried to take our struggle to ports outside this country. We looked what ports around the world did the most business with Liverpool. So it was decided we'd send delegations to Montreal, Sydney, New York, up and down the West Coast of America, and to Europe, too, in places like Bilbao in Spain, Norway, Turkey, Italy, and so forth ... I was on the delegation party to Montreal. Now, over 40 per cent of the cargo we handled here in

> Liverpool at that time came through the Port of Montreal. I'll never forget it for as long as I live. We were received so warmly by the dockers there. Their kindness and generosity was outstanding. Their union allowed us unlimited access to their membership, where we explained to them what our situation was like back in Liverpool. It received a lot of press in Canada, as did the other delegations in America, Australia and Europe. Much more than we ever received here in the UK ... this infuriated the dock management back here in Liverpool ... It was a huge success for us because we managed to create industrial actions in their ports which made for costly work stoppages. It also helped us raise a lot of needed revenue and financial support ... None of us had any experience with the Internet or computers at that time, but some people showed us, and we managed to get fax numbers and web addresses off the ITF [International Transport Workers' Federation] for dockers unions all around the world. We sent out faxes and we started getting a lot of positive replies. So we decided to call an international conference here in Liverpool, and the response was unbelievable ... There hadn't been an international workers' conference in Liverpool for many, many years, and now all of a sudden we were getting people coming in here from all over the world. It gave our cause even greater exposure, and it caused the British press and some British trade union leaders to finally take notice.[60]

By late December 1995, the British press eventually took note that something unique was happening in Liverpool:

> On a freezing dawn quayside in Newark, New Jersey, yesterday morning, three sacked Liverpool dockers formed a picket line at the berth of the Atlantic Container Line Ship, *Atlantic Companion*, and appealed for solidarity from the longshoremen of New York's main container port. For the second time in 12 hours, American dockers refused to work on a vessel loaded by 'scab' labour on Merseyside. Another Liverpool container flagship, the *Atlantic Cartier*, has been promised the same treatment when it arrives in Newark tomorrow ... They chase Liverpool-loaded ships back and forth between East Coast ports by aeroplane. For an industrial cause widely dismissed as hopeless, the dockers' campaign has succeeded in calling on a reserve of international solidarity which is causing significant damage to their employer. Emissaries have been sent all over the world to drum up practical support. In Canada – where strike breaking labour of the type employed in Liverpool is illegal – Michael Murray, president of the Montreal Longshoremen's Union, said last night the Quebecois dockers would not let their British counterparts down when a ship owned by Moline – the one-time Soviet shipping arm – arrives in Montreal from Liverpool on Thursday ... Ten thousand miles away in Sydney, the Maritime Union of Australia – which has donated £15,000 to the Merseyside dockers' support fund – is refusing to handle ships trading

> into Liverpool. Half a dozen ABC line vessels have already been hit by go-slows and other forms of industrial action in Sydney.[61]

The events that transpired during January 1997 were especially important in this international campaign. The Liverpool dockers designated 20 January 1997 as the day of international solidarity for their struggle. On that day, and the days immediately following, dockworkers in approximately twenty-seven countries and in 105 ports and cities around the world engaged in solidarity actions, including illegal work stoppages. These industrial actions proved successful, as the American press reported that the ports along the entire US West Coast came to a standstill during these protests. Dockers from other nations and ports gave not only moral support to the striking Liverpool dockers, but also financial assistance. Japanese dockers contributed one million yen (US $10,000) and the American West Coast longshoremen's union, the International Longshoremen and Warehouse Men's Union of America, donated almost $100,000.[62]

The major difficulty a union encounters in employing an international strategy is the large financial investment involved. One Liverpool strike activist recounted:

> The union, by law, could not give us strike pay. However, over the course of the twenty-eight-month strike they gave us a couple £50,000 payments in something they called hardship money. All told, I think they gave us something between £1 million and £2 million. Now, on the surface that may seem like a lot of money, but bear in mind we promised our membership we were somehow going to give them £50 in the hand every week. We also promised our people if there comes a point we can no longer give you £50 a week, we'll call it off. We also stated that if it gets to the point where people might be losing their homes, then we'll call it off as well. So, as you see, we had to give all our families £50 a week. Plus, we had to save anybody's mortgage that might be falling into default. Not only that, we had to fund anyone who came to us with a particular hardship. On top of this, we had to find the money for trips all around the world and the UK. Putting it all together, a conservative estimate is that we needed about £50,000 a week over the two and a half years in order to keep this strike going. So, if the central union kicked in say, £1.5 million, that's not a hell of a lot of money when you look at how much was needed.[63]

Support in the community

Dockers' families rallied to their support, and soon strikers' wives, girlfriends, sisters and mothers were coming to the forefront in this struggle.

In the second week of the strike they started the Women of the Waterfront (WOW) committee, taking an active role in all aspects of the struggle, including such duties as fundraising, picketing, organising marches, participating in conferences and public relations. They went and mounted picket lines at the homes of strike-breakers and company bosses, singing Jimmy Nail's hit song, 'Big river'.[64]

Most of these women were from the dockland community, and therefore many had vivid recollections of the degradations their fathers and brothers suffered under the old system of casual labour. This collective memory of infrequent pay packets and poor working conditions was instrumental in prompting many of the women to take active roles in this strike.[65] Doreen McNally, wife of a striking docker, is credited with forming WOW in October of 1995. She recalled how this came about:

> As wives, we knew this thing was something altogether different. Women were never asked to participate in our husbands' work lives before. However, one day one of the shop stewards asked me to speak at a rally being held on behalf of the dockers. I don't know why he singled me out. All I can think of is that maybe because I had telephoned a couple of our local radio call-in shows earlier on, and I made a case on the dockers' behalf ... Well in the area of town I was raised nearly everyone had a docker in the family. But as times progressed and people moved further out of the old neighbourhood there was less contact with other people going through similar circumstances. As we started coming together as one group, I can't tell you how therapeutic we found it by sharing our stories with one another. It was just what the doctor ordered. It must have helped because I am proud to say every single wife of those 400 striking dockers took part in one way or another. Whenever we had marches or rallies or whatever, everyone was there. You have to understand, our men had just been put through the shock of their lives. They were beaten down and many just felt absolutely castrated. We had to give them the needed support. It was up to us to see our families through this, and we needed to help our men get back on their feet and regain their confidence.[66]

Many of the striking dockers concurred with these sentiments. 'They were absolutely tremendous. Without their firm support we would have thrown in the towel within only a couple of weeks of that strike. We couldn't have taken that thing as far as we did without their help.'[67] Many of the dockers felt having women on board also helped raise the visibility of the dispute:

> First off, you have to realise that after a while when men don't have work they get weak. As the weeks of a strike go by, men need somebody to give

> them some inspiration to get out of their chair and get down to the picket line. The women were great because they were saying, 'Hey look this is my life being affected here too, you know'. We also noted what a boost it was for the miners' cause back in '84, when they asked their women to join in. At this time we couldn't get any of the media to touch our story with a ten foot barge pole. It wasn't till after the women helped out that anybody gave us any notice. Plus the women built a very effective organisation in their own right. They became very well organised. They also sent out delegations all around the world where they met with dockers' wives. They got our cause in the headlines and that was vital in a struggle like the one we were fighting. Without the Women of the Waterfront movement we would have sunk within a couple of months.[68]

It was at this juncture that the striking dockers were finally able to awaken a sleeping British left. Environmentalist organisations, such as Greenpeace and Reclaim the Streets (RTS), long thought to be bastions for radical middle-class youth, gave the strikers additional media exposure and financial support. Musicians and comedians such as Oasis, Chumbawumba, Billy Bragg and Jo Brand became vocal supporters of their cause. The celebrated Liverpudlian playwright, Jimmy McGovern, helped produce a critically acclaimed movie for television entitled *Dockers*, largely inspired by real life stories written by strikers.

One particularly memorable event was when Toxteth-born Liverpool FC striker Robbie Fowler defied the Football Federation's rules of conduct during an internationally televised football match and displayed for the network cameras a T-shirt under his official kit with the slogan in large letters: '500 Liverpool dockers sacked since 1995.'[69] According to a news report:

> Liverpool striker Robbie Fowler has shown his support for the sacked Merseyside dockers to millions of TV viewers. The 21-year old player lifted his top after scoring in last night's European Cup Winners' Cup match at Anfield to reveal a T-shirt with a slogan supporting the sacked men. The match was being broadcast live on TV to several European countries … Fowler made the gesture after scoring his second goal in the Reds' 3–0 win over SK Brann of Norway. A sacked dockers' spokesman said today: 'He's done it off his own back. We believe Steve McManaman gave him the top. They have both been very supportive and have made donations to our hardship fund. It's given the lads a lift'.[70]

Fowler, like his former teammate Steve McManaman, is a Liverpudlian of working-class origins, and the two shared family connections with

Liverpool's docks. The display of solidarity between millionaire footballers and the striking dockers illustrated the support these workers may have enjoyed locally, but lacked nationally. The Merseyside community proved staunch defenders:

> The people of Liverpool were absolutely fantastic. They were always in our corner. I can't begin to tell you how many local people gave their time to help us with all sorts of things. Whether it was walking a picket line with us, going on marches, attending rallies and fund raisers, Liverpool people were right there for us. The rest of the country might have ignored us, but not the people in this town. You could really pick up on this when you listened to the radio call in shows at the time. I'd estimate well over 90 per cent of those people dialling in to the Roger Phillips Show or whatever, were behind us and the strike . per cent. And that's all during the entire twenty-eight months too. You can always count on Scousers in a strike.[71]

Solidarity and defeat

The dockers remained steadfast in their demands. The MDHC made a number of offers during the dispute; all were voted down by the striking workforce. In October 1997, Morris ordered that the latest offer be considered by a secret postal ballot. The results demonstrated a firm resolve by the strikers. Most were still not prepared to sell their jobs for the £28,000 redundancy package offered. The company which administered the ballot for the TGWU reported:

> Number of ballot papers distributed 329
> Number of duplicate ballot papers distributed 11
> Number of ballot papers returned 316
> Number of invalid ballot papers (blank/spoilt/unsigned declaration) 6
> Thus, total number of valid ballot papers to be counted 310
> Rate of participation 91%
> Result:
> The question put to the membership was as follows:
> DO YOU ACCEPT THE COMPANY'S OFFER?
> Number voting YES 97 (31% of valid vote)
> Number voting NO 213 (69% of valid vote)[72]

The MDHC subsequently decided to make the same offer on an individual basis, with an assurance of confidentiality, but only for a limited period of time. Some felt this was the beginning of the end, as a number of beleaguered dockers accepted the offer: 'In the event they rejected the offer, the company then made the terms available to the men on an individual basis and claim that 67 have accepted it.'[73]

In the end, the Liverpool dockers lost their battle against the MDHC. After twenty-eight months many could hold out no longer. Most of the strikers had incurred an average of over £20,000 worth of debt at a time when many should have been planning their retirement. Others were concerned for their health, as a number of their colleagues had died in the preceding months from stress-induced heart disease.[74] There were also allegations that the TGWU headquarters had had enough of the dispute:

> Liverpool's sacked dockers were forced to end their 850-day fight after their own union threatened to stop paying hardship cash ... It was part of a behind-the-scenes deal thrashed out at the weekend, which led to the Mersey Docks and Harbour Company putting its £28,000 pay-off deal back on the table. A meeting of around 250 sacked men in Liverpool voted by 4 to 1 to accept the pay-off for each of the 329 former Mersey Docks and Harbour Company workers. A TGWU official denied the union had tried to engineer a settlement by threatening to withdraw hardship payments ... There was a problem coming up on the question of the men's pensions' surplus and the pension fund in which they haven't put any money into for a long time and which could have been lost under the regulations governing the scheme ... One docker, fighting back tears as helped pack up the picket line today, said: 'It's a bad day. It's a sell-out'.[75]

A leading activist summarised the causes behind the dispute's termination:

> After twenty-eight months our support from our own union had dwindled to the point that our struggle had become more of a fight with them than with our employer. Our arguments with Morris were becoming headlines more and more in every major newspaper. We suffered five deaths on the picket line from heart attacks – and they weren't old men. All their coronaries were attributed to stress. I mean people were becoming tired of it. Every day, for twenty-eight months you were up at 6 o'clock in the morning and down to the picket line. The frustration was terrible. We started getting a lot of young aggressive policemen monitoring our pickets. It was getting to the point where there were men getting arrested who never had a run in with the law in their entire lives, but now all of a sudden they were getting criminal records. So there was an accumulation of all these things. On top of that, the employer played out a card I was terrified they would do, and I'm surprised it took them so long to finally do it. What they did was they made an open-ended offer. They said we'll give you a six-month window to accept our offer of a £28,000 buy-out agreement

> for your job. They also said it would be done in total privacy. All you had to do was phone this number, and they'd set up an interview, and you would then receive your money. We had refused their offers before in open votes amongst the membership. People wanted their jobs back, full stop – not some cash pay-off. I sensed trouble though when in September 1997 they made this open-ended offer to people on an individual basis ... Now where the fear factor comes in with it was the employer also said this offer would only be on the table for a limited time, so if you wait too long you won't be eligible for the money. So that started breaking up the ranks a bit. Then the union started making threats against us if we didn't settle, so we realised Morris was going to sell us out.[76]

Morris refused to accept criticism from the left for his role in ending the dispute. In a letter to the *Guardian*, he defended the stance he and his union had adopted:

> There are, however, three points which everyone should understand. Firstly, calls for solidarity action, defiance of the law and so on, would have been no more than rhetoric. There was no support for solidarity action whatsoever within the T&G – indeed, over 800 T&G members employed by Mersey Docks, workmates of those dismissed, continued working normally throughout the dispute, which was called without their involvement. I have as much responsibility to them as to the dismissed 320. Secondly, the legal threats faced by the union were not abstract ones. A judgment was made in a New Jersey court which would have fined the union $1 million a day if we lent public support to the dismissed dockers. Fines of that magnitude, which could have been repeated in Britain itself, would have left the T&G incapable of functioning – a high price to pay for rhetoric. If it was a matter of individual sacrifice, I would have been happy to make it. But I was not prepared to sacrifice the interests of every T&G member and their families and see our organisation smashed up to no avail. Thirdly, it is ironic that those who normally shout loudest about rank-and-file democracy in trade unions should overlook the point that the course of action urged by several of your correspondents was explicitly rejected by the T&G's conference. This conference, which is exclusively composed of lorry drivers, car workers, building workers, catering workers, etc., has a better sense of the realities of both the legal dangers and the dockers' dispute itself. Not surprising since it is they, not the comfortable middle-class, who would carry the can for any misjudgement.[77]

The end of the dockers' battle was a disappointment to their supporters. Left-wing Labour MP and outspoken critic of the New Labour project, Tony Benn, lamented the plight of Liverpool's dock workers:

> The plain blunt truth is that the men and women of the waterfront fought a magnificent fight on the principle that you do not betray people who have been sacked for crossing a picket line. They have been let down by the Labour government – the Labour government after May, which could have dealt with this problem quite easily. They ran the most brilliant campaign. All around the world the Liverpool docks dispute was well known ... The dispute will be remembered in the history of the Labour movement on the same scale and with the same honour as the Tolpuddle Martyrs and the miner's dispute of 1984/85. I'm bitterly disappointed they did not get the backing which would have allowed them to get their jobs back. The union was in a position where it would have had to take what it believed to be illegal action. But we wouldn't have any of our liberties if we did not take illegal action. If the suffragettes had not chained themselves to railings, gone on hunger strike or gone to prison, then women would not have had the vote. If the union would have broken the law in support of the Liverpool dockers I would have given them 100 per cent support.[78]

Although defeated, there was a lasting class-consciousness rekindled out of this situation which manifested itself in one final collective action. A number of friends involved in the strike invested their redundancy money in a dilapidated night-club on Liverpool's Hope Street, and turned it into what is now called the Casa Club, a restaurant, bar and community centre. Named in honour of the socialists who fought in the Spanish Civil War, the club serves not only as a viable commercial enterprise, but also as a focal point for organised labour on Merseyside today. Its function room and upstairs offices have become home to numerous adult education classes, job training seminars, and places where community activists can congregate in a welcoming environment. In many ways the Casa Club has taken the place of the former MTUCURC in Hardman Street, which was born out of the unemployed struggles of the 1980s.

Thus, it can be submitted that long-time working-class values of mutuality and solidarity manifested themselves once again on Merseyside, despite the defeat of the dockers' strike. The renowned social historian, E. P. Thompson, posited that these same values were particularly cherished amongst England's emerging working class in the early nineteenth century. Not surprisingly, these were also the ideals that sustained and motivated the striking Liverpool dockers, some 200 years later. If the dockers failed to win their original demands, the public sympathy and outpouring of support they received from fellow workers during this struggle reminded them of the vital importance of traditional notions of working-class solidarity, even in this post-industrial age. It demonstrated that class-consciousness and working-class agency retained their salience even in this modern era of unregulated global capital.

One docker summed up the source of such cherished principles brilliantly: 'Growing up working-class in Liverpool means you're taught two things in life: always help your friends and neighbours when they're in need, and never cross a picket line.'[79]

Notes

1 Peter Turnbull, Charles Woolfson and John E. Kelly, *Dock Strike: Conflict and Restructuring in Britain's Ports* (Aldershot, 1992), pp. 13–14, 18. See also: Andrew Charlesworth, David Gilbert, Adrian Randall, Humphrey Southall and Chris Wrigley, *An Atlas of Industrial Protest in Britain* (London, 1996), pp. 196–7.
2 *The Times*, 28 December 1964.
3 Interview with Tony Nelson. See also: David F. Wilson, *Dockers: The Impact of Industrial Change* (Bungay, 1972), p. 50.
4 Gordon Phillips and Noel Whiteside, *Casual Labour: The Unemployment Question in the Port Transport Industry 1880–1970* (Oxford, 1985), p. 235.
5 Phillips and Whiteside, *Casual Labour*, p. 159; Wilson, *Dockers*, p. 102.
6 Baron Patrick Arthur Devlin, *Final Report of the Committee of Inquiry under the Rt. Hon. Lord Devlin into Certain Matters Concerning the Port Transport Industry* (London, 1965), pp. 1–11.
7 Devlin, *Final Report*, pp. 125–9.
8 Wilson, *Dockers*, p. 181.
9 Jim Phillips, 'Decasualisation and Disruption: Industrial Relations in the Docks, 1945–1979', in Chris Wrigley, ed., *A History of British Industrial Relations, 1939–1979* (Cheltenham, 1996), pp. 169–71. See also: *The Times*, 2 October 1967; Wilson, *Dockers*, p. 178.
10 Charlesworth *et al.*, *Atlas*, p. 97; Wilson, *Dockers*, pp. 17, 178, 189.
11 *The Times*, 16 October 1967.
12 Interview with Jimmy Nolan.
13 Tony Lane, *Liverpool – City of the Sea* (Liverpool, 1997), p. 25.
14 Lane, *Liverpool*, p. 25.
15 Interview with Tony Nelson.
16 Lane, *Liverpool*, pp. 25–6; *The Times*, 29 November 1969 and 21 August 1971.
17 Jon Murden, 'City of Change and Challenge: Liverpool since 1945', in John Belchem, ed., *Liverpool 800: Culture, Character & History* (Liverpool, 2006), pp. 430–1; *The Times*, 14 October 1980.
18 *The Times*, 21 January 1993.
19 Murden, 'City of Change', p. 431.
20 Interview with Tony Nelson.

21 Peter Stoney, 'The Abolition of the National Dock Labour Scheme and the Revival of the Port of Liverpool', *Economic Affairs*, vol. 19, no. 2 (2000), p. 19.
22 Peter Turnbull and Victoria Wass, 'The Greatest Game No More – Redundant Dockers and the Demise of "Dock Work"', *Work Employment & Society*, vol. 6, no. 4 (1994), pp. 487, 489–90, 493–4.
23 *Guardian*, 2 August 1989.
24 *Independent*, 2 August 1989.
25 Chris Carter, Stewart Clegg, John Hogan and Martin Kornberger, 'The Polyphonic Spree: The Case of the Liverpool Dockers', *Industrial Relations Journal*, vol. 34, no. 4 (2003), pp. 292–4; Turnbull *et al.*, *Dock Strike*, pp. 184, 221–6.
26 Hansard, House of Commons, 17 April 1989, c. 45.
27 Hansard, House of Commons, 17 April 1989, c. 46.
28 Hansard, House of Commons, 17 April 1989, c. 80.
29 Michael Lavalette and Jane Kennedy, *Solidarity on the Waterfront: The Liverpool Lock Out of 1995/96* (Rock Ferry, 1996), p. 26.
30 Turnbull and Wass, 'The Greatest Game No More', pp. 487–8, 491–2.
31 Lavalette and Kennedy, *Solidarity*, pp. 7, 26.
32 Interview with Billy Jenkins.
33 Turnbull and Wass, 'The Greatest Game No More', pp. 499–503.
34 Interview with Tony Nelson.
35 Interview with Tony Nelson.
36 Interview with Bobby Morton.
37 Interview with Doreen McNally.
38 Noel Castree, 'Geographic Scale and Grass Roots Internationalism: The Liverpool Dock Dispute, 1995–1998', *Economic Geography*, vol. 76, no. 3 (2000), pp. 277–9.
39 Lavalette and Kennedy, *Solidarity*, p. 31. See also Turnbull *et al.*, *Dock Strike*.
40 Turnbull and Wass, 'The Greatest Game No More', p. 499.
41 Merseyside Port Shop Stewards Committee, *Submission on Behalf of Sacked Liverpool Dockworkers to the Employment Sub-Committee*, House of Commons, May 1996, p. 5: www.labournet.net/docks2/other/topdock.htm.
42 Stoney, 'Abolition', p. 20.
43 Jane Kennedy and Michael Lavalette, 'Globalisation, Trade Unionism and Solidarity: Further Reflections on the Liverpool Dock Lockout', in Ronaldo Munck, ed., *Labour and Globalisation: Results and Prospects* (Liverpool, 2004), p. 210; Carter *et al.*, 'Polyphonic Spree', p. 294
44 Castree, 'Geographic Scale', p. 277; Richard Saundry and Peter Turnbull, 'Mêlée on the Mersey: Contracts, Competition and Labour Relations on the Docks', *Industrial Relations Journal*, vol. 27, no. 4 (1996), p. 275; *Guardian*, 30 August 1995.
45 Lavalette and Kennedy, *Solidarity*, Ch. 2.

46 Carter *et al.*, 'Polyphonic Spree', p. 291.
47 *Liverpool Echo*, 29 September 1995.
48 Interview with Terry Teague.
49 Interview with Bobby Morton.
50 *Lloyds List*, 8 December 1995.
51 Carter *et al.*, 'Polyphonic Spree', p. 293.
52 Interview with Bobby Morton.
53 Interview with Bobby Morton.
54 Interview with Terry Teague.
55 *Guardian*, 14 December 1996.
56 Interview with Billy Jenkins.
57 Interview with Terry Teague.
58 Kennedy and Lavalette, 'Globalisation', pp. 206–8, 210, 212, 225; *Guardian*, 23 November 1996 and 14 December 1996; *Independent*, 3 December 1995 and 8 December 1996.
59 Carter *et al.*, 'Polyphonic Spree', p. 298.
60 Interview with Terry Teague.
61 *Guardian*, 20 December 1995.
62 Castree, 'Geographic Scale', p. 282.
63 Interview with Bobby Morton.
64 Lavalette and Kennedy, *Solidarity*, p. 45.
65 Lavalette and Kennedy, *Solidarity*, p. 47.
66 Interview with Doreen McNally.
67 Interview with Billy Jenkins.
68 Interview with Terry Teague.
69 Carter *et al.*, 'Polyphonic Spree', p. 292.
70 *Liverpool Echo*, 21 March 1997.
71 Interview with Terry Teague.
72 Labour.net – Liverpool Dock Dispute Ballot: www.labournet.net/docks2/9710/ballot3.htm.
73 Labour.net Interview with Terry Teague: www.hartford-hwp.com/archives/61/066.html.
74 Carter *et al.*, 'Polyphonic Spree', p. 294.
75 *Liverpool Echo*, 27 January 1998.
76 Interview with Terry Teague.
77 *Guardian*, 4 February 1998.
78 *Liverpool Echo*, 27 January 1997.
79 Interview with Jimmy Nolan.

Conclusion

It has been said that on the terraces of both Anfield and Goodison football grounds in Liverpool only one chant is shared by both sets of supporters in the vast repertoire of singsongs shouted out on match day. That melody is an adaptation of the traditional folk tune, 'We shall not be moved'. And when this old labour protest song is sung from the terraces, some say the locals shout it with an intensity which can't be described in words. Therefore, I will abstain from attempting such a literal portrayal. However, in many ways this tune serves as a reminder of the history, and indeed, the unique culture of a population who through their own tenacity and talent have endured a long painful history of poverty, alienation, sectarian bigotry and, most hurtful of all, unrelenting joblessness.

This book has tried to demonstrate that this fighting spirit which Liverpool is known for emerged from a unique past. It has illustrated, first, that levels of unemployment in the two decades after 1979 on Merseyside were extraordinarily high in relation to other British conurbations; and second, that the responses by Liverpool workers to redundancy and industrial closure were expressly unique with respect to frequency, intensity and, above all, in their originality.

Once again, this is not to suggest that any particular tactic in the struggle against unemployment was utilised exclusively on Merseyside. Indeed, all of the reactions to joblessness in this critique occurred in other regions of Britain as well, whether they were strikes against factory closures, the establishment of unemployed centres, mass urban strife, the election of radical left-wing Labour councils, workplace occupations as well as others not discussed in this study, such as workers' cooperatives and workers' alternative plans.

However, it was on Merseyside that *all* these weapons in this arsenal of resistance were deployed, and they generated far greater publicity with, arguably, better effect than in any of Britain's other industrial centres. Moreover, some of these tactics were pioneered in Liverpool. It was the wide range of initiatives implemented and the free use of experimentation when they were utilised, as well as their sequential or synchronic adoption over a relatively short period of time, which underpins the conclusion that Liverpool was different from the rest, or indeed, maybe to some degree it was 'exceptional'.

This study has argued that large segments of Liverpool's working class, both organised and unorganised, drew upon a long established oppositional culture that had its roots in the city's past traditions. In contrast to many economic or sociological accounts of unemployment during the age of Thatcher, which most always treat the unemployed as passive, nameless victims, this historical analysis, informed by a Thompsonian perspective, shows that workers in Liverpool drew upon this tradition of defiance and workplace militancy in order to actively recreate and reinvigorate that culture. If the often innovative strategies they used to combat unemployment were not always successful, which most were not, that still does not detract from due recognition of the agency with which some elements of Liverpool's working class pursued these endeavours.

Therefore, it is hoped that this study has contributed to the debate by offering a fresh look at working-class activism during the age of Thatcher. Through its Thompsonian perspective, it explored the agency asserted by a group, who up to this point in the historiography were almost always portrayed as passive victims, or even worse, as mere statistics. In particular, the oral testimony given in this research proves that many of these displaced workers and the long-term unemployed refused to accept the situation as it was handed to them. Whether it was triggered by the highly restrictive labour laws passed under Thatcher and continued under Blair, or in reaction to the closure of large manufacturing establishments, this critique has demonstrated that large segments of Liverpool's working class responded vigorously and were not merely acted upon. They fought back, and they fought back with ferocity and imagination.

Whatever the changes that have since occurred on Merseyside, contemporary Liverpool has transformed itself in both its landscape and its economy. Nevertheless, the events of the 1970s, 1980s and 1990s charted in this study made a unique contribution to the city as it stands today. The 'Scouse' sense of identity remains a vital part of the consciousness of many Liverpudlians, and while this notion draws heavily on a history scarred by joblessness, sectarianism and poverty, this self-awareness of who and what they are derives as much from the acts of resistance used in fighting these injustices, as the injustices themselves. Indeed, perhaps this is why in Liverpool they choose to sing, 'We shall not be moved'.

Select bibliography

Primary sources

Archival sources

Liverpool and Merseyside Record Office – Liverpool

352 MIN City of Liverpool, *Proceedings of the Council – 1981–1982*, vol. 2, July–November, p. 130.

Merseyside Maritime Museum Archives and Library – Liverpool

Merseyside Docks and Harbour Board Collection, Dockers' Registers – Various Years

Modern Records Centre – University of Warwick

MSS.126/TG/59/11 'Minutes of the Merseyside Transport and General Workers' Composite District Committee Meeting', 10 July 1986.

MSS.292/1980 *Report of 112th Annual Trades Union Congress*, Brighton Centre, Brighton, September 1st to 5th 1980 (Enfield and Welshpool: Macdermott & Chant, 1980).

MSS.292D/90/4 TUC Consultative Conference: Services for the Unemployed, Opening Speech by Lionel Murray, TUC General Secretary, 4 November 1980.

MSS.292D/10.13/2 Lionel Murray, General Secretary, and Brendan Barber, Press Officer, Trades Union Congress, London, UK, 26 May 1982: Press Release.

MSS.292D/135.56 Lionel Murray, General Secretary, Trades Union Congress, 12 December 1980, Circular No. 85 (1980–1981).

MSS.292D/135.58/1 *Report of Consultative Conference on 'Services to the Unemployed'*, North West Regional Council of the T.U.C., 20 December 1980.

MSS.292D/135.58/1 Meeting minutes from a conference by the North West Regional Council of the Trades Union Congress held in Manchester on 28 February 1981.

MSS.391/3/66 Transport and General Workers' Union Biennial Delegate Conference Papers (Annotated by Alan Thornett), July 1979.

MSS.391/3/67 Transport and General Workers' Union Biennial Delegate Conference Papers (Annotated by Alan Thornett), June 1981.
MSS.393D/135.58/1 Private and Confidential Memorandum Services for the EPOC 5/3 Unemployed, Employment Policy and Organisation Committee of the Trades' Union Congress, 21 January 1981.

People's History Museum – Manchester

Ref. No. 331.861 Pamphlet Collection, Miners' Strike 1984–85.

Public Records Office – Kew, London

HO3106/48ptE Personal letter from Michael Heseltine to the Prime Minister, 13 August 1981, 2 pages.

Unite the Union Archives Office – Holborn, London

MSS.126/TG/1887/28 Transport and General Workers' Union 28th Biennial Delegate Conference, Scarborough, 9–13 July 1979: Minutes and Record of the Proceedings.
MSS.126/TG/1887/29 Transport and General Workers' Union 29th Biennial Delegate Conference, Brighton, 22–26 June 1981: Minutes and Record of the Proceedings, Souvenir Programme and Press Cuttings.

Working-Class Movement Library – Salford

5000092 Stand by our men: the story of the women of the Women of the waterfront supporting the sacked Liverpool Dockers, 1996.
36005357 2 million plus: rally and march against unemployment, 1980.
36012212 Liverpool: lessons for the left – Socialist Workers Party, 1987.
36017614 Jobs!: what jobs? – A survey of jobs registered and publicly displayed in Liverpool Job Centres one week in May 1989.
36017665 People's march for jobs: May 1981 Liverpool-London – Salford Committee, 1981.
36018147 People's march for jobs: May 1981 Liverpool-London – official souvenir, 1981.
36018147 Marxism on Trial: Defend the Liverpool Socialists (no date given).
AG-Unemployment Merseyside Trade Union Community and Unemployed Resource Centre – Information Folder (no date given).
(Uncatalogued) British Leyland File – Triumph Motor Company (Liverpool) Limited Employee Handbook (no date of publication).

Newspapers and periodicals

Belfast News Letter
Belfast Telegraph
Big Flame

Bristol Evening Post
Daily Mail
Daily Mirror
Financial Times
Guardian
Herald Scotland
Independent
Irish Times
Liverpool Daily Post
Liverpool Echo
London Evening Standard
Lloyd's List
Mirror
Morning Star
New York Times
Northern Echo
Observer
Scotsman
Telegraph
The Times

Oral interviews

Billy Albertina – Cammell Laird occupation leader and GMB steward – Interview: 11 April 2011.
Mohamed Ali – Former Liverpool city councillor – Granby Ward and community activist in the Toxteth area – Interview: 15 July 2010.
Anonymous Former Cannell Laird worker – Interview: 13 April 2011.
Phil Ash – Former TGWU steward at Standard-Triumph – Interview: 7 October 2008.
Bob Braddock – Coordinator of the People's Centre (formally known as the Merseyside Trade Union and Community Unemployed Resource Centre – MTUCURC) – Interview: 1 October 2009.
Greg Coyne – Unemployment activist and co-organiser of the TGWU 6/612 branch – Interview: 13 April 2010.
Kevin Coyne – Activist in MTUCURC, member of TGWU 6/612 Branch, co-organiser of the 'People's March for Jobs' – Interview: 1 April 2010.
Clive 'Dixie' Dean – Retired Merseyside Police Constable – Interview: 14 June 2010.
Lol Duffy – Cammell Laird occupation co-organiser – Interview: 8 April 2011.
Mike Evans – Retired Merseyside Police Inspector – Interview: 20 June 2010.
Joe Farrag – Director of the Liverpool 8 Law Centre – Interview: 13 November 2014
Bob Fisher – Retired Merseyside Police Sergeant – Interview: 16 June 2010.

Jimi Jagne – Toxteth resident – Interview: 13 November 2014.
Billy Jenkins – Former Liverpool docker – Interview: 15 January 2008.
David Leach – Former Liverpool city councillor – Granby Ward – Interview: 11 May 2011.
Ian Lowes – Retired Liverpool city council worker, GMB convenor, Chairman of the Liverpool City Council Joint Shop Stewards' Committee – Interview: 9 November 2010.
Ian MacDonald – Retired Merseyside Police Assistant Chief Constable – Interview: 16 June 2010.
Eddie Marnell – Cammell Laird occupation co-organiser – Interview: 6 April 2011.
Doreen McNally – Wife of Liverpool docker and founder of Women of the Waterfront – Interview: 14 January 2009.
Tony McQuade – Former TGWU 6/612 shop steward at Standard-Triumph and activist for the unemployed – Interviews: 24 October 2008 and 5 October 2009.
Gill Monglione – Activist in MTUCURC, participant in the 'People's March for Jobs' – Interview: 1 October 2009.
Bob Moreton – Unite official and former docker – Interview: 15 January 2009.
Tony Mulhearn – Former Liverpool city councillor, past president of the local Liverpool Labour Party and member of the Militant Tendency – Interview: 1 November 2010.
Tony Nelson – Former docker, TGWU activist and strike committeeman – Interview: 19 November 2008.
Jimmy Nolan – Former Liverpool docker and TGWU official – Interview: 21 November 2008.
David Potts – Retired Merseyside Police Constable injured during Toxteth riots – Interview: 9 June 2010.
Jimmy Rafferty – Retired Merseyside Police Detective Constable – Interview: 15 June 2010.
Eddie Roberts – Retired TGWU official and union convenor at Ford Motor Company's Halewood facility – Interview: 28 October 2008.
Ken Routledge – Former shop steward and trade union activist at Standard-Triumph – Interview: 26 September 2008.
Jack Spriggs – Former Liverpool city councillor, chairman of the 'One Fund for All' mutual aid society and coordinator of the 1972 sit-in strike at Fisher-Bendix – Interview: 17 October 2009.
Terry Teague – Former Liverpool docker and trade union activist, and manager of the Casa Club in Liverpool – Interview: 14 January 2009.
Bob Towers – Participant in the 'People's March for Jobs', political activist and member of the TGWU 6/612 Branch of the Unemployed – Interview: 1 October 2009.
Ann Trevor – Retired Merseyside Police Constable – Interview: 19 June 2010.
Frank Trevor – Retired Merseyside Police Sergeant – Interview: 19 June 2010.

Personal papers

A personal letter written from Merseyside Police Detective Constable Brian Smith to his mother. Date: Exact date unknown, but thought to be in the summer of 1981.

Government publications

Castle, Barbara. 'In Place of Strife: A Policy for Industrial Relations', Cmnd. 3888, London: HMSO, 1969.
Census 1951, England and Wales. 'County Report: Lancashire', London: General Registers Office, 1954.
Census 1961, England and Wales. 'Occupation, Industry, Socio-Economic Groups County Reports: Lancashire', London: General Registers Office, 1963–64.
Census 1971, England and Wales. 'County Report: Lancashire', London: HMSO, 1973.
Census 1971, England and Wales. 'Report for the County of Merseyside as Constituted as of 1 April 1974', London: HMSO, 1975.
Census 1981, Great Britain. 'County Report: Merseyside', London: HMSO, 1982.
Census 1981, Great Britain. 'Economic Activity: Merseyside', London: HMSO, 1983.
Census 1981, Great Britain. 'Key Statistics for Urban Areas: The North – Cities and Towns', London: HMSO, 1984.
Census 2001, Great Britain. 'Key Statistics for Urban Areas: The North – Cities and Towns', London: HMSO, 2004.
Central Policy Review Staff. *The Future of the British Car Industry*, London: HMSO, 1975.
Department of Employment. *Employment Gazette* February 1951 – March 1987, London: HMSO.
Department of Employment. *Employment Monthly Digest of Statistics*, London: HMSO (published annually).
Department of Employment. *New Earnings Survey* 1970–1984, London: HMSO.
Devlin, Baron Patrick Arthur, *Final Report of the Committee of Inquiry under the Rt. Hon. Lord Devlin into Certain Matters Concerning the Port Transport Industry*, London: HMSO, 1965.
Donovan, Baron Terence. 'The Report of the Royal Commission on Trade Unions and Employers' Associations', London: HMSO, 1968.
Office of National Statistics. *Census of Employment* 1971–1995, London: HMSO.
Office of National Statistics. *Labour Force Survey* 1979–1998, London: HMSO.
Ryder, Baron Don. *British Leyland, the Next Decade: An Abridged Version of a Report Presented to the Secretary of State for Industry*, London: HMSO, 1975.
Scarman, Rt. Hon. Lord. *The Brixton Disorders, 10–12 April 1981*, London: HMSO, 1981.

Published works of a primary nature

Memoirs and autobiographies

Edwardes, Michael. *Back from the Brink*, London: William Collins & Sons, 1983.

Hatton, Derek. *Inside Left*, London: Bloomsbury Publishing, 1988.

Heffer, Eric. *Never a Yes Man: The Life and Politics of an Adopted Liverpudlian*, London: Verso, 1991.

Heseltine, Michael. *Life in the Jungle: My Autobiography*, London: Hodder & Stoughton, 2000.

O'Mara, Pat. *Autobiography of a Liverpool Irish Slummy*, New York: Vanguard Press, 1933.

Thatcher, Margaret. *The Downing Street Years*, London: HarperCollins, 1993.

Trade union publications

Beynon, Huw. *What Happened at Speke?*, Liverpool: 6/612 Branch TGWU, 1978.

Leyland Combine Trade Union Committee. 'British Leyland, the Edwardes Plan and Your Job', Kidderminster: Leyland Combine Committee, 1980.

Merseyside Port Shop Stewards' Committee. 'Never Cross a Picket Line: The Story of 500 Sacked Liverpool Dockers', International Conference Pamphlet, 17–23 February 1996, Liverpool.

Political pamphlets and literature

Institute for Workers' Control. 'Lucas an Alternative Plan', IWC Pamphlet No. 55, Nottingham: Institute for Workers' Control.

Liverpool Black Caucus. *The Racial Politics of Militant: The Black Community's Struggle for Participation in Local Politics, 1980–1986*, London and Liverpool: The Runnymede Trust/Merseyside Area Profile Group, 1986.

Merseyside Community Relations Council. 'Racial Discrimination and Disadvantage in Employment in Liverpool: Evidence Submitted to the House of Commons Select Committee on Employment, 1986', Liverpool: Merseyside Area Profile Group, 1986.

Passingham, Bernie and Danny Connor. 'Ford Shop Stewards on Industrial Democracy', IWC Pamphlet No. 54, Nottingham: Institute for Workers' Control.

Local authority publications

Evans, E. S. P., City Planning Officer. 'Census 1981: Liverpool City: Key Statistics: Standard Data Zones', Liverpool: Liverpool Planning Department, 1983.

Evans, E. S. P., City Planning Officer. 'Census 1981: Liverpool City: Key Statistics: 100% Ward Data', Liverpool: Liverpool Planning Department, 1983.

Gifford, Lord Tony QC, Wally Brown and Ruth Bundey. *Loosen the Shackles: First Report of the Liverpool 8 Inquiry into Race Relations in Liverpool*, London: Karia Press, 1989.

Hayes, Michael G. *Past Trends and Future Prospects: Urban Change in Liverpool 1961–2001*, Liverpool: Liverpool City Council, February 1987.

HM Inspectors, Department of Education and Science. *Educational Provision by Liverpool Educational Authority in the Toxteth Area*, March 1982.

Liverpool City Council. *The Toxteth Survey: Technical Report*, February 1982.

Liverpool City Planning Department. *Liverpool's Economy: Employment and Unemployment: Changes and Trends, 1978–1991*, 1992.

Liverpool City Planning Department. *Unemployment in Liverpool: Unemployment Change, 1982–1985*, 1985.

Nevin, Brendan, Peter Lee and Jenny Phillimore. *Measuring the Sustainability of Neighbourhoods in Liverpool*, Liverpool: City of Liverpool, 2001.

Websites containing primary sources

Austin Rover Online, Facts & Figures, History: www.aronline.co.uk/index.htm?ryderreportf.htm.

Austin Rover Online, The Cars, Triumph TR7: www.aronline.co.uk/index.htm?tr7storyf.htm.

Ferguson, Kenneth. 'Jobless Unionists Fight Unemployment'. *New Internationalist*: www.newint.org/issue117/jobless.htm.

Hansard, House of Commons and House of Lords Debates, 1803–2005: http://hansard.millbanksystems.com/.

Keter, Vincent. 'Trade Union Legislation: Labour's Changes to the Conservative Reforms', House of Commons Library, Standard Note: 7N/BT/596, Business and Transport Section (7 October 2010), pp. 2–7: www.parliament.uk/briefing-papers/.

Labour.net Interview with Terry Teague: www.hartford-hwp.com/archives/61/066.html.

Labour.net – Liverpool Dock Dispute Ballot – Labour.net: www.labournet.net/docks2/9710/ballot3.htm.

Libertarian Communism Society at libcom.org – Interview with Tony McQuade: http://libcom.org/library/an-interview-with-tony-mcqade-former-shop-steward.

Merseyside Port Shop Stewards Committee. 'The Case for the Reinstatement of the Sacked Liverpool Dockers': www.labournet.net/docks2/9707/booklet.htm.

Merseyside Port Shop Stewards Committee. *Submission on Behalf of Sacked Liverpool Dockworkers to the Employment Sub-Committee*, House of Commons, May 1996: www.labournet.net/docks2/other/topdock.htm.

Morning Star on Line – The Flying Picket – Liverpool: www.morningstaronline.co.uk/news/features/people-s-pub-history19.

Top of the Docks – Labour.net: www.labournet.net/docks2/9708/canliv1.htm.

Trades' Union Congress – Blog for Stronger Unions: www.strongerunions.org/2008/12/04/unemployed-workers-centres/.
United Kingdom Census – Office of National Statistics: Census 1991, Census 2001: www.statistics.gov.uk/hub/index.html.

Secondary sources

Books

Ayers, Pat. *The Liverpool Docklands: Life and Work in Athol Street*, Birkenhead: Liver Press, 1987.
Bagguley, Paul. *From Protest to Acquiescence: Political Movements of the Unemployed*, London: Macmillan, 1991.
Batstone, Eric, Ian Boraston and Stephen Frenkel. *Shop Stewards in Action: The Organisation of Workplace Conflict and Accommodation*, Oxford: Basil Blackwell, 1977.
Belchem, John. *Before the Windrush: Race Relations in 20th-Century Liverpool*, Liverpool: Liverpool University Press, 2014.
Belchem, John. *Irish, Catholic and Scouse: The History of the Liverpool-Irish, 1800–1939*, Liverpool: Liverpool University Press, 2007.
Belchem, John. *Merseypride: Essays in Liverpool Exceptionalism*, Liverpool: Liverpool University Press, 2000.
Bevins, Reginald. *The Greasy Pole: A Personal Account of the Realities of British Politics*, London: Hodder & Stoughton, 1965.
Beynon, Huw. *Working for Ford*, 2nd edition, Harmondsworth: Penguin Books, 1984.
Burnett, John. *Idle Hands: The Experience of Unemployment, 1790–1990*, London: Routledge, 1994.
Charlesworth, Andrew, David Gilbert, Adrian Randall, Humphrey Southall and Chris Wrigley. *An Atlas of Industrial Protest in Britain*, London: Macmillan Press, 1996.
Church, Roy. *The Rise and Decline of the British Motor Industry*, Cambridge: Cambridge University Press, 1995.
Coates, Ken. *Work-Ins, Sit-Ins and Industrial Democracy: The Implications of Factory Occupations in Great Britain in the Early 'Seventies*, Nottingham: Spokesman, 1981.
Crick, Michael. *The March of Militant*, London: Faber & Faber, 1986.
Cronin, James E. *Industrial Conflict in Modern Britain*, London: Croom Helm, 1979.
Cronin, James E. *Labour and Society in Britain, 1918–1979*, London: Batsford Academic and Educational, 1984.
Croucher, Richard. *We Refuse to Starve in Silence: A History of the National Unemployed Workers' Movement, 1920–46*, London: Lawrence & Wishart, 1987.

Darlington, Ralph. *The Dynamics of Workplace Unionism: Shop Stewards' Organisation in Three Merseyside Plants*, London: Mansell, 1994.

Darlington, Ralph and Dave Lyddon. *Glorious Summer: Class Struggle in Britain 1972*, London: Bookmarks, 2001.

Davies, Sam. *Liverpool Labour*, Keele: Keele University Press, 1996.

Dickson, Tony and David Judge. *The Politics of Industrial Closure*, London: Macmillan Press, 1987.

Evans, Eric J. *The Shaping of Modern Britain: Identity, Industry and Empire, 1780–1914*, London: Routledge, 2011.

Evans, Eric J. *Thatcher and Thatcherism*, 2nd edition, London: Routledge, 2004.

Fine, Sidney. *Sit-Down: The General Motors Strike of 1936–1937*, Ann Arbor: University of Michigan Press, 1970.

Foster, John and Charles Woolfson. *The Politics of the UCS Work-In*, London: Lawrence & Wishart, 1986.

Frost, Diane and Richard Phillips. *Liverpool '81: Remembering the Riots*, Liverpool: Liverpool University Press, 2011.

Fukuyama, Francis. *The End of History and The Last Man*, New York: Penguin, 1992.

Garside, W. R. *The Measurement of Unemployment: Methods and Sources in Great Britain 1850–1979*, Oxford: Basil Blackwell, 1980.

Goodman, J. F. B. and T. G. Whittingham. *Shop Stewards in British Industry*, London: McGraw-Hill, 1969.

Greenwood, J. *Worker Sit-Ins and Job Protection*, Farnborough: Gower Press, 1977.

Gretton, John. *Students and Workers: An Analytical Account of Dissent in France, May–June 1968*, London: Macdonald, 1969.

Hanson, Charles G. *Taming the Trade Unions: A Guide to the Thatcher Government's Employment Reforms, 1980–90*, London: Macmillan, 1991.

Harvey, David. *A Brief History of Neoliberalism*, Oxford: Oxford University Press, 2005.

Hayek, Friedrich A. *The Road to Serfdom*, London: Routledge, 1944.

Hindess, Barry. *The Decline of Working-Class Politics*, London: MacGibbon & Kee, 1971.

Hobsbawm, Eric. *Worlds of Labour: Further Studies in the Histories of Labour*, London: Weidenfeld & Nicolson, 1984.

Hobsbawm, Eric and George Rudé. *Captain Swing: A Social History of the Great English Agricultural Uprising of 1830*, New York: Pantheon Books, 1969.

Hunter, Bill. *They Knew Why They Fought: Unofficial Struggles and Leadership on the Docks, 1945–1989*, London: Index Books, 1994.

Kelly, John. *Rethinking Industrial Relations: Mobilization, Collectivism, and Long Waves*, London: Routledge, 1998.

Keynes, John Maynard. *The General Theory of Employment, Interest, and Money*, London: Palgrave Macmillan, 1936.

Lane, Tony. *Liverpool – City of the Sea*, Liverpool: Liverpool University Press, 1997.

Lavalette, Michael and Jane Kennedy. *Solidarity on the Waterfront: The Liverpool Lockout of 1995–96*, Birkenhead: Liver Press, 1996.

Laybourn, Keith. *British Trade Unionism, c.1770–1990*, Stroud: Alan Sutton, 1991.

Lloyd, P. E. *Manufacturing Industry in the Inner City: A Case Study of Merseyside*, North West Industry Research Unit, Working Paper Series No. 2. School of Geography, University of Manchester, June 1977.

Marsden, David, Timothy Morris, Paul Willman and Stephan Wood. *The Car Industry: Labour Relations and Industrial Adjustment*, London: Tavistock Publications, 1985.

Marsh, Arthur. *Managers and Shop Stewards: Shop Floor Revolution?*, London: Institute of Personnel Management, 1973.

McIlroy, John. *The Permanent Revolution? Conservative Law and the Trade Unions*, Nottingham: Spokesman, 1991.

Parkinson, Michael. *Liverpool on the Brink*, Hermitage: Policy Journals, 1985.

Phillips, Gordon and Noel Whiteside. *Casual Labour: The Unemployment Question in the Port Transportation Industry 1880–1970*, Oxford: Clarendon Press, 1985.

Piven, Frances Fox and Richard A. Cloward. *Poor People's Movements: Why They Succeed, How They Fail*, New York: Pantheon Books, 1977.

Riddell, Peter. *The Thatcher Era and its Legacy*, Oxford: Blackwell, 1991.

Shaw, Eric. *Discipline and Discord in the Labour Party*, Manchester: Manchester University Press, 1988.

Sherry, Dave. *Occupy! A Short History of Workers' Occupations*, London: Bookmarks Publications, 2010.

Spencer, Bruce. *Remaking the Working Class? An Examination of Shop Stewards' Experiences*, Nottingham: Spokesman, 1989.

Steiger, Manfred B. and Ravi K. Roy. *Neoliberalism: A Very Short Introduction*, Oxford: Oxford University Press, 2010.

Taaffe, Peter and Tony Mulhearn. *Liverpool – A City that Dared to Fight*, London: Fortress Books, 1988.

Taylor, Robert. *The Trade Union Question in British Politics: Government and Unions since 1945*, London: Basil Blackwell, 1993.

Thompson, E. P. *The Making of the English Working Class*, New York: Vintage, 1966.

Thompson, E. P. *The Poverty of Theory and other Essays*, London: Merlin Press, 1980.

Thompson, Willie and Finlay Hart. *The UCS Work-In*, London: Lawrence & Wishart, 1972.

Thornett, Alan. *Inside Cowley*, London: Porcupine Press, 1998.

Todd, Selina. *The People: The Rise and Fall of the Working Class, 1910–2010*, London: John Murray, 2014.

Touraine, Alaine. *The May Movement: Revolt and Reform: May 1968, the Student Rebellion and Workers' Strikes, the Birth of a Social Movement*, New York and Toronto: Random House, translated 1971.

Turnbull, Peter, Charles Woolfson and John E. Kelly. *Dock Strike: Conflict and Restructuring in Britain's Ports*, Aldershot: Avebury, 1992.

Turner, Rachel S. *Neo-Liberal Ideology: History, Concepts and Policies*, Edinburgh: Edinburgh University Press, 2008.

Turok, Ivan and Nicola Edge. *The Jobs Gap in Britain's Cities: Employment Loss and Labour Market Consequences*, Bristol: The Polity Press, 1999.

Wainwright, Hilary. *Labour: A Tale of Two Parties*, London: The Hogarth Press, 1987.

Waller, P. J. *Democracy and Sectarianism: A Political and Social History of Liverpool 1868–1939*, Liverpool: Liverpool University Press, 1981.

Wapshott, Nicholas. *Keynes Hayek: The Clash that Defined Modern Economics*, New York: W.W. Norton & Company, 2011.

Westergaard, John, I. Noble and A. Walker. *After Redundancy: The Experience of Economic Security*, Cambridge: Polity Press, 1989.

White, Michael, ed. *The Social World of the Young Unemployed*, London: Policy Studies Institute, 1987.

Whiteside, Noel. *Bad Times: Unemployment in British Social and Political History*, London: Faber & Faber, 1991.

Williams, Karel, John Williams and Colin Haslam. *The Breakdown of Austin Rover*, Leamington Spa: Berg Publishers Limited, 1987.

Willman, Paul, Tim Morris and Beverly Aston. *Union Business: Trade Union Organisation and Financial Reform in the Thatcher Years*, Cambridge: Cambridge University Press, 1993.

Wilson, David F. *Dockers: The Impact of Industrial Change*, Bungay: Fontana/Collins Publishing, 1972.

Wrigley, Chris. *British Trade Unions, 1945–1995*, Manchester: Manchester University Press, 1997.

Edited collections

Altena, Bert and Marcel van der Linden, eds. *De-Industrialization: Social, Cultural and Political Aspects*, Cambridge: Cambridge University Press, 2003.

Belchem, John, ed. *Liverpool 800: Culture, Character & History*, Liverpool: Liverpool University Press, 2006.

Belchem, John, ed. *Popular Politics, Riot and Labour: Essays in Liverpool History 1790–1940*, Liverpool: Liverpool University Press, 1992.

Belchem, John. 'Liverpool in the Year of Revolution: The Political and Associational Culture of the Irish Immigrant Community in 1848', in John Belchem, ed., *Popular Politics, Riot and Labour: Essays in Liverpool History 1790–1940*, Liverpool: Liverpool University Press, 1992.

Benyon, John. 'The Riots, Lord Scarman and the Political Agenda', in John Benyon, ed., *Scarman and After: Essays reflecting on Lord Scarman's Report, the Riots and Their Aftermath*, Oxford: Pergamon Press, 1984.

Benyon, John. 'The Riots: Perceptions and Distortions', in John Benyon, ed., *Scarman and After: Essays Reflecting on Lord Scarman's Report, the Riots and Their Aftermath*, Oxford: Pergamon Press, 1984.

Blackaby, Frank, ed. *De-Industrialisation*, London: Heinemann Educational Books, 1978.

Bohstedt, John. 'More than One Working Class: Protestant-Catholic Riots in Edwardian Liverpool', in John Belchem, ed., *Popular Politics, Riot and Labour: Essays in Liverpool History 1790–1940*, Liverpool: Liverpool University Press, 1992.

Bradley, Pauline and Chris Knight, eds. *Another World is Possible: How the Liverpool Dockers Launched a Global Movement*, London: University of East London Radical Anthropology Group, 2004.

Bryer, Rob, Stan Brignall and Allen Maunders. 'The Origins of Plant Closures', in Hugo Levie, Denis Gregory and Nick Lorentzen, eds, *Fighting Closures: De- Industrialization and the Trade Unions 1979–1983*, Nottingham: Spokesman, 1984.

Campbell, Alan, Nina Fishman and John McIlroy, eds. *The Post-War Compromise: British Trade Unions and Industrial Politics, 1945–64*, Monmouth: Merlin Press, 2007.

Crick, Bernard, ed. *Unemployment*, London: Methuen, 1981.

Fineman, Stephen, ed. *Unemployment: Personal and Social Consequences*, London: Tavistock Publications, 1987.

Gallie, Duncan, Catherine Marsh and Carolyn Vogler, eds. *Social Change and the Experience of Unemployment*, Oxford: Oxford University Press, 1994.

Hindess, Barry. 'The Decline of Working-Class Politics – a Reappraisal', in Chris Cook and Ben Pimlott, eds, *Trade Unions in British Politics: The First 250 Years*, 2nd edition, London: Longmans, 1991.

Hoyles, Andrée, 'The Occupation of Factories in France: May 1968', in Ken Coates, Tony Topham and Michael Barratt Brown, eds, *Trade Union Register, 1969*, London: The Merlin Press, 1969.

Hyman, Richard. 'Workers' Control and Revolutionary Theory', in Ralph Miliband and John Saville, eds, *The Socialist Register*, vol. 11, London: Merlin Press, 1974.

Johnson, Christopher H. 'Introduction: De-industrialization and Globalization', in Bert Altena and Marcel van der Linden, eds, *De-Industrialization: Social, Cultural and Political Aspects*, Cambridge: Cambridge University Press, 2003.

Joshi, Chitra. 'On "De-Industrialization" and the Crisis of Male Identities', in Bert Altena and Marcel van der Linden, eds, *De-Industrialization: Social, Cultural and Political Aspects*, Cambridge: Cambridge University Press, 2003.

Kennedy, Jane and Michael Lavalette. 'Globalisation, Trade Unionism and Solidarity: Further Reflections on the Liverpool Dock Lockout', in Ronaldo Munck, ed., *Labour and Globalisation: Results and Prospects*, Liverpool: Liverpool University Press, 2004.

Levie, Hugo, Denis Gregory and Nick Lorentzen, eds. *Fighting Closures: De-Industrialization and the Trade Unions 1979–1983*, Nottingham: Spokesman, 1984.

Lyddon, Dave. 'The Car Industry, 1945–79: Shop Stewards and Workplace Unionism', in Chris Wrigley, ed., *A History of British Industrial Relations*, Cheltenham: Edward Elgar, 1996.

McIlroy, John. 'A Brief History of British Trade Unionism and Neoliberalism: From the Earliest Days to the Birth of New Labour', in Gary Daniels and John McIlroy, eds, *Trade Unions in a Neoliberal World*, Abingdon: Routledge, 2009.
McIlroy, John. 'A Brief History of British Trade Unionism and Neoliberalism in the Age of New Labour', in Gary Daniels and John McIlroy, eds, *Trade Unions in a Neoliberal World*, Abingdon: Routledge, 2009.
McIlroy, John. 'Britain: How Neo-Liberalism Cut Unions Down to Size', in Gregor Gall, Adrian Wilkinson and Richard Hurd, eds, *The International Handbook of Labour Unions: Responses to Neo-Liberalism*, Cheltenham: Edward Elgar, 2011.
McIlroy, John, Nina Fishman and Alan Campbell, eds. *The High Tide of British Trade Unionism: Trade Unions and Industrial Politics, 1964–1979*, Monmouth: Merlin Press, 2007.
Murden, Jon. 'City of Change and Challenge: Liverpool since 1945', in John Belchem, ed., *Liverpool 800: Culture, Character & History*, Liverpool: Liverpool University Press, 2006.
Phillips, Jim. 'Decasualisation and Disruption: Industrial Relations in the Docks, 1945–1979', in Chris Wrigley, ed., *A History of British Industrial Relations, 1939–1979*, Cheltenham: Edward Elgar, 1996.
Taylor, Stan. 'The Scarman Report and Explanations of Riots' in John Benyon, ed., *Scarman and After: Essays reflecting on Lord Scarman's Report, the Riots and Their Aftermath*, Oxford: Pergamon Press, 1984.

Journal articles

Bagguley, Paul. 'Protest, Acquiescence and the Unemployed: A Comparative Analysis of the 1930s and 1980s', *The British Journal of Sociology*, vol. 43, no. 3 (September 1992), pp. 443–61.
Barker, Allan, Paul Lewis and Michael McCann. 'Trade Unions and the Organisation of the Unemployed', *British Journal of Industrial Relations*, vol. 22, no. 3 (1984), pp. 391–404.
Bean, Ron and Peter Stoney. 'Strikes on Merseyside: A Regional Analysis', *Industrial Relations Journal*, vol. 17, no. 1 (March 1986), pp. 9–23.
Carter, Chris, Stewart Clegg, John Hogan and Martin Kornberger. 'The Polyphonic Spree: The Case of the Liverpool Dockers', *Industrial Relations Journal* vol. 34, no. 4 (2003), pp. 290–304.
Castree, Noel. 'Geographic Scale and Grass-Roots Internationalism: The Liverpool Dock Dispute, 1995–1998', *Economic Geography*, vol. 76, no. 3 (2000), pp. 272–92.
Christian, Mark. 'An African-Centered Approach to the Black British Experience: With Special Reference to Liverpool', *Journal of Black Studies*, vol. 28, no. 3 (January 1998), pp. 291–308.
Clutterbuck, Richard. 'Terrorism and Urban Violence', *Proceedings of the Academy of Political Science*, vol. 34, no. 4 (1982), pp. 165–75.
Cooper, Paul. 'Competing Explanations of the Merseyside Riots of 1981', *The British Journal of Criminology*, vol. 25, no. 1 (January 1985), pp. 60–9.

Darlington, Ralph. 'Shop Stewards' Leadership, Left-Wing Activism, and Collective Workplace Activism', *Capital & Class*, vol. 26, no. 76 (Spring 2002), pp. 95–126.

Darlington, Ralph. 'Workplace Union Militancy on Merseyside since the 1960s: Extent, Nature, Causes, and Decline', *Historical Studies in Industrial Relations*, vol. 19 (Spring 2005), pp. 123–52.

England, Joe. 'Shop Stewards in Transport House: A Comment upon the Incorporation of the Rank and File', *Industrial Relations Journal*, vol. 12, no. 5 (1981), pp. 16–29.

Forrester, Keith and Kevin Ward. 'Organising the Unemployed? The TUC and the Unemployed Workers Centres', *Industrial Relations Journal*, vol. 17, no. 1 (1986), pp. 46–56.

Gall, Gregor. 'Resisting Recession and Redundancy: Contemporary Worker Occupations in Britain', *Working USA – The Journal of Labor and Society*, vol. 13, no. 1 (2010), pp. 107–32.

Green, A. E. 'The Likelihood of Becoming and Remaining Unemployed in Great Britain, 1984', *Transactions of the Institute of British Geographers*, New Series, vol. 11, no. 1 (1986), pp. 37–56.

Green, A. E., D. W. Owen and C. M. Winnett. 'The Changing Geography of Recession: Analyses of Local Unemployment Time Series', *Transactions of the Institute of British Geographers*, New Series, vol. 19, no. 2 (1994), pp. 142–62.

Hobsbawm, Eric. 'The Forward March of Labour Halted', *Marxism Today* (September 1978), pp. 279–286.

Lane, Tony. 'Merseyside under the Hammer', *Marxism Today* (February 1981), pp. 18–21.

Lane, Tony. 'The Unions: Caught on an Ebb Tide', *Marxism Today* (September 1982), pp. 6–13.

Leslie, Derek, Joanne Lindley and Leighton Thomas. 'Decline and Fall: Unemployment among Britain's Non-White Ethnic Communities 1960–1990', *Journal of the Royal Statistical Society: Series A (Statistics in Society)*, vol. 164, no. 2 (2001), pp. 371–87.

Lyddon, Dave. 'British Leyland: The Shop Stewards and Participation', *International Socialism*, 1st series, no. 102 (October 1977), pp. 20–6.

Lyddon, Dave. 'Strike Statistics and Militancy: A Comment', *Historical Studies in Industrial Relations*, vol. 19 (Spring 2005), pp. 153–70.

Pritchard, Colin. 'Unemployment, Age, Gender and Regional Suicide in England and Wales 1974–90: A Harbinger of Increased Suicide for the 1990s?', *The British Journal of Social Work*, vol. 25, no. 6 (1995), pp. 767–91.

Rose, Ed. 'The "Disorganised Paradigm" British Industrial Relations in the 1990s', *Employee Relations*, vol. 16, no. 1 (1994), pp. 27–40.

Rose, Vanessa and Elizabeth Harris. 'From Efficacy to Effectiveness: Case Studies in Unemployment Research', *Journal of Public Health*, vol. 26, no. 3 (2004), pp. 297–30.

Saundry, Richard and Peter Turnbull. 'Mêlée on the Mersey: Contracts, Competition and Labour Relations on the Docks', *Industrial Relations Journal*, vol. 27, no. 4 (1996), pp. 275–88.

Smith, David. 'Tonypandy 1910: Definitions of Community', *Past & Present*, no. 87 (May, 1980), pp. 158–84.

Smith, Richard. "Gissa Job": The Experience of Unemployment', *British Medical Journal*, vol. 291 (1985), pp. 1263–6.

Spencer, Bruce. 'Post-War Trade Unionism: Its Role and Significance', *Studies for Trade Unionists*, vol. 13, no. 52 (December 1987), pp. 7–21.

Spencer, Bruce. 'The Case for Workers' Take-Over: G.E.C. and U.C.S.', *The Political Quarterly*, vol. 43, no. 4 (24 August 2005), pp. 425–36.

Squiers, Neil F., Nick J. Beeching, Bernard J. Schlecht and Sue M. Ruben. 'An Estimate of the Prevalence of Drug Misuse in Liverpool and a Spatial Analysis of Known Addiction', *Journal of Public Health Medicine*, vol. 17, no. 1 (1995), pp. 103–9.

Stoney, Peter. 'The Abolition of the National Dock Labour Scheme and the Revival of the Port of Liverpool', *Economic Affairs*, vol. 19, no. 2 (2000), p. 19.

Terrill, Richard J. 'Margaret Thatcher's Law and Order Agenda', *The American Journal of Comparative Law*, vol. 37, no. 3 (Summer 1989), pp. 429–56.

Thompson, E. P. 'The Moral Economy of the English Crowd in the Eighteenth Century', *Past and Present*, vol. 50 (1971), pp. 76–136.

Turnbull, Peter and Victoria Wass. 'The Greatest Game No More – Redundant Dockers and the Demise of "Dock Work"', *Work, Employment & Society*, vol. 6, no. 4 (1994), pp. 487–506.

Unsworth, Clive. 'The Riots of 1981: Popular Violence and the Politics of Law and Order', *Journal of Law and Society*, vol. 9, no. 1 (Summer 1982), pp. 63–85.

Willman, Paul. 'The Reform of Collective Bargaining and Strike Activity in BL Cars, 1976–1982', *Industrial Relations Journal*, vol. 15, no. 2 (June 1984), pp. 6–17.

Zack-Williams, Alfred B. 'Africa Diaspora Conditioning: The Case of Liverpool', *Journal of Black Studies*, vol. 27, no. 4 (March 1997), pp. 528–42.

Unpublished theses

Carden, Michael J. 'Union Democracy and Incorporation: A Case Study of the T.G.W.U. Merseyside Division with Particular Reference to the Dock Industry', MA diss., University of Liverpool, 1996.

Mills, A. J. 'Worker Occupations, 1971–1975: A Socio-Historical Analysis of the Development and Spread of Sit-Ins Work-Ins and Worker Cooperatives in Britain', PhD thesis, Department of Sociology, University of Durham, 1982.

Unpublished papers

Richardson, Michael, Paul Stewart and Andy Danford. 'Managerial Strategy and Conditions at Work in the British Automobile and Aerospace Industries 1950–1982', paper presented to AUTO21 Conference, Workers and Labour

Markets in the Global Automotive Industry, McMaster University, Hamilton, Ontario, Canada, 22–23 October 2004.

Tuckman, Alan. 'Occupation, Worker Co-Operatives and the Struggle for Power: Britain in the 1970s', unpublished academic paper given at the 28th International Labor Process Conference at Rutgers – The State University of New Jersey, 15–17 March 2010.

Index

Note: *Italicised* page numbers indicate passages of oral testimony by person listed.